90 0689714 3

Traditional Cures for Modern Conflicts

SAIS African Studies Library

General Editor
I. William Zartman

Traditional Cures for Modern Conflicts

African Conflict "Medicine"

edited by
I. William Zartman

LYNNE RIENNER PUBLISHERS

BOULDER
LONDON

Published in the United States of America in 2000 by
Lynne Rienner Publishers, Inc.
1800 30th Street, Boulder, Colorado 80301

and in the United Kingdom by
Lynne Rienner Publishers, Inc.
3 Henrietta Street, Covent Garden, London WC2E 8LU

Library of Congress Cataloging-in-Publication Data
Traditional cures for modern conflicts : African conflict "medicine" /
edited by I. William Zartman.
Includes bibliographical references.
ISBN 1-55587-876-8 (hc : alk. paper)
1. Ethnicity—Africa. 2. Culture conflict—Africa. 3. Social conflict—Africa. 4. Conflict management—Africa. 5. Political customs and rites—Africa. 6. Africa—Social life and customs. 7. Africa—Politics and government. I. Zartman, I. William.
GN645.T65 1999
303.6'9'096—dc21 99-24150
CIP

British Cataloguing in Publication Data
A Cataloguing in Publication record for this book
is available from the British Library.

Printed and bound in the United States of America

The paper used in this publication meets the requirements
of the American National Standard for Permanence of
Paper for Printed Library Materials Z39.48-1984.

5 4 3 2 1

To Mohamed Sahnoun and Kofi Annan,
makers of peace by traditional and modern methods

Contents

Acknowledgments

The African Studies Program at the Paul H. Nitze School of Advanced International Studies, Johns Hopkins University, would like to acknowledge its deep gratitude to the United States Institute of Peace for its generous support of this project, and also to the U.S. Army War College for its participation and cosponsorship of the initial conference. We would also like to thank Colonel Dan Henk, Noa Davenport, and Laura Nader for their stimulating contribution to the conference on which this book is based. I also want to express my personal gratitude to Theresa Taylor Simmons for the hard work and masterful direction that she put into the organization of the conference and the preparation of the manuscript; to Ben Fred-Mensah for organizing the bibliography; and to Kwaku Nuamah for proofreading and preparation of the index.

—I.W.Z.

1

Introduction: African Traditional Conflict "Medicine"

I. William Zartman

Traditional societies in Africa and elsewhere are reputed to hold secrets of peacemaking locked in their ways, formed from centuries of custom before the disruption of colonization. In places and practices that modernization has passed by, these traditions are often claimed to be still in use, keeping the heart of society in harmony while imported overlays such as states and currencies are collapsing in conflict around them. Some of this smacks of the "noble savage" of romantic literature, and other aspects may merely be the invention of a current conflict management fad that ignores the pervasiveness and creativity of conflict. But some of Africa's reputation in conflict management has historic and even contemporary footnotes, and there are also other, less well-known claims to a non-Western approach to conflict management. A clearer picture is needed.

In recent times, medical scientists have turned attention to medicines and healing practices used in precolonial Africa in order to understand the bases of their effectiveness in modern scientific terms (de Souza 1997; Ahyi 1997). In some cases, such study has brought to light new chemical compounds and psychological effects, enriching the scientific repertory with previously unknown substances and practices. Without the benefit of modern science, Africans discovered chemical substances through their effects and used them effectively for medical purposes (Githens 1949; Kerharo and Bouquet 1950; Kerharo 1974; Kokwaro 1976; Radji 1987; Movich 1997–1998; Adjanohoun 1980; Bep 1986; Mortabo Degbe 1991; Diemé 1992). In the same way, healing practices were developed that now provide new insights into different ways of dealing with illness (Lambo 1961; Field 1960; Laplatine 1976; Sow 1977; Adjido 1984; Good 1987; Lewis 1988).

In other cases, it turned out that the substances and practices of African traditional medicine were the same as those used today, independently discovered and developed in Africa and in other parts of the world. Here, the contribution of contemporary research is to show these similarities and to identify practices and products from diverse sources with a common name. In both cases, research globalizes knowledge, whether by adding African discoveries to the world repertory or by bringing African inventions under the universal names of things already known. African traditional conflict "medicine" invites the same kind of attention.

With the end of the systems of world order that colonialism and the Cold War provided, Africa is experiencing a greater degree of conflict than it has seen in a long while. While this conflict is frequently noted to be primarily internal in nature (Smock 1993; Copson 1994; Zartman 1995), the fact—not as frequently noted—is that domestic political conflict does not remain self-contained, nor is it self-generated. The stakes of Africa's conflicts in the post–Cold War era are indeed internal, but their origins and ramifications involve entire regions. African conflict in the 1990s is not only more prevalent than in earlier periods; it is more virulent and destructive because its implications lie within both the state and the region. More than ever, Africa needs effective conflict management practices.

In response, international attention has focused on ways of dealing with African conflicts. The United Nations Security Council has sent nine peacekeeping missions to Africa in the 1990s alone—the UN Transition Assistance Group (UNTAG) in Namibia from 1989 to 1990; the UN Mission in Western Sahara (MINURSO) from 1991 to (presumably) 1999; the UN Operations in Mozambique (UNOMOZ) from 1992 to 1994; the UN Aouzon Strip Observer Group (UNASOG) in 1994; the UN Assistance and Verification Mission (UNAVEM I, II, and III) from 1989 to 1997; the UN Observer Mission in Angola (MONUA) from 1997 to 1998; the UN Operations in Somalia (UNOSOM I and II) from 1992 to 1995; the UN Mission in Rwanda (UNAMIR) from 1993 to 1996; the UN Mission in Liberia (UNOMIL) from 1993 to 1997; and the International Mission Supervising the Agreements of Bangui (MISAB) from 1996 to 1999—under chapters VI and VII of the Charter. Special representatives of the UN Secretary General (SRSGs) have been sent to Rwanda, Burundi, Zaire, Sierra Leone, Liberia, Western Sahara, Congo (Brazzaville), Mozambique, Angola, and South Africa in the same decade. Individual countries, such as the United States and France, have sent peacekeeping missions to Somalia (Operation Restore Hope) in 1990 and Rwanda (Operation Turquoise) in 1994, and evacuation or protection missions to Liberia in 1990, Sierra Leone in 1997, Central African Republic in 1996, Congo (Brazzaville) in 1997, and Zaire in 1991, 1993, and 1996.

Within the continent itself, the Organization of African Unity (OAU) has also sent special representatives of the Secretary-General to conflict areas such as Congo in 1993 and 1997, and Zaire in 1997, and peacekeeping forces in Rwanda (NMOG) in 1994. The Economic Community of West

African States (ECOWAS) sent a military monitoring group (ECOMOG) to Liberia in 1990 and Sierra Leone in 1997 and repeatedly mediated the regional conflict centered on the two countries. The Inter-Governmental Agency for Development (IGAD) had attempted to mediate the Sudanese conflict in 1994 and thereafter, and the Front Line States/Southern African Development Community (FLS/SADC) mediated the conflict in Lesotho in 1994. Former Tanzanian President Julius Nyerere single-handedly seized the mandate of the international community to mediate the Burundi crisis after 1995; then-president Mobutu Sese Seko of then-Zaire tried to mediate the Angolan civil war in 1990; and France more successfully mediated the Senegal-Mauritanian dispute in 1993.

Even private agencies have become involved in seeking to bring peace back to Africa. The International Negotiation Network (INN) of the Carter Center of Emory University has worked on regional conflicts in the Horn of Africa, the Great Lakes, Congo-B, and Liberia. International Alert in London brought its good offices to Sierra Leone. The Liberian Council of Churches was the first of many unsuccessful mediators in its country's civil war. A Kenyan businessman, Washington Okumu, put the final piece of the agreement to end the South African conflict in place.

Yet African conflicts remain impervious to these attentions. Though they involve the activities of seasoned peacemakers using the best of personal skills and recently developed knowledge about ways of managing and resolving conflicts, international efforts at conflict management have not been particularly effective or efficient in overcoming the disasters that have brought them to the continent. Some of these conflicts—Mozambique, Liberia—have indeed been brought under control after lengthy and multiple efforts (Hume 1994; Msabaha 1995; Olson and Stedman 1995), but their occurrence and duration and the persistence of the other conflicts show that improvements are needed in conflict management.

The weaknesses are twofold. The outburst and persistence of violent conflict means that homegrown measures at dampening escalation and preventing violence have failed. Before the conflicts rise to an intensity that justifies international attention, domestic measures would be expected to come into play, and they have not, at least not effectively. Governance is conflict management (Zartman 1997); if some areas of Africa have kept their conflicts under control, many have not and have seen the original attempts at building a national community at independence become chewed into pieces and spat out in subnational ethnic violence. Traditional African conflict management practices have proven ineffective against contemporary—if not modern—challenges. Contemporary challenges may be of the same type of internal contests of authority or clashes between governed communities that Africa has always known. But modern challenges indicate new types of conflicts that contest state authority along with its commonality of values and its respect of venerable leaders, and that reject community solidarity destroyed by a combination of globalizing experience and parochial ambitions. Whether it is the specifically different nature of these conflicts as a modern phenomenon, or simply their contemporary occurrence as a broader challenge, today's conflicts elude traditional management methods, and it is no use blaming the inadequacies or machinations of foreign actors for the fact.

At the same time, the persistence of violent conflict in Africa indicates that modern international methods are also defective in facing the challenge. Despite the increased attention and improved knowledge about conflict management in the post–Cold War era (Crocker, Hampson, and Aall 1996; Zartman and Rasmussen 1997), African conflicts elude international as well as domestic efforts to bring them under control. The methods are often faulted for their foreignness and non-African nature and for ignoring the wisdom of traditional African conflict management practices, but even when examined in their own terms according to modern concepts of conflict management, they tell more from their shortcomings than from their successes (Hampson 1996; Zartman 1997).

The conclusions to be drawn are not clear, since failure is usually overdetermined. As noted, conflicts today may be different in nature—modern and therefore impervious to traditional methods, yet African and thus resistant to international methods. Both traditional and international practices may be sound but poorly applied. Probably most telling but most difficult to deal with, methods—but especially traditional methods—may be operating effectively in keeping large numbers of conflicts under control but therefore also out of reach of the analyst, leaving only the exceptionally difficult cases to escalate their way onto the headlines. The only conclusion that does ring clear is that more work is required on the nature of both conflict and conflict management methods in Africa so as to improve the fit between the two.

■ Identifying Traditional Practices

The first step is to identify the kinds of practices that have been used in African societies to deal with conflict. Africa's reputation may (or may not) be exaggerated, but in precolonial societies as well as in their continuation under colonial and now independent rule, methods did exist to deal with conflict. This fact is characteristic of all societies. To recognize it is merely to make an empirical generalization, not necessarily to take an interpretative position on either the African anthropological thesis that societal harmonization is an African characteristic (Rose 1992) or the broader sociological thesis that equilibrium is a universal societal characteristic (Parsons

1937). While it is impossible to inventory all conflict management methods across the whole continent, some salient and representative accounts would bring the richness of African experience to light. While some such accounts have been made (Kenyatta 1938; Evans-Pritchard 1940; Bohannan 1957; Swartz 1966; Middleton 1966; Rose 1992), they tend to present one small part as a microcosm of the whole, thus asserting what needs to be demonstrated and epitomizing what needs to be compared. The first task, then, is to acquire some data.

Admittedly, even data collection poses some problems and begs some assumptions. Other than by the luck of the random, there is no way of knowing how salient or representative selected cases may be until all the cases have been examined. Yet of course all the cases cannot be examined. Not only does this pose a methodological problem; it also constitutes an ontological problem that has long dogged the subject (Penel 1997, 170). Africa has too frequently been presented as a continent where peacemaking is a universal characteristic and palaver a common practice. In conflict management as in many other activities, any case is assumed to be representative because Africa is assumed to be a homogeneous unit, with its own peculiar universalities.

Although this effect might be dismissed as a case of the resemblance of the stranger, in which foreigners or out-group members are often assumed to all look alike, it is in fact the result of the activities of the in-group. Africanists in African studies programs writing about African subjects implicitly or even explicitly propagate the impression that their subject has similarities that outweigh its differences, and that the whole is merely the repetition of some of its parts. Africa tends to be portrayed by a number of cases whose only sure commonality is their location on the same continent, with no certainty or control to assure that they represent more than just isolated examples.

Unfortunately, there is little that can be done about the problem, other than to be very careful in the choice of language. On one hand, there are not only similarities but also identities associated with habitation on the African island, dual categories of commonalities that are important to understanding the nature of the subject. It is meaningful to a certain degree to talk of African conflict management practices, in the sense that such practices exhibit both similarities and differences that are used as references by people who identify by the generalization "African." To some extent, Africans share similar practices, but more importantly and to an increasing extent, they claim as their own and draw inspiration from practices at home and elsewhere on their continent.

On the other hand, such claims and references do not indicate that the practices are either common or exclusive to all African societies. Commonality is a challenge to any analysis. Any student of the subject faces the decision whether to rise to the level of abstraction where the generalization can cover the entire subject or to stay at a lower level of meaning where coherence is greater and coverage smaller. Or, in other words, how many exceptions does it take to prove a rule? A practice scattered throughout the continent and not limited to a single subregion can be called African even though not all Africans practice it, as long as this is clearly understood to be the case.

Exclusiveness is a challenge too, although it is less often taken up. Much discussion of the concept of culture is plagued by the assumption that identifying characteristics are the sole property of the identified group, or that commonality means exclusivity. Yet one group's characteristics may be found in other groups as well, yet are in no way diminished by the discovery that they are shared: The fact that both Arabs and Latinos use cilantro (coriander) in their cooking does not diminish its savor.

The authors in this study examine traditional conflict management practices that can be found on the African continent, not claiming that such practices are typical, representative, or universal on the continent. They also examine similar practices elsewhere, notably in the Middle East and China, for comparison. They make no claims about either homogeneity or exclusivity associated with being African. Examples of African conflict management practices are presented, and then their characteristics are discussed in the context of both internal meaning and external comparisons. At best, this attempt to confront the subject can produce some observations about approaches and methods used in Africa that will stand as hypotheses that other studies can test, and it will make its greatest contribution if it inspires such tests.

In the end, this attempt is a way of dealing with the mercurial subject of culture and of cutting through the raucous debate between the poles of cultural relativism and human universalism (Faure and Rubin 1993; Aurach 1999; Cohen 1997). As noted, even while recognizing the original contributions and autonomous inventions coming from the African continent, it seeks to avoid false claims about the uniqueness of the whole culture that produced them. It also seeks to avoid the loftiness of analysis that makes the local terrain far below featureless, leveling all the parochial peculiarities in the search for a scientific assertion of the oneness of human behavior the world around. Instead, it begins with an inductive and much more sound approach, without limiting assumptions of essential uniqueness or universality, looking for characteristic behaviors and then comparing them with patterns of behavior observed elsewhere. To Geertz's (1983, 16) observation that "the interpretive study of culture represents and attempts to come to terms with the diversity of the ways human beings construct their lives in the act of leading them," it is necessary, honest, and evenhanded to add—as Geertz does in practice—"*and* unity" to the observation of diversity. A search for both the particular within the universal and the universal across the particulars is the only way to apprehend the richness and comprehend the solidarity of humanity.

■ Known or New, Outmoded or Relevant

The second step in examining African traditional conflict management practices is therefore to determine what is new and needs to be recognized as different, as distinguished from that which is universal and needs to be recognized by its name. Unlike chemical compounds and medical practices, conflict management techniques are not unambiguously identifiable by specific formulas and prescriptions, nor can they be examined in isolation from their context. So the accounts need to be interpreted in order to ascertain what is really going on, how conflicts are managed, what the contextual societal conditions are that allow the mechanisms and practices to operate, what kinds of conflicts can be handled, and so on.

Like the problem of identifying representative accounts, the task of distinguishing the new from the known raises its own inherent problems of terminology. Most open to question is the notion of tradition itself, a term that has occasioned vast discussions and inspired great ambiguity. There is no need here to enter into the clouds of connotations that surround the concept (see Hountondji 1997, 15–19); the term is used here precisely, neutrally, and unabashedly, without quotation marks because as Houtondji (1997, 17) nicely points out, they are "not sounds likely to be heard." Conflict management practices are considered traditional if they have been practiced for an extended period and have evolved within African societies rather than being the product of external importation. Tradition continues to exist, even in the contemporary—or modern—period, and the traditional practices considered here all are practiced today; it is quite another matter to revive practices from history that have fallen into disuse and therefore would have to be readjusted and refurbished to fit into a modern context. At the same time, tradition is likely to have been updated, adjusted, and opened to new accretions in order to stay alive through changing times. Traditional does not mean unaltered or archaic.

It is the third step that constitutes the justification of the enterprise, and that is the determination of the relevance of traditional African conflict management practices to modern conflicts. Not all conflicts are the same, and the appropriateness, the methods, and the name or newness of the approach vary according to the type of conflict it is addressing. Two different categorizations are important. The first distinguishes between conflicts between communities, systems, or states, and those within them. Conflicts between systems occur in relations of anarchy, as theories of international politics point out (Waltz 1954). There is no order among the parties, other than that provided by their power relations. While relations between them may matter, there is an absence of overarching authority and of common values. The units are neither within nor under anything; they can pull away from each other because they are not contained in a common organization, so no sanctions of exclusion and no appeals to relationships are possible. Conflict management methods must treat the parties as formally equal and sovereign units, find commonalities between them and seek an overlap in their positions, and develop relations that hold the parties to their agreement. Such requirements point to methods of negotiation, although there may be some mediation possibilities as well (Walton and McKersie 1965; Zartman and Berman 1982; Mastenbroek 1989; Pruitt and Carnevale 1983; Druckman 1997).

Conflicts within a system occur in the context of a sociopolitical structure, under an institution of authority, and within a community of values. Here conflicts tend to pit a deviant member or members against a part or all of the body politic, against or under the normative structure of the community. Using the traditional anthropological distinction between cephalic and acephalic societies, the sociopolitical order may be hierarchical or communal, although usually some elements of both are present (Evans-Pritchard 1940; Gluckman 1956, 1963, 1965a; Montagne 1973). Conflict management in these cases can take advantage of referents in values, authority, and community to anchor its efforts; it is essentially calling the offender to order, preserving the community and hierarchy and restoring the harmony of society. This context is particularly important; as noted by an African medical practitioner in a related field, "the basic difference between traditional healers and us, modern doctors, is that they heal relationships, we heal bodies" (Ahyi 1997, 237). Mediation, arbitration, and even adjudication are appropriate forms of management for this type of conflict, and also in some cases multilateral negotiation as consensus building (Berckovitch 1997; Bilder 1997; Touval and Zartman 1985).

Further distinctions over the nature of internal structure, authority, and values may be useful but are secondary; the important distinction concerns the existence of a community within which the conflict occurs. However, an additional distinction must be noted within the category of internal conflicts, between within-system and against-system conflicts. Generally, internal conflicts already described can be contained within the sociopolitical system and do not challenge or threaten it directly. Their resolution reinforces community and authority, as the deviant party is brought to order—even if the main problem of the conflict is to ascertain which of the conflicting parties has deviated from established norms and authority.

There is another category of internal conflicts, however, that explicitly challenges the internal order—and even those that do not do so initially may turn into the second type if mismanaged. Here the grievance is not between members of the community within the community, under the ruler, but between members and the ruler or political system as a whole, whose legitimacy the grievants contest. These conflicts have the characteristics neither of interstate nor of the usual internal conflicts, that is, they are not among equals outside a common framework nor are they hierarchical within a common framework. In other terms, they are neither authority-neutral nor authority-reinforcing but authority-destroying. As such, they are the hardest to handle, since neither the conditions of equality favoring negotiation nor those of hierarchy and community favoring arbitration or consensuation exist (Zartman 1995). These characteristics, typical of the current conflicts in Africa, explain the difficulties of both traditional and modern methods for their management and underline the need for more work on both counts to improve the ability to handle them.

As noted, much of that work is being done on modern methods, almost by definition, but little is done on traditional methods. The need leads back to previously indicated questions, with renewed insistence. What kinds of conflicts did traditional conflict management practices handle best, and how do those kinds compare with contemporary conflicts? What have been the characteristics in contemporary action? Can traditional methods yield insights and approaches that can enrich the work either of African or of international peacemakers? In the end, what is the role of traditional conflict management practices today—should it take over the field, should it be combined with modern and foreign methods, or should it leave the field to newer and better methods? These are the questions that guide this study.

■ Cases and Comparisons

To begin to attack these questions, testimonies have been gathered from the three corners of the continent (the cultural traditions of North Africa being quite different from the sub-Saharan part of the continent, the fourth corner has been left out of this study). While they tend to focus on conflict management in a single community or set of communities, they all seek to address the question of external conflict as well in some way. And while they seek to bring out the characteristics of traditional practices, they all examine these practices' relevance to the contemporary era beyond the traditional context. Four of the studies deal with West Africa. Uwazie presents social relations and peacekeeping practices among the Igbo in Nigeria; Wilson-Fall compares the way in which the Fulani in the Sahel prevent and manage conflicts among themselves compared to those that involve them with other ethnic groups; Fred-Mensah analyzes mediation, arbitration, and adjudication among the Buem as they deal with land disputes occasioned by a clash between established land-tenure systems and newcomers in Ghana; Kouassi details diplomatic practices within and among West African communities and states between Ghana and Nigeria, emphasizing the role of moral, legal, and ethical principles, the use of more formal mechanisms such as arbitrators, treaties, and family ties, and above all the institution of the ombudsman as a mediator that could still be relevant in the present. Two other studies discuss different traditions within East Africa. Tuso presents a particular social system within the Oromo in Ethiopia, where age groups take on different assigned roles in decisionmaking and conflict managing, thus serving to perpetuate the structure of the social system by handling the challenges that arise within it; and Deng discusses the internal system for handling conflict as practiced at the hands of an exceptionally wise Dinka chief and its extension to the management of relations between the Dinka and neighboring Arabs in Sudan, ending with an examination of the applicability of these practices to the contemporary identity crisis in the country. In each instance, the practices and the sociopolitical system within which they function are presented and their modus operandi analyzed, with particular attention to the ways in which traditional practices are used in the three types of conflicts.

The issue is then discussed within an expanding context, to show the similarities between traditional measures in Africa and conflict management in other parts of the non-Western world—Lebanon, Palestine, and China—compared with Western practices in the United States. King-Irani presents a reconciliation and conflict management ritual of widespread occurrence throughout the Arab world, and shows its resonance in conflict transformation terms newly introduced (or newly rediscovered) in the West. Abu-Nimer presents practices developed in the Palestinian Mideast and those used in the American Midwest as the basis of a comparison between a broader categorization of non-Western and Western conflict management methods. Faure brings out the basic similarities between African traditional conflict management practices and those found in China, and then goes on to find in their communitarian nature a broader element of distinction from Western conflict and conflict management.

Finally, the relevance of traditional conflict management in the modern world is reviewed and evaluated. In an account from southern Africa, Masina discusses the various ways of handling different types of conflicts in the internal and external relations of the Xhosa in South Africa, and then examines the application of the underlying spirit of *ubuntu* to the management of contemporary disputes in a way that serves to create a new identity group of all South Africans. Menkhaus shows how African institutions and practices were used in Somalia and could have been used more, but he also shows how such methods were sometimes subverted by conflicting actors who were able to turn their attributes against them. Osaghae evaluates more broadly the use of traditional methods to see where they are applicable and where their relevance is limited by the nature of the conflict. The conclusion highlights the universal characteristics of conflict management measures invented in Africa, but also shows the special forces and particular requirements of African efforts. This juxtaposition in turn permits identification of the peculiar contributions of traditional approaches to modern conflicts and the directions indicated by old methods.

PART 1

Managing Conflict in Traditional African Societies

2

Social Relations and Peacekeeping Among the Igbo

Ernest E. Uwazie

Traditional African legal-anthropological research focused on differentiating between custom and law (Gluckman 1955, 1956; Bohannan 1957; Gibbs 1963). For the most part, the absence of written codes or statutes in indigenous (precolonial) Africa was a major defining characteristic of custom—an immemorial traditional social order, largely immutable and closely linked to the cultural system. The view of simpler or indigenous societies dominated by integrated traditions of maintaining peace and order distinguished them from modern states with law (Bohannan 1957; Michalowski 1985; Weber 1954; Vinogradoff 1925). Hence, statutes or judicially declared rules of social control—deliberately, reflectively, and rationally made by law-trained professionals—became the essence of justice in both colonial and independent African nation-states. However, persistent and serious problems in the present formal or official (modern) legal system throughout Africa have caused a type of "law-nostalgia"—a search for rediscovery and adaptation of traditional or indigenous African conflict management systems (Uwazie 1991; Ayittey 1991; Albert et al. 1995; Comaroff and Roberts 1981).

This chapter focuses on the varying uses of indigenous and formal legal systems for managing conflicts and the interactions among them. It examines conditions under which disputants choose from the various modes of conflict management, and why each mode may be more amenable to resolving certain kinds of conflicts. In essence, it is about the complex strategies of dispute management in a pluralistic legal environment in Igboland, eastern Nigeria.

Relevant literature on dispute processing and conflict resolution (e.g., Abel 1973, 1982; Merry 1979, 1982; Black and Baumgartner 1978; Nader and Todd 1978) proposes conflict-handling forums and procedures of disputing typologies such as mediation, negotiation, arbitration, litigation, self-help, avoidance, and "lumping it" (see also Felstiner 1974; Danzig

1973; Goldberg et al. 1985; Tomasic and Feeley 1982). Variables such as the nature of relationships, socioeconomic status, the nature of the dispute, and the disputant's past experiences allow for explanations of the choice of various conflict management strategies (Merry 1979, 1982; Moore 1978; Starr and Yngvesson 1975; Gibbs 1963; Howell 1954). The findings are based on both civil and criminal disputes, gathered from personal observations, interviews, and surveys.

■ Relationships and Disputing

In the condition of legal pluralism, disputants make their disputing choices partly as a result of the relationship between the litigants. For Black (1976, 1987), a disputing mode is isomorphic to the disputants' social environment. Whether law has a penal, compensatory, therapeutic, or conciliatory style, it depends on the rank relations between the disputants and their degree of intimacy or relationship. However, Merry (1982) posits that the future of the disputants' relationship is more crucial than its past in selecting a particular disputing process. My study suggests that except in situations of dispute over scarce resources, selection of a disputing mode is informed by ongoing, long-term relationships.

□ *Dispute Settlement in the Family*

The scene inside the family's zinc-roofed hut may resemble a battle of the sexes to a stranger: the female and male groups sat opposite each other on the four wooden benches facing the center; some younger groups sat on the cement floor in the same arrangement. The Umuada (married daughters) and the other adult members of the Dozie-Iwu family, including "Mmadie's" (husband's pride)[1] parents, were present to settle a domestic matter. The family head (Onyi'si) welcomed the assembled audience with six white and red kola nuts. After the welcoming remarks, he admonished those gathered to reconcile this couple: "There is no need to decide guilt or innocence in spousal cases, only to reconcile the husband and wife because of the sacredness of marriage."

Holding a six-by-two, one-inch-thick wooden object, covered with multicolored bird feathers, the Onyi'si beckoned the family ancestors to hover around those who had gathered to resolve the family matter. He ceremoniously seated the family "Ofo" (oath object) in the center of the floor and swore the people to be unbiased and to ensure family unity in their judgment. After a brief proverbial introduction of the case, he asked Mmadie to stand next to the Ofo and present her complaint.

Mmadie, a forty-year-old peasant farmer, complained that her marriage, after eighteen years and seven children, had become too abusive to bear. She told the gathered family members that her husband, Dozie, fifty, neglected to provide food for his immediate family, and that he was having an affair with a widow in the village. She reported that Dozie had physically abused her when she confronted him with his infidelity and his neglect. Mmadie stressed that she wanted the physical abuse to stop. She de-emphasized the infidelity allegation to the extent that it did not interfere with Dozie's ability to provide adequately for the family. She reiterated similar past complaints to the Onyi'si and threatened to report the matter to the entire village, or to Dozie's age group, if it was not resolved at the family level.

In his response, Dozie countered that his wife had neglected him, either by preparing his food late or by not preparing it at all. He retorted that he had stopped buying goat meat for the house because Mmadie had complained that it was an insufficient meal for a family of twelve. Apparently Dozie also supported his aged mother and two other relatives. He contended that Mmadie did not understand that their farm had not produced enough to generate extra cash for certain soup ingredients. He said he had tried to supplement the family income by climbing palm trees and gathering palm nuts, a primary source of cooking oil, for interested customers.

Dozie's customers were mostly widows who did not have able males to fetch them palm nuts. He stated that he had come home late on many occasions because he was trying to collect fees from customers who could not pay on time. The best time to collect these debts was in the late evening after people had returned from selling in the markets. Dozie contended that because his customers were mostly widows and his debt collection occurred in the evenings, Mmadie suspected adultery. Without expressly denying it, he baited his wife to present evidence of adultery.

After invoking the god of thunder (Amadioha) and the ancestors to punish any persons (mediators) who might cause Mmadie and Dozie to sever their marriage and break up the family, the Onyi'si rephrased the dispute as a case of spousal abuse and neglect, pointing to Dozie's wife beating and Mmadie's refusal or reluctance to prepare food for her husband. Most of the males in the audience questioned the disputing couple. The women urged the men to resolve the case without finding fault. The questions were aimed at a reconciliation. Mmadie's parents and Dozie himself reiterated a commitment of reconciliation and to keeping the family together.

The deliberations ended when the family head announced that both Mmadie and Dozie were equally responsible for the quarrel. Fines of a cock and a hen were imposed on Dozie and Mmadie, respectively; the birds' blood would be spilled on the ground to appease the gods and goddesses of the ancestors that may have been offended by the couple's quarrel. Further, the couple would provide food for those who were present. Mmadie gave them two big trays of foo-foo (made of pounded cassava root), including her "best-ever-made" vegetable and cocoyam soup. Dozie provided the goat meat for the soup and four calabashes, or gallons, of palm wine. The family head used the last wine dregs to pour libations, invoking an ancestral enchantment to solidify their decision. He swore the couple to comply with it and avoid future conduct that would upset the family harmony. The session ended with a reiteration of marriage vows of mutual responsibility and care for each other and their children.

The mediative role of the family head, as well as the other adult members reiterating the sacredness of marriage in resolving this case, emphasizes two important sociolegal phenomena. First, the mediators or dispute handlers paid little or no attention to the adultery accusation. The villagers are usually ambivalent about adultery unless it involves a married woman, or when liaisons interfere with a husband's responsibility to provide for his family. By Igbo custom, a man can marry as many women as he can maintain. However, adultery and polygamy are forbidden by the state law. Second, this is a case of "inside washing of one's dirty laundry" (see Griffiths 1985), a strongly held view in Igboland. This principle was frequently mentioned during the disputing process, and everyone seemed to share a common concern to hold the family together. Traditionally, the Igbos distrust outside groups. Each family attempts to resolve intrafamily disputes within, lest "enemies" or outsiders use such disputes to undermine family security.

In this cultural context, a sense of reconciliation is the paramount goal, not necessarily punishment. Even when fault is attributed, punishment is aimed at reintegration. The disputants' representatives and other adult members participate in the resolution. The web of socioeconomic relations between disputants (e.g., spouses, family and village members, or business partners) is rationally considered in choosing a system of justice that would not upset the status quo (Van Velsen 1964). Contrary to Merry (1979), the past duration and frequency of disputants' relationship is as important as its future in disputing. Eighty-one percent (N=224) of my survey respondents indicated that they would consider long-term relationships with the other party in selecting a disputing mode (see further Table 2.1). Even in the supposedly fragile market relationships in the urban areas (cf. Gluckman 1955; also Merry 1979), indigenous modes of justice are used in resolving cases where the disputants are nonstrangers or fellow villagers. Eighty percent of those in the urban sample (N=84) reported that they have, at least once, used some form(s) of indigenous justice. In contrast, formal law tends to be used in situations (e.g., involving strangers) when such informal, indigenous forms of law are absent or ineffective (cf. Merry 1979; see also Uwazie 1994).

Table 2.1 Nature of Disputants' Relationships: "To whom would you complain if you have a case with . . . ?"

Type of Relationship	Percentage Formal[a]	Percentage Indigenous	Valid N
Spouse	33.3	66.7	177
Family Member	1.4	98.6	215
Neighbor	12.0	88.0	213
Village Member	3.3	96.7	215
Another Villager	16.3	83.7	203
Total Stranger	46.3	53.7	190
Total N (Urban and Rural)=			226

Note: [a] Formal includes police and court, while Indigenous includes village/family tribunals (Amalia), chief (eze), age grade, married daughters (Umuada), oracle priest (dibia), etc.

The belief that many family matters are better resolved through reconciliation than by litigation (see further Starr and Yngvesson 1975) is held by 64 percent (N=198) of those surveyed who said they would report spousal grievances first to the family head. Indeed, 77 percent (N=224) of the respondents said that they would first report any disputes with a family member to the family head. The lower percentage use of the family head in spousal cases, compared with a family member, could have two explanations. First, domestic disputes are so intimate that the couple seek outside intervention after exhausting such unilateral actions as toleration, avoidance, or negotiation; this was reiterated by Mmadie. Secondly, a couple usually use their respective parents to resolve their disagreement before going to the family head. In contrast, conflicts between separate households in the family fall under the jurisdiction of the family head, for example, land matters between married brothers, or uncle versus nephew.

Airing one's dirty laundry in public (at the village square) may attract shame to the disputants to the extent that it compromises the privacy of their association or intimacy. It also undermines the prestige and honor of a family because it challenges the symbolic influence of the family head. In fact, the Dozie family had a long-standing rule to report all cases, especially civil and minor criminal offenses, to the family head before taking them to an outside agency. Similarly, the village mandates that all cases be brought to the attention of the village head before a complaint is filed with the police or court. Any villager or family member who violates this rule receives severe sanctions, ranging from stiff fines[2] to a conditional period of ostracism. The "inside resolution" approach to spousal and other intrafamily conflicts ensures that a dispute does not disrupt the ongoing relationships or undercut the group's unity and solidarity.[3]

■ The Nature of a Dispute

The nature of a case is another factor in the selection of a dispute mode (Goldberg et al. 1985; Fuller 1978). For example, polycentric disputes have underlying implications, and they require a disputing mode that involves solutions beyond the immediate problem. Such disputes may not be properly resolvable by the rules of court procedures. My study suggests that the formal legal system may serve as a token response to disputes over scarce resources by pretending to have control while actually deferring to a more amenable means of settlement. For example, court or police case referrals to the indigenous, or less formal, social control mechanism may coerce the disputants to accept the latter's decision, while the former appears to be the actual source of resolution. My study suggests that the police and court and the village tribunal respectfully cooperate in the management of disputes, also revealing that the indigenous justice system does not necessarily defer to state law in case of conflicts of laws.

□ *The Case of Land and Assault*

The villagers called her *Nwanyiukwu* (big, bad woman) because of her reported disrespect for several village judgments against her. She had been heavily fined for deriding the Amalia, or village elders, and the traditional ruler or chief (*eze*), uttering taboo curse words, and for disorderly conduct—publicly flashing her buttocks at the elders. After ten years of contemptuous behavior, the villagers ostracized her.

On the night of March 22, 1989, Nwanyiukwu, with her two sons and a daughter, confronted and assaulted her husband's brother, Oma, and his family. The confrontation occurred over disputed land that had been temporarily allocated to Nwanyiukwu's late husband.[4] Oma testified before the village tribunal that he had reclaimed the land after the death of his brother, partly to show his dislike for Nwanyiukwu's disruptive behavior, whom he described as "a mad, troublesome woman." Reportedly, Oma had never liked his brother's wife, especially since the villagers suspected her of contributing to her husband's death by manipulating him to swear a false oath regarding the theft of a chicken in 1968.

Other members of Oma's family offered contemptuous, negative descriptions of Nwanyiukwu's disruptive and quarrelsome behavior in the village. They cited several village and family judgments against her, stating that she had been ostracized from both her family and the village for not abiding by prior decisions. Consequently, Nwanyiukwu, having realized her reputation in the village, filed criminal charges of aggravated assault with the police. Oma was arrested and, after spending five hours in the police cell, released to the custody of the village chief. Six months after this incident, the police advised both parties to resolve their decision through the village moot. Also, the parties were required to report to the police station upon request. At the time the villagers gathered to hear this case in November 1989, both parties reported countless visits to the police station, ten miles away. The parties also reported that an undisclosed large amount of cash had been paid to the police as a bribe. As the police had expected, the village tribunal, including the disputants' own representatives,[5] resolved the case after two hearings over a two-week period (personal interview with Police Investigator, November 25, 1989). The police decision to refer this case to the village tribunals and the villagers' subsequent decision reveal a situation of "mutual deference" between the two competing legal spheres.[6]

Interestingly, the natives also de-emphasized the assault charges; instead, they concentrated on resolving the underlying or precipitating land dispute. Nwanyiukwu was orally censured for starting the fight, but each party was responsible for its own medical expenses stemming from the assault. In addition, in an unprecedented move, the Oma family agreed to divide their family land into individual family allocations.[7] Subsequently, a final agreement was submitted to and accepted by the police as a final resolution of this case.

Police or court referral of certain cases to the indigenous legal order is a common practice in the Nigerian legal system. Twenty-nine percent (N=76) of the disputants who have used the formal legal (i.e., police/court) system reported that their cases were at one time referred to the native tribunals. For example, 98 percent (N=222) of the respondents reported that they would rather use the indigenous justice system than the court or police to resolve land matters; only 7 percent (N=194) of those who have used the indigenous system reported that they appealed the decision.[8]

However, disputes over scarce resources may force a single-issue disputing intervention like the court. In such situations, the disputed resource is ranked higher, or held to be of greater importance, than any existing relationships (Starr and Yngvesson 1975; Forman 1972). Thus disputants may be willing to sacrifice the social relationship in order to gain access to, or exclusive use of, the resource. Scarcity of land appears to have caused Nwanyiukwu's physical confrontation with her brother-in-law, thereby forcing a readjustment of the entire family landholding.

However, an appeal for a court resolution of such a land dispute is only symbolic; it subtly coerces the disputants to seek resolution at the village moot. For example, the police in *Nwanyiukwu vs. Oma* used subtle coercion by referring the case to the village tribunals while retaining jurisdiction until an acceptable decision was reached. The numerous "invitations" to the police station also may have been a police strategy to discourage the use of formal law in the case. A senior magistrate told me that 99 percent of the land cases in his court were appealed from the village moot, and that he usually referred a majority of them back to the native tribunal.

□ *The Case of the Family Iroko Tree: "Life-Wire" of the Family*

The oracle or voodoo priest (*dibia*) had told Chukwu's family to consecrate a particular tree, at a certain location, for their family worship. The location had to be kept secret and carefully disguised from the public, lest enemies desecrate it. The iroko tree, known as "Ozondu" (life-wire), forms the past, present, and future of this family: it is the center of ancestral worship and sacrifices, as well as healing.

The Chukwu family acquired this tree from Ako in a rather complex and confusing manner, prompting a disgruntled member of the Ako family, Ejim, to resell it to Agim Ohihi after the death of the Ako family head. The Chukwu family was very surprised when this tree was felled to be sawed into planks in 1978 by Agim. The action prompted a lawsuit against Agim and Ejim.

After ten years of countless court delays and changes of attorneys and venues, the magistrate advised the parties and their respective attorneys to seek a resolution of the case in the village. And, as in *Nwanyiukwu vs. Oma,* the court asked to be informed of the village decision. The disputants recollected that both the defense and plaintiff counsels observed two of the several village moot sessions (personal interview: December 10, 1989).

This case provides another insight into land custom in Igboland. The Chukwus acquired this iroko tree from Iwuoha Ako, the head of the Ako family, but without the land on which the tree was located. No outsider witnessed this transaction, as this would undermine the necessary secrecy; no written contract existed. Upon Iwuoha's death, his eldest son, Ihiala, thirty-six, inherited his title as well as this case.

By custom, the family head, though entrusted with all family land, can conduct sales transactions only with the unanimous consent of other entitled family members. However, Ihiala testified before the village moot that his uncle, Ejim, was not at home when his father sold the tree to the Chukwu family. He also explained that his father was solely responsible for the burial of his grandfather, without any help or compensation from any of his uncles, thereby justifying his father's conduct in selling the tree to Chukwu.

Ejim was living in the southeastern city of Calabar when his parents died, and they were buried by Iwuoha. Ejim returned to his ancestral home after the Nigerian civil war and requested a parcel of family land for farming. Iwuoha refused the requested land until he was compensated for their parents' funeral expenses. Ejim protested that Iwuoha's condition was unreasonable, and demanded a full account of the funeral expenses minus all the benefits that Iwuoha might have gained from their family land over a twelve-year period. Ejim resented Iwuoha's apparent sole control of their family land, but thought he was unable to dispute with the family head. However, after ten years away from home, he began to gather some information from other villagers about the family land.

Ejim learned of the sale of the iroko tree soon after Iwuoha's death, and confronted the heir, Ihiala, about his or Iwuoha's failure to disclose such information to him. Ihiala reiterated his father's demand for compensation before disclosing such information about their family land. He also reiterated the oath of secrecy between Chukwu and his father. Ejim stated that he sold the tree to protest Iwuoha's conduct, but it was also a challenge to Ihiala's leadership. As the Amalia (village tribunal) deliberated over this case, they recounted several past land disputes between Iwuoha and Ejim, revealing what seemed to be a feud between the two brothers.

The Amalia first decided that the initial and the second transactions were invalid because they lacked the consent of the other family members. They reasoned that Iwuoha, despite the need for secrecy, could have merely leased the tree for a specified period of time, instead of selling it outright. A lease transaction would have allowed a negotiation about consecrating another family tree, or a renewal of the lease on some family consensual terms. Also, the Amalia said that Iwuoha should have sworn Ejim to secrecy about the iroko sale, with the requirement that Ejim could share in the proceeds after compensating Iwuoha for the funeral expenses. However, the Amalia strongly condemned Ejim's resale of a family tree as "homicide," and as a provocation of conflict. They rebuked him for not seeking reconciliation, given that he did not perform the required funeral rites for his parents.

Agim Ohihi was blamed for knowingly buying and felling a family tree, for as a native (*nwa ala*), he should have respected the Igbo custom that forbids one from buying disputed property. However, Agim's behavior coincided with the village rumors about past land disputes between the Ohihi and Chukwu families, reportedly a constant source of conflict.

In the lawsuit, the Chukwus had asked for an unspecified amount of punitive and compensatory damages from Ejim and Agim. This suggests that social relationships could be sacrificed where the object of dispute is invaluable or where the available native options, for example, self-help violence, may be socially or legally unattractive. At the Amalia, the Chukwus went beyond the court claims to accuse Agim and Ejim of intentional genocide; this reflects the dire consequences of desecrating a family tree, a consideration that would not be relevant in a court proceeding. As Merry (1979, 908) states, "As disputants became more emotionally committed to the dispute, their moves and reactions . . . intensify and escalate"; they may seek recourse to court or self-help.

Nonetheless, the various circumstances of the iroko case seemed to have informed the Amalia judgment: (1) Ihiala should designate another tree for the Chukwu family or pay for all expenses to perform another consecration ceremony; (2) Agim and Ejim must perform certain sacrifices to appease the gods and ward off any evil that might befall the Chukwu family; and (3) the iroko should not be used for any purpose. At the time of judgment, the tree had almost decayed into compost soil (after twelve years of disputing), and the Chukwu family retorted that their ancestral spirit had rightfully consumed it. It was expected that the Mba East Magistrate court would accept the judgment of the Amalia, with the assured approval of the disputants.

The final question in this case reveals another condition of interactions between competing laws, which describes the "law of convergence (and divergence) of norms" (Griffiths 1985, 223). The substantive norms of competing disputing processes may converge because "neither (form of justice) can afford that the other appears to offer a higher quality" of justice—for fear of loss of potential cases (Griffiths 1985, 224). In this regard one system of law may trade its effectiveness in substance for its ineffectiveness in procedure. Generally, the Nigerian courts hold indigenous justice decisions valid and binding if the disputants willingly and voluntarily requested it, agreed to accept the decision, and if the procedures and outcomes conform to the particular custom or native law (see Nigerian Supreme Court Justice Karibi-Whyte in *Agu vs. Ikewibe* 1993; *Okere vs. Nwoke* 1991).

□ *The Villagers Versus the School Committee*

By 11 P.M. on December 12, 1989, the village "town crier" or messenger had visited every kindred to make a public announcement of a village meeting at 6 A.M. the following morning. Later, about two hours before the appointed time, he beat the wooden bell several times to remind the villagers of this very important meeting, and threatened to fine any adults who did not attend.

The villagers formed a quorum (as each of the ten kindred groups was represented) as the meeting began about an hour later than scheduled, reflecting a common mockery of "Igboman's time." About sixty adult villagers, mostly males, had gathered at the village square to hear a case between the Umuofo kindred and the Ezeala School Committee. The village chairman introduced the case, stating that he had received a complaint from the Umuofo group protesting a plan to acquire their land for secondary school construction. On the heels of the chairman's introduction, the Umuofo group leader narrated how the "Go-menti" (government) had surveyed several acres of their family land without their unanimous approval or adequate compensation.

The school committee chairman responded that the committee had adhered to the state land use decree in its effort to acquire the disputed land. He explained the financial constraints imposed by the large compensations demanded by the complainants. He also reiterated the community development benefits from building the only secondary school in Ezeala village. However, the case posed a direct conflict between custom and state law.

By custom, unanimous approval from the various family groups must be granted to acquire their land. This custom is in contrast to the land use decree that has its own set standards for compensation. Also, the Umuofo people alleged that the school committee gained approval of some of their members through bribery and co-optation, a likely action that may have been aimed at undermining a more unified, populous challenge to acquiring the land. Nonetheless, the villagers had to decide whether the lack of unanimity in granting the land outweighed the community interest in building an educational institution. After seven hours of marathon moot sessions, the village chairman privately disclosed to the leader of the plaintiffs the decision to slightly increase the compensation, to be paid in installments over a one-year period. The Umuofo group shouted "No!" to this final offer and subsequently sought a court restraining order against any trespass on their land.

During the hearing for a temporary injunction, the magistrate heard testimony from some of the villagers who had decided the case at the village moot. In court, the plaintiffs reiterated their protest, threatening to perform dangerous charms (voodoo) and to destroy any structures erected on the disputed land. After the hearing, the magistrate issued an interim injunction, but strongly advised the parties to seek a resolution at the village level (Mba East Magistrate court, January 12, 1990). Although the land use decree has been criticized by the courts as unfair, corrupt, and uncustomary (personal interviews with Justice Achi-Kanu, December 18, 1989; Chief Magistrate Elkuma-Nkama, November 10, 1990), the court must decide the issue of "equity" in the amount of compensation to the plaintiffs.

Ala (land) forms the central core of Igbo consciousness. In fact, the totality of Igbo life—culture and customs—revolves around it (Isichei 1976). The people worship *ala,* and their food and water come from it. Famine or low agricultural productivity and illness come from human offenses against gods of *ala,* and they usually attract heavy penalties and sacrifices.

The ubiquitous prominence of land, coupled with its scarcity in most parts of Igboland, make it almost impossible to assess adequate monetary compensation in land disputes. For these reasons, land disputes are very frequent, and many involve very dangerous and feared means of settlement such as voodoo or witchcraft, or other types of self-help. The use or threat of voodoo and vandalism is a practical limitation in enforcing any resented action or judgment by the court, and this seemed to have informed the presiding magistrate's advice about seeking a village resolution. On the other hand, the prospect of a lengthy and costly court process may force the disputants to reconcile through the village tribunal.

■ Socioeconomic Status

Disputants' selection of a disputing mode is isomorphic to their social environment or relative social status or power, for example, sex, education, and income (see also Nader 1969b; Lowy 1971; Merry 1982). Since legal structures affect the distribution of power in many societies, we need to understand the behavior of disputants in legal systems, relative to their status.

Minority groups use the formal legal system for resolving such disputes as property (Abel 1973), especially in simple societies; this also seems to reflect the justice expectations of litigants in Western courts. Merry (1982), for example, states that mediation in nonindustrialized societies is beneficial or fair only when the disputants are "equals." My analysis examines how two possible indicators of power (income and education) affect the use of the indigenous and formal legal systems.

It has been argued that the formal legal system is a litigious arena dominated by those with higher income and education (Cappelletti 1978; Goldberg et al. 1985), especially when inequalities in income and education exist between disputants. This view implies that disputants with lower income and education might use mechanisms other than the formal law to seek redress. Higher income helps to ensure access, while a more educated disputant tends to better understand the intricacies of the formal legal system. Therefore, formal or state law supposedly equalizes the differences between disputants (Nader and Todd 1978), and indigenous law is viewed negatively by such disputants.

However, my data suggest that the effects of income and level of education may depend on the types of cases and relationships between disputants. It has been stated earlier in the chapter that the use of police is forbidden by the village tribunal because it is viewed as "bad" and disruptive of the social network. An Igbo proverb, "Whoever cheats the poor would answer to the god," reflects a conscientious deterrence to the use of the police, especially when the parties are not equals. It is believed that the ancestors protect the poor and would punish any powerful person or group that mistreats them. In fact, the villagers resent wealthy or powerful natives who resort to the court or police in disputes with a party who is not as powerful. A wealthy man who harasses the poor, for example, is contemptuously referred to as *Nwokeukwu* (big, bad man); his misfortunes are blamed on his disregard or unfairness toward the not-so-rich members. For example, the villagers attributed the sudden death of the first son of a veteran village political leader to his father's "sins" against the poor. Perception of a "big, bad man" seems to be worrisome to those who receive such social labels.

In a court case observed, a retired magistrate, Akuobi, was sued by some of his family members over a land dispute. By the time the case was appealed to court, it had been decided by the Umuada and the village tribunal. Akuobi, who also was the family head, insisted that he was to inherit the family land as the sole surviving legitimate child. The other family members, he contended, were "bastards" or born out of wedlock, and by custom, though unconstitutional, they had no inheritance rights in the family. But each time he tried to sell this four-acre land, the family members obstructed the sale. However, the court recognized Akuobi's role as the family head as well as the plaintiff's legal rights by awarding a half acre of the land to Akuobi, while the remaining three and a half acres would be equally divided among the five family members, including Akuobi.[9]

Despite the relatively high level of education among the Igbo, they respect custom. It is very common to see college-educated Igbos with strong loyalty to the culture, evidenced by their participation in the various native organs of disputing and government, or as disputants in the indigenous justice (Uwazie 1991). Also, the presence of voodoo or other forms of self-help may make use of the police or court culturally unattractive, forcing the powerful to be responsible or to seek native reconciliation. A weaker party may resort to other competitive, indigenous avenues to seek or to forestall justice (see further Nader 1969b). During my fieldwork, a wealthy educated villager told me that a poor fellow villager was responsible for his undiagnosed illness that had baffled both native and medical doctors for five years. He believed he was bewitched by the other party after winning a land case in court. Other villagers told me that they had complained to the village tribunal after a party had threatened them with voodoo to protest judgments.

■ Experiences of Disputants

Positive and negative attitudes and experiences of disputants about a particular justice mode affect their frequency of use (Merry 1979; see further Table 2.2). The informal forms of dispute management arguably provide better access, cost, efficiency, satisfaction, and therapy than the formal

Table 2.2 Comparative Attitudes and Experiences: "Which system do you think is more . . . ?"

Variable	Percentage Formal	Percentage Indigenous	Valid N
Costly (time and money)	99.0	1.0	221
Accessible	16.0	84.0	220
Satisfactory	33.0	67.0	190
Total N (Urban and Rural) =			226

legal system (Cain 1985; Tomasic and Feeley, eds., 1982; Danzig 1973). I expect that indigenous justice is used because it offers certain better alternatives than the formal legal system (police and court).

Disputants have much quicker and easier access to any of the types of indigenous justice than to the police or court. A disputant simply orally complains to the family head or village chief/chairperson. In cases where both disputants are women, the aggrieved party complains by loud shouts of "*egbe-ee!*" during the particular incident, to be echoed by other women as they rush to the scene. A case may be resolved immediately upon such a complaint, or a date is set for a public hearing at the village square or at another neutral site.

In contrast, the bureaucratic maze of filing petitions in the formal legal system may be so frustrating that it discourages potential clients. The rules and legal jargon of the English-based legal system are often too confusing. The distance of the police station or courthouse from the disputants further inhibits the access. The cost of access to the formal legal system may be prohibitively high, for example, hiring an attorney or bribing the police or court registrar before one's complaint is filed.

■ Conclusions

In sum, an assessment of the Nigerian legal culture reveals a condition of multiple legal orders, encompassing both state and nonstate modes of justice; they also vary in their forms of disputing: mediation, negotiation, arbitration, self-help, gossip, divination, or avoidance and toleration. The modes of conflict resolution or settlement vary from the comparatively well organized Hausa-Fulani Islamic justice in the north, through the advanced judicial chieftaincy institutions of the Yoruba in the southwest, to the highly decentralized Igbo legal arrangements. Each mode of indigenous justice assumes that law is a functional element of society, a means of social ordering and practical solutions to inevitable normal human conflicts. Hence, the primary purpose of the law or traditional conflict management is peacekeeping and maintenance of the social equilibrium in the community (Uwazie 1991).

The leaders or chiefs and their council of elders have a holistic view of their society and often conceive their role in terms of the community welfare. Dispute management is seen as reconciliation of divergent interests, which preserves the physical existence and spiritual well-being of the whole society (see also Albert et al. 1995; Uwazie 1994). While problems of the complexity and varieties of custom or tradition exist, and their interactions with formal law seem uneasy, legal coexistence remains inevitable, necessary, and mutually beneficial. Although attempts or suggestions to incorporate or codify customary law may be futile and unnecessary, there is need to develop certain consensual criteria for balancing the attendant conflicts of laws. Future study should focus on methods for developing and analyzing such criteria. It also suggests the critical need for curriculum reforms in Nigeria's legal education and training that respect the proper place of the indigenous justice.

■ Notes

1. For purposes of confidentiality, all personal and place names are pseudonyms, though they are indigenous names. Any coincidences are highly regretted.

2. I observed a case where a prominent villager was fined 50 naira (U.S.$13) for calling the police to report a young man who had connected (public) electricity through the villager's line without his consent.

3. Most of the villagers stressed to me the need for maintaining social harmony; most view the use of police/court as harassment (see Merry 1979) or "very bad." Also, the elders enhance their reputation and prestige from their ability to manage such village/family conflicts.

4. Information was gathered from police reports and interviews with the disputants and other family members. In fact, as a neutral literate observer, I was asked to write up the terms of the native decision to be forwarded to the police.

5. Villagers would assemble at the village square after a town crier's early morning notice. The case is heard with disputants' representatives participating in a secret deliberation to render judgment.

6. The investigating police officer told me that none of the potential witnesses was willing to testify in court on behalf of Nwanyiukwu.

7. Land ownership is communal, and individual allocation is temporary, with the family head presiding over all transactions concerning family land. Land sale or mortgage must be by consensus of the adult male family members.

8. This view was confirmed by my interviews with judges and magistrates. They told me that most land cases come to the court by way of appeals, implying that they must have been heard first at the native level.

9. The 1978 Nigerian Land Use Decree asserts eminent domain. This decree has been criticized for its alleged tribalistic and corrupt motivations. Some argue

that it was initiated by Nigerian soldiers who, after retirement, returned to settle in the attractive federal capital, Lagos, but were resented by the mostly Yoruba land- and homeowners. In protest, others allege these powerful army veterans used the decree also to enrich themselves.

3

Bases of Traditional Conflict Management Among the Buems of the Ghana-Togo Border

Ben K. Fred-Mensah

This chapter presents and examines the bases of traditional conflict management practices among the Buem people of the Ghana-Togo border, ranging from general socialization processes through adjudication procedures to the invocation of transcendental powers. The various modes, mechanisms, and forums that the Buems employ to prevent, resolve, or control conflict situations are examined against the background of the people's concept of social harmony and the limitations of their traditional political order. The analysis takes into account the local variables that may facilitate, detain, or even totally prevent conflict resolution, including relationships between disputants, the bases of the disputes, geographical proximity of the disputants, and the willingness of disputants to have the dispute resolved.

■ The Buems of the Ghana-Togo Border

Buem-Kator (eastern or upper Buem), along the central part of the Ghana-Togo border, is a cluster of farming communities that constitutes the eastern portion of the larger Buem Traditional Area in the Jasikan District of the Volta region of Ghana, and marks the eastern limit of the Bia-Akwapin-Togo mountain ranges that run across the middle of the country.

The soils were formed from the rich volcanic rocks of the mountain ranges and are some of the best agricultural soils in Ghana. However, due to extensive cultivation of both food crops such as rice, cassava, and plantain and cash crops, of which cocoa and coffee are the principal ones, the area is significantly depleted of the original forest cover (Darkoh 1964a, 1964b).

The Buem Traditional Area as a whole is the largest and politically dominant ethnic group in the northern portion of the Volta region. Kinship, politics, and conflict management are inextricably intertwined.

The largest kinship unit in Buem-Kator is the agnatic clan (*kodua*). Most Buem settlements were founded by clans and in most cases the names of the clan leaders have been stamped on such settlements. Next to the clan is the lineage (*letifo*), which also originated from a remote male ancestor whose name is applied to the group. The functional significance of kinship in Buem is felt more at the lineage than at the clan level. Lineages serve as the social frame of reference for their members and form the basis of communal life and individual and group identities. Lineages hold ancestral properties, and lineage heads are thus assigned the responsibility of allocating land to lineage members for the purpose of farming and housing. Buem lineages are also expected to offer eligible members to be recruited into the various political and ritual offices, including the traditional judicial councils.

The Buem Traditional Area is a politically centralized chiefdom, though there is a wide devolution of powers and functions to administrative and geopolitical constituents. The highest political authority is represented by a paramount chief (an *omanhene*), the life president of the traditional council, recognized by the government as a first-class chief, and judicial head of the area. The superior court of the traditional area is thus the paramount chief's court, which is situated in an open-air space in his palace in the traditional capital, Borada.

The paramount chief discharges his judicial functions with the assistance of a council of elders. His court is normally composed of the queen mother, senior divisional chiefs, the chief farmer (*muosenioga*), and the chief fetish priest (*orfouo kpani*) of the chiefdom. He is represented in the various Buem towns and villages by divisional chiefs. Like the paramount chief's court, the court in every subchiefdom is administered by the divisional chief, who presides over and is assisted by a similar council of elders. A town chief's court, normally situated in his house or in an open-air space in front of his house, is the last court of appeal in the town. Serious cases such as sacrilege, murder, and infringement of any of the town's well-known taboos are reported directly to the town chief's court.

■ Nature and Sources of Conflicts in Buem-Kator

Even though Buems insist on social harmony as the overriding ideology of their community, people do not follow the dictates of the rules of community with "slavish, fascinated, passive obedience" (Malinowski 1959, 9–10; Gluckman 1965a, 202). As in any other community, conflicts are part of Buem-Kator social life. Conflicts occur within lineages, between members of different lineages, and between sections of Buem-Kator and their non-Buem neighbors. In defining their conflict situations, Buems distinguish between anger (*konyi*), quarrel (*kador*), fighting or dueling (*bekpeligiti*), and war (*kekpe*). Disputes in the community commonly involve breach of contract, slander, and witchcraft and sorcery accusations. Conflicts can also result from marital misunderstandings, injuries against persons, damage against property, and disparaging statements, particularly against a public official or against another lineage. Buems also commonly argue or fight over inheritance, land boundaries, and rights of access and control over land. Conflicts with non-Buem neighbors are commonly over land along their common borders or over territorial security issues.

■ Conflict Management Practices in Buem-Kator

Kanye Ndu Bowi. Anthropologists who apply structural-functionalist perspectives to the study of social control have provided some understanding of conflict management and the maintenance of social order in precolonial African societies. Attention has been drawn to the use of coercion and the mediating role of conventions, norms, and moral principles as mechanisms through which political authority is upheld and social order maintained (Fortes and Evans-Pritchard 1940; Gluckman 1956). Coercion and morality are thus viewed as the mechanisms of social control. Buems maintain that the overriding concern of their normative order is to sustain social harmony in the social systems.[1] The philosophical foundation of this worldview is encapsulated in the phrase *kanye ndu bowi,* "the ingredients of harmony."

Kanye ndu bowi is a broad ideological orientation that encompasses all manner of social control and modes of conflict management in the area. One important means by which Buems translate *kanye ndu bowi* into practical reality is through the imposition of "intrinsic sanctions," the subtle but pervasive means by which members of the Buem-Kator community are molded into complying with the rules of social control—the moral code, the normative order, and the belief and value systems (Nukunya 1992, 81; Radcliffe-Brown 1952, 205; Gluckman 1965a, 202–207). Intrinsic sanctions are both positive (the psychic rewards that the people receive when they conform to the approved mode of behavior) and negative (the feeling of moral discomfort that the people experience when they default).

The Buem creation of an ideology of social harmony involves the manipulation of social relationships through the use and strengthening of myths, beliefs, values, and motives (Cohen 1974, 81). The inculcation of the ideology of social harmony, as the Buem elders maintain, is an ongoing process and an integral part of the Buem socialization process—the culturally approved means by which the people strive to achieve conformity to the rules of conduct and ensure the continuity of the community.

Individuals in Buem-Kator are essentially compelled to comply with the rules of conduct, settle disputes, and abide by the outcomes of mediations or court settlements. Buem elders hold the view that a failure to comply with the rules of social control undermines the social order and is tantamount to an assault on the community as a whole. Such failures are often met not only with the imposition of fines but also with strong condemnation by the public, whose duty it is to provide public officials with loyalty and support in enforcing community rules. The need to settle disputes and abide by terms of dispute settlement is also motivated by the fact that members of the community are invariably in ongoing social and economic relationships and must necessarily deal with each other in the future.

Because Buems are often inextricably related by blood and marital ties, distance does not normally make people eschew settlement of disputes. Buems generally believe that they all have descended from common ancestors who originally lived at Korbuja, the first Buem settlement in Buem-Kator. From Korbuja, they migrated to found their present settlements. The founders of the three youngest Buem settlements—Kute, New Ayoma, and Odumase—were said to have descended from clans in the older Buem settlements.

Crosscutting ties derived from marriage are another reason that Buems are motivated to settle disputes. Buems generally believe that marriages are social contracts that transcend the relationship between the married couples. As the elders often insist, "marriages are not between a man and a woman. They are between lineages." Buems thus believe that a fight between any two Buems is ipso facto a fight between blood relations. In line with this, Buems often say that *ortorkeme li temi,* or "house matter must not be allowed to be heard by outsiders." This is a case of the prohibiting of "outside washing of dirty linen." They also often say that *kesiade kayor na bulie,* or "peace should prevail for us to live in." The desire here is to contain all manner of conflicts among themselves at the lowest possible level of the social and the political order.[2]

The individual in Buem-Kator is often viewed as the chief determinant of conflict prevention. This thinking finds expression in the saying that "it is the crooked leg that draws mud and smears it unto the straight one." Buems are aware that most conflicts that tend to assume extralineage or community-level dimensions originate with recalcitrant and recidivous individuals. In this regard, the relationships between the individual and his or her lineage regarding conflict management are twofold: as a bearer of the lineage name, the individual is expected to uphold a positive image of the lineage through his or her social conduct; lineage members are also expected to stand unfailingly by a member who is involved in any manner of dispute. Lineage heads play an extra role by making sure that any member of the group who is summoned for any form of wrongdoing attends the court hearing and pays the court fines that may be imposed. The socialization processes of individuals are thus manipulated by lineage members in particular and the larger community as strategies of inculcating the culturally approved attitudes and conduct in their members.

☐ *Buem-Kator Dispute-Handling Forums*

Benyaogba Ukpikator. The most common conflict-handling forum in Buem-Kator is *benyaogba ukpikator,* which literally means "to say no to a case between adversaries." The closest English equivalent for *benyaogba ukpikator* is mediation. *Benyaogba ukpikator* provides adversaries the forum to underplay conflicts and amicably convince each other that whatever may be the matter between them is of no significance. This procedure of conflict management is expected to eschew the adversarial deliberations and winner-loser mentality that are associated with adjudication and arbitration. *Benyaogba ukpikator* is a generally flexible and adaptable method of resolving disputes between kin members and between neighbors who live close to each other and are involved in ongoing social and economic relationships. It is thus considered to be the most desirable mode of dispute settlement. As Merry (1989, 82) puts it,

> Mediation is most likely to succeed between disputants whose various residential and kinship ties require them to deal with one another in the future. In other words, it is a phenomenon of communities. When social relationships are enduring, disputants need to find a settlement to continue to live together amicably.

The Buem managers of *benyaogba ukpikator* are usually lineage elders, medicine men, priests, and influential individuals who are known for their wisdom, skills, and trustworthiness in dispute settlement. They normally enjoy a wide reputation within their communities and have the capability to persuade and even manipulate individuals who have been summoned to attend the hearing.[3] Lineage heads or individual Buems who have excelled in the art of negotiation and the handling of *benyaogba ukpikator* are often called upon to mediate conflicts outside their communities. This is the case of the current Chief Farmer of New Ayoma. This man is an elder from the Agbo lineage whose ancestry is traced to the Obuosia Clan, one of the four founding clans of New Ayoma. Among his successes in mediation was the resolution of a chronic land boundary dispute between two farming sections of Baglo and Old Ayoma. This mediation has been deemed successful by the fact that it is ten years now since the dispute was mediated and none of the parties has raised any objection to the process or returned to a conflictual relationship.

Bate Kate. Buems use the phrase *bate kate* to refer to either arbitration or adjudication. *Bate kate* can be conducted either at a lineage head's court or in a town chief's court, depending upon the gravity of the offense (Swartz 1966, 100). Buems say that they always try to avoid *bate kate,* which they consider to be time-consuming, not only to the adversarial parties, but also to their respective kinsfolk who are customarily obliged to accompany them to hearings. *Bate kate* is a more elaborate process than *benyaogba ukpikator* because the former proceeds in stages and normally involves intensive cross-examination and assembling of witnesses and, when necessary, exhibits. In terms of monetary outlay, *bate kate* can be expensive, because fines and, in some cases, costs are imposed on convicted parties. Cases that are submitted for *bate kate* include those that either have failed to be resolved by *benyaogba ukpikator* or are constitutionally defined as criminal. Criminal cases include murder, treason, and disparaging statements against chiefs or public officials. Infringements of well-revered taboos of the chiefdom are also criminal and must be settled at a town chief's court. Appeals from lower courts have to be sent to the next higher court (Busia 1951; Boahen 1966).

In practice, however, most disputes are settled at the town level. Participants usually detest the costs (in terms of time and physical resources) that are incurred when cases are allowed to go through a number of steps before they are finally settled. There is the notion among the Buems that if a dispute can be settled at all, it must be possible to settle it at the lowest level. Since kinfolk of disputing parties are traditionally expected to support kin members and accompany them to all courts, they tend to prevail upon kith and kin to accept a settlement at the lowest possible court.

Deliberations at *bate kate* can be an elaborate process. In line with the usual procedure of *bate kate,* each disputant, without interruption, presents his or her version of what has occurred. After both have been heard, adjudicators closely question each disputant on the basis of what he or she has said. The objective is to reach an agreement on a single story by eliminating ambiguous elements in the statements of the adversaries. There is extensive use of evidence, witnesses, and cross-examination. Court deliberations are usually opened to the general public and everyone present has the privilege to cross-examine any of the disputants. Order at court is strictly enforced and the use of abusive language is discouraged and can lead to contempt of court.

Adzina. *Adzina,* "going into seclusion to meditate on an issue," provides a miniforum to arrive at a verdict (*badunkortor*) from *bate kate,* the Buem version of "trial by jury." *Adzina* works this way: to arrive at a verdict in all manner of cases that come before a town chief or a lineage head, some attendants at the court who have been present throughout the court hearing and have been following the proceedings are appointed at the end of the hearing to deliberate and return a verdict. The "jury" is normally made up of representatives of the presiding judge (a chief or a lineage head), the adjudicating council, and the disputing parties. The "jury" will leave the courtroom and find a place out of sight where they will deliberate until they reach a verdict. In doing so, they are said to be consulting with the *abrewa*. The *abrewa* is a fictitious old woman endowed with wisdom and mystical powers that enable "her" to arrive at impartial judgments. Judgment is either accepted wholly and a fine is imposed on the convicted party, or it is rejected and the case is forwarded to a higher court. Through the returning "jurors," the *abrewa* will send a message of admonition to the convicted party and words of consolation to the innocent.

Witchcraft, sorcery, and ordeal. Buems commonly resort to the use of witchcraft (*kabor*) or sorcery (*kuve*) to settle conflict when they do not want to bring their grievances into the open *benyaogba ukpikator* or *bate kate*. In Buem thought, witchcraft refers to nonmaterial mystical means of attacking one's adversary, whereas sorcery involves both nonmaterial mystical means and material objects. The most prevalent mystical object used in sorcery is a substance literally called "black powder." To target one's victim, black powder, believed to contain malevolent spirits capable of causing damage, will secretly be sprinkled across his or her path while incantations are made. The desired effect is achieved when the targeted person becomes indisposed, or even dies, after coming into contact with the black powder. Whereas witchcraft is directed only at persons with whom the witch has a consanguine relationship, sorcery can be an effective mystical means of causing harm to any adversaries.

Kemuikadiakor, trial by ordeal, can also refer to oath-taking in the course of *bate kate*. Buems would traditionally resort to the use of *kemuikadiakor* as an adjunct to *bate kate* to determine guilt or innocence, particularly in theft cases in which evidence is so conflicting that adjudicators find it difficult to come to a decision by secular means (Assimeng 1981, 93; Kenyatta 1938, 225; Radcliffe-Brown 1940, xviii). Witchcraft and sorcery accusations also normally call for *kemuikadiakor* because the truth in the accusation is often difficult to determine by the secular processes of mediation and adjudication.

In the first stage of the *kemuikadiakor* process, the town chief will order the disputing persons to consult a medicine man, a fetish priest, or an oracle. The disputing parties will be accompanied by appointees of the chief and the heads of their respective lineages. Whoever is found guilty by the metaphysical consultant will immediately have his or her hair shaven to the skin and be made to settle all the costs related to the travel and the trial, plus fines imposed by the town chief on their return.

□ *Imposition of Banyinkortu*

Fines (*banyinkortu*) are normally imposed on the convicted parties. Fines are traditionally in kind, involving alcoholic beverages and livestock. The size of the fine depends on the gravity of the offense, the manner in which the convicted party has conducted himself or herself throughout the deliberation, and his or her previous record. Once the fines are paid, it is assumed that the settlement has been accepted by the disputants. With a calabash of drinks in hand, the local fetish priest will pour libation and close the deliberation this way: He will first address the gods and the earth: *Oh! Atibluku atsa kator* ("the almighty God up in the heavens") *kalor kemenge* ("the earth on which we stand"):

> According to the Old Woman's verdict, to which we the panel members have agreed, this party has been found guilty. We sympathize with the other party, the innocent party. With this drink, we beseech the gods to help us to restore peace between the adversarial parties. As both parties drink from this calabash, none should nurse malicious intentions against the other. Strike down whoever will nurse malicious intention toward the other, flout the authority of the judges, and attempt to bring calamity into the community.[4]

□ *Organized Fighting*

Exchanges of angry words (*kador*) and dueling (*bekpeligiti*) are common among Buems, though such situations are not usually allowed to progress into violent conflict. Individuals or groups may fight each other when it is impossible to submit themselves for a settlement through a third-party intervention. Buems maintain that they do not wage war (*kekpe*) against each other. Their custom is totally opposed to the spilling of blood on their soil, particularly the blood of Buems. Violent settlement of disputes among Buems is supposed to be restricted to the use of the fist. Weapons of any kind—stones, knives, clubs, sticks, spears, and guns—are banned and must not be used by Buems against each other. Whoever uses any form of weapon beyond the fist and spills the blood of a fellow Buem is liable to a fine of livestock, usually a ram (*kofonu*). This fine is imposed whether the individual is found guilty of the offense or not. Recently, a man inflicted cutlass injuries on his brother over a piece of their lineage land. Even though this man was found to be the rightful holder of the land and the injured brother a persistent trespasser, a fine of a ram and a quantity of alcoholic beverages was imposed on him for spilling the blood of a fellow Buem on Buem soil. With a ritual ceremony involving libation and the ram, the earth and the offender are believed to have been cleansed.

☐ *Fission*

Fission as a means of conflict management is similar to what Merry (1989) refers to as "moving away from conflict." Protracted disputes between or within clans of the same town are settled when one clan or a section of the clan breaks away from the others to found a new settlement elsewhere. Two towns in Buem-Kator—Odumase and Dzolu—were said to have been founded this way. The people of Dzolu were part of the larger Korbuja, the first Buem settlement in Buem-Kator. After a long quarrel between some sections of Korbuja over the control and use of oil palm trees, some clans decided to break away from Korbuja. Under the joint leadership of two men, Edze and Kpogadzi, these clans moved eastward to found the present town of Dzolu.

Odumase, the smallest Buem-Kator town, was also founded when one of the clans of Baglo, the Kpala Kuda Clan, broke away from the other clans (the Ordzormia Clan, the Ordormia Clan, the Orditia Clan, and the Kudubi Clan) and moved a few miles to the north of Baglo to found a new town. Until the Kpala Kuda Clan broke away, both the chief and the queen mother of Baglo were recruited from the Kpala Kuda Clan. Sometime in the 1950s members of the other four clans began to question the basis of the Kpala Kuda Clan's monopoly control over the sources of recruitment of both the town chief and the queen mother.

The other clans suggested that the queen mother be recruited from another clan while the Kpala Kuda Clan retained its status as the source of the recruitment of the town chief. Finding it impossible to resolve the matter in the subchiefdom, the leaders referred the case to the paramount chief's court at Borada, where it was settled in favor of the other clans. The court suggested that the queen mother be recruited from another clan while the Kpala Kuda retained its royal status as the source of recruitment of the town chief. The Kpala Kuda Clan appeared to have accepted the terms of the settlement and was accordingly pacified by being offered a ram and a quantity of alcoholic beverages.

At this stage, the conflict appeared to have been resolved. However, after consuming the food and the drinks, the Kpala Kuda Clan began to resent the paramount chief's ruling. The conflict intensified. To prevent an imminent bloodshed, the Kpala Kuda Clan decided in 1958 to break away to found its own town, Odumase, sometimes called Baglo Odumase.

Second-Order Conflicts

In Buem-Kator, cases are traditionally brought before either lineage heads or town chiefs for mediation or adjudication. However, there often is a question as to who is competent to handle a particular type of case. The traditional Buem constitution explicitly spells out the hierarchical order of the Buem politico-judicial system, showing the judicial powers and functions of chiefs and lineage heads. The constitution broadly distinguishes between criminal and civil cases and the courts that are competent to handle criminal cases. Treason, murder, and the spilling of blood are criminal cases and must be directly reported to the chief's court. Other cases like adultery and sex in the bush are civil cases, which can be settled at either a chief's court or a lineage head's court. The constitution has not, however, made it clear which civil cases must go to the chief's court and which cases can be settled at a lineage head's court. The constitution is also silent on the judicial role of influential individuals on whom people often rely for settling disputes.

This raises an important question: Can cases that involve public senior officials be reported to a lineage head's court, or to a conflict-settling forum to be headed by an influential individual whose constitutional status may be inferior to that of the public officials involved in the case? In other words, should senior public officials submit themselves to hearing before their juniors? The constitution is vague on this issue, and this gives rise to what I refer to here as *second-order* conflicts or conflicts about conflict resolution. Second-order conflicts refer to conflicts that emanate from the constitutional definition or lack thereof of the appropriate modes of conflict resolution.

Evidence from Buem-Kator shows that a second-order conflict can pose a greater problem to the social order than the initial conflict that gave rise to it. For example, a chief's spokesman (*okyeame*) accused the local fetish priest of making disparaging statements about him and reported the case to an influential individual for mediation. The fetish priest objected to the mediation on the grounds that he, as the town fetish priest, and the plaintiff, as the town chief's spokesman—two senior public officials—could not submit themselves to a hearing before their junior. He maintained that he would attend the hearing of the case only when it was removed from the proposed mediator's house to the town chief's court.

To complicate the matter further, the proposed mediator had sent for the town chief to attend the hearing. The chief did not disapprove, but sent an appointee with an explanation that he would be out of town and could not attend in person. The apparent failure of the chief to register his disapproval was interpreted by the proposed mediator as the recognition of his competence to hear the case. In an attempt to forestall setting a precedent over senior public officials' submission to hearings at their juniors' courts, the fetish priest appealed to the town chief to order the case to be removed to the latter's court.[5] The fetish priest maintained that he would appeal to the chief of Dzolu, the most senior chief in Buem-Kator, if the local town chief failed to act on his complaint. Judging from the nature of emotions involved in the case, an early intervention by the town chief was necessary to forestall a disruption of the social and the normative order.

□ *Buems and Their Neighbors*

Warfare (*kekpe*) is the usual means by which conflicts between Buems and their neighbors are settled. Most of the wars between Buems and their neighbors have been over scarce resources, notably land. Interests at stake in such wars are often so great that they are never resolved. They normally continue until both groups grow tired of the inconvenience of fighting or the pains of losing their men in the battle. There is always the possibility that such wars will continue in the future. The continuing hostilities between a section of New Ayoma and their neighbors at Akpafu and between Kute and Akposso in Togo over land boundaries are examples of such stalemates.

Buems say that they also fight when they perceive their neighbors' behavior to be a threat to their territorial security. They say they will fight a neighbor who they believe has provided military or any other form of assistance to another territory with which they were previously at war. Unlike wars over land, these forms of conflicts can be brought to an end by a third-party intervention. In this case, prestigious men from within any of the two fighting groups, or from a different territory, can be called upon to seek resolution through mediation and conciliation. An instance of this mode of conflict resolution was demonstrated in the war between a section of Buem-Kator and Ahlor in Togo. This war was brought to an end through the negotiating skills of a renowned and highly charismatic Roman Catholic priest named Father Dogli.

The Buem-Ahlor War began in 1938 and lasted until 1941. Today, it is difficult to establish the real cause of the war, though speculation suggests that the war was the result of an attempt by Buems to punish the people of Ahlor for assisting their enemies in an earlier war between the Buem Traditional Area and some of their northern neighbors in a cash-cropping area called Dzindzin. After three years, it became apparent to both parties that victory would be difficult to achieve by either of them. Some elders from the two warring communities thus began to seek other means to end the war. A recourse was thus made to Father Dogli. The mediation was accepted by both parties, and the settlement was sealed when the leaders of the warring groups drank water from the same calabash. Since then no open conflict has been reported between the two groups.

■ Nature of Enforcement

The choice of mechanisms by which Buems attempt to enforce their judicial decisions in order to achieve conciliation between adversarial parties and maintain social order is influenced by the frailty of their political order and their limited capability for enforcement. Does the absence of separation of powers between the Buem political and judicial personnel constitute a recipe for abuse of community power by such public officials? The search for answers lies in the motivation of public officials to strive to enhance institutional legitimacy and personnel trustworthiness, the need for *lelorkalorbunu* (or concurrence in court decisions), the threat of ostracism, and the functional importance of traditional religion and community rituals.

In Buem-Kator, the top political officials—chiefs, fetish priest, and lineage heads—are also the judicial officials. However, contrary to the modern expectation that such a concentration of state or community power can be a recipe for autocracy and despotism, power concentration in Buem-Kator has given rise to a strong emphasis on truth, openness, institutional trust, and transparency in all manner of dispute settlement in the chiefdom. In Buem-Kator, conflict mediation and adjudication provide political officials the opportunity to demonstrate their skills, capabilities, and trustworthiness and, in doing so, to enhance their legitimacy and political standing before their people.[6] Buems say that any community leader—a chief, a lineage head, or an elderly person—who cannot be relied upon in settling interpersonal disputes and community squabbles is *kwesia panin,* a stupid and worthless elder.

Until both parties have agreed on what has occurred, no resolution will be suggested. Buems believe that the primary objective of their forums of conflict resolution is to achieve *lelorkalorbunu,* a mutual understanding and acceptance of the disputing process by the adversarial parties. Buem mediators and adjudicators are compelled by tradition to ensure that parties to disputes concur in both the judicial procedures and outcomes for the conflict to be considered resolved. Once this is achieved, the managers of the disputing process can then begin to suggest courses of action to repair whatever might have caused the dispute and to return relations between the disputants to a conflict-free basis. In a similar observation among the Bena of Tanzania, Swartz notes that once the "agreement on facts is achieved, there is usually little difficulty in gaining agreement on a solution, since the solution is the obvious one in terms of what has been agreed upon as having happened."[7]

Buems use the expressions *bedieon lebor* and *bedieon lekpa*[8] to refer to the ostracizing of incorrigible criminals. It is a procedure by which recidivous individuals—the habitual criminals who constantly steal, rape, and murder but often fail to submit themselves to the orders of the courts—are dealt with. An ostracized person is an individual who Radcliffe-Brown calls "the bad lot" and whose societal position Llewellyn and Hoebel refer to as "the status of the finally intolerable."[9] The fear of ostracism among Buems generally offers the conflict managers the opportunity to exert their influence and utilize community pressure[10] to persuade intransigent parties to attend a hearing when summoned and to accept settlements.

The process of ostracizing is a public one in which every member of the community may take part. The individual who is to be ostracized is forced to walk the lengths and breadths of the town, amidst singing and drumming, and is subjected to all manner of deprecative and abusive statements, and songs such as

> Has been removed from the group!
> Has been removed from the group!
> The mother is weeping!
> The father is weeping!

To Buems, ostracizing is the traditional equivalent of life imprisonment. Once ostracized, a party cannot be talked to by members of the community, cannot be visited when sick, and cannot be buried in the public cemetery. The ostracized individual is a pariah, an outcast, "stripped of his or her soul," and existing in the community only in the "mundane body." Buems thus believe that the psychological impact of ostracizing is so devastating to the victim that he or she is bound to die of it. The relatives of the ostracized individual may associate with him or her, though they do it at the risk of incurring the wrath of the public. My informants, however, claimed that as far as human memory could go, this punitive measure has not been used in the area. One reason is that kin members of prospective victims normally intervene to bring pressure to bear on them to conform. Kin members also often intervene on behalf of prospective victims by meeting the community obligations such as the paying of court fines, the chronic default of which normally leads to ostracizing.

One other way of enforcing judicial decisions is through supernatural sanctions. If a person refuses to abide by a decision of the court, the chief and his elders may, as Radcliffe-Brown (1952, xviii) puts it, "by imprecation or the threat thereof, compel him to do so." Curses are verdict enforcement mechanisms. They can serve as powerful sanctions to ensure obedience to a court's decision. Buem conflict-resolving forums thus become the media through which the gods influence the conduct of the recalcitrant elements. After resolution of a case, the adversarial parties are expected to drink an alcoholic beverage, usually palm wine (*kube nte*), or water (*ntsu*) from the same calabash. This is a Buem version of peace pipe smoking, signifying acceptance of amends and reconciliation. The community gods and ancestral spirits are invoked and implored through the pouring of libation to be alert so as to deal sternly with any of the parties who will flout the verdict and the enforcement authority of the adjudicators.

Conclusion

The colonial experience brought to Buem-Kator significant alterations in political, judicial, economic, and sociocultural structures. Among the obvious facets of these changes are the emergence of the centralized modern nation-state of Ghana, the introduction of Western-style education, the proselytization into the Christian faith, the adoption of monetized economy, and the provision of modern infrastructural facilities such as road transportation and telecommunication services. As should be expected, these changes have had significant impacts on the traditional conflict management practices of the area. Today, Buems are economically and geographically more mobile, owe allegiance and submission to authority structures beyond their territorial borders, and have a wider range of choice in the areas of group (whether political, social, economic, or religious) affiliation and conflict resolution. Buems say that the presence of the national government's judicial and security officials in the area and the alternatives that they offer in conflict management have undermined their traditional conflict mediation system, including their reliance on supernatural sanctions for determining truth in court and enforcing court decisions.

One important source of change and tension in the traditional Buem conflict management system is in the continuing impact of cash cropping, based principally on cocoa and coffee, in the area. The production of cocoa and coffee was adopted in Buem-Kator immediately following the end of World War I, giving rise to a large influx of migrant farmers from other parts of Ghana, Togo, Benin, and Nigeria. Individual Buems and lineage heads transferred large tracts of land to the migrant farmers, who now control the use of over 70 percent of all cultivable land in the area. This has led to a significant shift in the local economic power to the migrants, who now question the legitimate basis of the exercise of the traditional Buem political and judicial authority over them (Fred-Mensah 1996).

There have often been discussions about the effectiveness of the control that was exercised formerly by indigenous authorities over communities and their resources. Most contemporary development experts on Africa are calling for the recognition and incorporation of Africa's indigenous roots in the attempt to build the region's economic, political, and sociocultural future (Lawry, Riddell, and Bennett 1984; Ayittey 1991). In Ghana, as in Nigeria and other places (as Uwazie notes in the previous chapter), the national judicial system not only recognizes the existence of traditional conflict management systems and their relative competence in matters of local traditions and customs, but also refers cases from the national courts to these traditional courts.[11] The traditional courts are deemed more competent in cases that demand knowledge in local customs and history, since much of this has not been written and it is the chiefs and their elders who could be relied upon as sources of such knowledge.

While acknowledging the importance of utilizing traditional Buem institutions in the area's development efforts, some important questions need to be addressed. To what extent are traditional conflict management structures capable of meeting the challenges of the changing context of the area's political economy? For example, in matters relating to land, how appropriate is it to apply traditional Buem institutions to the management of conflicts that are emanating from land transactions between Buems and the migrant farmers in the area? The previous controls that were exercised by Buem chiefs and lineage heads over the land during the precolonial era were tailored to the requirements and circumstances of the time—relative land abundance and subsistence food production of the pre-cash-cropping era. The test of whether a particular standard of law should be adopted by a particular community should depend on the prospect of the respect and conformity that the law will generate and inspire among the people. The development of a modern conflict management system for Buem-Kator, in particular, must begin by looking for avenues through which relevant aspects of the precolonial customary laws of the area could be harmonized with the appropriate aspects of the modern judicial and administrative systems of Ghana.

■ Notes

I am grateful to the Rockefeller Foundation for the generous financial help that made it possible for me to travel and live in Buem-Kator; this chapter is a spin-off of the materials that I collected during my visits to the area between 1993 and 1995. I am also thankful to the African Studies Program at the Paul H. Nitze School of Advanced International Studies, Johns Hopkins University, for funding the last minute research in Buem-Kator in February and March 1996, research that enabled me to unearth many of the details of the traditional Buem-Kator conflict management practices that are presented here.

1. Until recently, the dominant analytical perspectives on the ideology of harmony had been influenced by the Durkheimian notion of cultural cohesion and the maintenance of social order in nonindustrial communities. Nader challenges the tendency among anthropologists to insist that "disputing among non-Western peoples aims to restore harmony to social relations, that harmony is either functional in the face-to-face societies or the product of their specific social organization." Rose too notes that the ideology of harmony has often been interpreted by scholars to imply that conflict is bad and its absence is good. She notes that harmony could

mean different things to different people. Rose provides a guide to the interpretation of harmony by classifying perspectives on harmony into "offensive" and "defensive" perspectives. According to Rose, from the offensive perspective, harmony "advances the interest of the stronger party in a dyadic relationship, whereas from the defensive perspective, harmony protects the interest of the weaker party in a dyadic relationship" (Nader 1990, 10–11; Rose 1992, 80–81; also Leach 1954).

2. Gluckman's works generally suggest an equilibrium model of social processes in which he sees communities as coherent, self-contained systems in which economic, political, social, and religious practices complement and reinforce one another in a harmonious and well-ordered fashion. He believes that traditional systems are organized in such a way that conflicts that arise from contact between individuals are neutralized by societal norms, values, and belief systems that emphasize tendencies toward social equilibrium. According to this thinking, multiple interests that develop from marriages between different ethnic or descent groups tend to evolve into certain forms of institutions that impose constraints upon community members who would choose to utilize the option of violence in situations of conflict of interest. The function of such institutions therefore is to "weaken the incentives to cause harm to others" (Bates 1983, 7–20; Gluckman 1965a, 195; Gluckman 1956; Colson 1970, particularly, the essay on "Social Control and Vengeance in Plateau Tonga").

3. To Touval and Zartman, manipulation is one principal means that mediators use to bring about reduction in conflict. The authors explain that manipulation requires leverage—"the power, influence, and persuasion that can be brought to bear on parties to move them to agreement" (Touval, Saadia, and I. William Zartman 1985, 12; see also, Touval and Zartman 1989, 115–137).

4. This was cited by a group of Buem elders that the author interviewed in a small town called New Ayoma in Buem-Kator on March 15, 1996. It has been translated into English by the author.

5. Fines are a form of punishment that are imposed on guilty parties. Buems refer to punishment as *kortuborni,* which literally means "pulling of the ear." Ear pulling is a common way by which younger members of Buem families are punished. It is the older—a parent, a brother, a sister, an aunt, or an uncle—who is customarily permitted to pull the ear of the younger as a form of punishment. A younger member of the family cannot pull the ear of an elder person. In other words, Buem customs do not permit juniors to punish seniors.

6. Swartz notes among the Bena of Tanzania that by "achieving settlements, the political official meets not only the expectation of the disputants that their difficulties will be resolved, he also reinforces the general expectation that he can bring about the resolution of significant disputes." Merry also observes that in nonindustrial societies the reputation mediators "earn for skillful negotiation, [their] expertise in community norms and genealogies, and [their] fairness and impartiality brings them more cases and political influence" (Swartz 1966, 106; Merry 1989, 81).

7. Swartz (1966, 102). Other authors too have stressed that in adjudicating processes there is always the need for the disputing parties to concur in decisions of the courts if the conflict is to be considered resolved. Bohannan observes among the Tiv of Nigeria that "a good judge does not force a decision on the parties but gets them to concur if he can." Evans-Pritchard notes among the Nuer that there is always the need for parties to conflicts to agree to settling the conflict and concurrence by disputing parties in the verdict reached by the mediators for mediation to be of any effect (Bohannan 1957, cited by Gluckman 1965a, 185; Evans-Pritchard 1940, 164).

8. The word *bedieon* means "to remove" and *lebor* is used here figuratively. *Lebo* is a type of an earthenware pot that is placed under a felled oil palm tree to collect its juice (the palm wine). I have already indicated the importance of palm wine in Buem culture. It thus follows that the removal of the earthenware pot from under a functioning oil palm tree signifies the denial of the precious palm wine (societal support) to the pot (the ostracized individual). The word *lekpa* means "society" or "group," hence the expression *bedieon lekpa* means to remove (someone) from a society or a group.

9. Both cited by Gluckman (1965a, 190).

10. Radcliffe-Brown observes that some aspects of "law" in nonindustrial communities are concerned with conflicts whose resolution is obtained by the collective action of the community on behalf of injured persons. Injured persons may obtain satisfaction by the community taking forcible action against the aggressor. If such public sentiment is sustained, the conflict will be resolved in a way that is regarded as just, and so satisfies the community (Radcliffe-Brown 1940, xvii). This observation does not, however, mean that public pressure does not play a role in enforcing judicial decisions or maintaining social control in modern societies. As Cooter notes in a recent work, when the state "enacts a social norm into law, private citizens can help enforce the underlying obligation by reporting violators to the authorities." He notes further that the "mere possibility of such a report often deters violators" (Cooter 1989, 22).

11. The recognition of the customary laws of the various ethnic units of Ghana is spelled out in the country's statute book. Customary laws in Ghana consist of rules of law that by custom are applicable to particular communities in the country. A customary law is included in the national common law only when it is intended to be generally applied in the country as a whole (Ghana, 1960. *Interpretation Act, 1960,* C.A.4, p. 8).

4

Conflict Prevention and Resolution Among the Fulbe

Wendy Wilson-Fall

In discussions and readings regarding conflict management in Africa, there are several recurrent characteristics. One characteristic is that strategies to manage or reduce conflict within a society differ from those used to avoid, lessen, or otherwise manage conflict between the society and others. This chapter addresses both phenomena as they pertain to the Fulbe (popularly known as the Fulani) of West Africa, using examples from Senegal, Niger, and northern Nigeria.

Most state-level conflicts in the Sahelian and savanna pasture zones in precolonial times resulted from power struggles over natural resources and labor. The control and maintenance of pastures and water sources have been imperative to the reproduction of Fulbe society, which has as its base the management of cattle herds. The Fulbe's origin as a people is tied in with their role as keepers of cattle. In Fulbe ideology and mythology, they came into existence as caretakers of cattle, and the future existence of Fulbe culture and identity is intimately related to the continued association of Fulbe people with their animals. The punishment for cattle theft, for example, is a prime example of conflict management and the centrality of livestock to Fulbe society.

Prior to and during the early part of the colonial era in West Africa, indigenous peoples practiced traditional methods of conflict management characterized by a concern for long-term rather than short-term solutions. Many of these methods were also preventive or meant to minimize conflict. When the colonial regime replaced the power base of local political structures, the use of traditional methods of conflict management dwindled. Especially in terms of land use and access to other natural resources, the colonial governments made it clear that they were the ultimate authority. When conflicts arose, Africans went directly to the colonial authorities, especially when they perceived that there was a likelihood that the decision would fall to their advantage. This was particularly the case for land use disputes between farmers and herders, which were most often resolved to the farmers' benefit. In spite of this, many of the conditions of peace that were established in the precolonial period persist today, which is a good reason for scholars to return to these processes to see what can be learned from them. As a matter of fact, when formal governmental solutions fail, it is often the traditional perspective that is used as a model to resolve conflicts over pasturelands and water sources.

The resolution or management of conflict takes place on various levels of corporate behavior, levels at which decisionmaking and initiation of action customarily take place in Fulbe society. These are the individual, the patrilineal, the maximal lineal, and the extramaximal group, that is, the ethnic/occupational group that is best defined, in a historical and spatial analysis of Fulbe social behavior, in geographic and demographic terms. Although the Fulbe do not place as much importance on the clan as East African pastoralists, clan identity and recognition of a common putative ancestor is important, particularly in relation to conflicts with other Fulbe over natural resources. These levels of social and economic organization respond to conflict differently.

■ Conflicts Internal to Fulbe Society

□ *Wife Capture*

Within and between pastoral Fulbe groups, one conflict that occurred on the household, or patrilocal, level was that resulting from wife capture, or elopement practiced as kidnapping. It may occur as a complete surprise to everyone but the couple concerned (*teegal*) or it may occur as a planned event (*koobgal*).

During the colonial and precolonial periods, serial marriages ranging from first marriage to cousins to later marriage to persons from other, "stranger" lineages were more common than they are now, though this practice still exists. Although wife capture in the case of *teegal* is in fact an outlaw act of sorts, it existed as an outlaw act with rules (Dupire 1969). The rules of wife capture are that the man kidnapping the woman and the woman herself must absent themselves from the woman's community for a specified amount of time, depending on local custom. In fact, most often the wife-to-be is aware of the impending kidnapping, and may often be a coconspirator. The point here is that she has been captured from some male relative's family unit, usually her father's, her older brother's, or her current husband's household.

In the case of the Wodaabe of Niger, which I observed, the woman and her new husband must absent themselves, in fact, hide from her family, for at least a year or until the woman is noticeably pregnant. Should they be found by men from her family before that time, the woman's family have the right to beat the captor to the extent that they feel appropriate. However, if they do not find the couple until after the established limits have passed, they are expected to accept the fact and to leave them in peace. This is stylized, ritualized kidnapping. It provides a release valve for social tensions that otherwise could negatively affect the cooperation that is needed on the patrilocal level.

In the case of *koobgal,* a marriage has been planned according to tradition, involving all family members. Only the date of the stylized capture has not been revealed. When the day comes, the groom arrives at the home of the unknowing wife in the company of his close male friends and relatives. Their purpose is to take the new bride to the home of the groom. However, various members of the wife's immediate family, particularly her siblings, are expected to demand various gifts and favors along the way. They present a stylized resistance.

Such operations may seem to have an ultimately benign character. However, Fulbe are known for their violent reactions to any threat of nuptial intervention. Many men today continue to carry their knives, which are a regular part of herders' gear, and in cases where adherence to custom breaks down, violent confrontations between Fulbe men do take place in small towns and in villages. Since Fulbe society in general is characterized by first marriage to cousins, the marriage to cross cousins is often not one of romance. Couples are usually fairly young, and in the past these first marriages did not usually last. Wife capture allows a man to take a wife while avoiding both the gifts associated with marriage and marriage to an undesired relative. This option means escape from a potentially dangerous conflict between the young husband and his father or other relatives that would be linked to a more closely related wife. The second marriage is considered much more up to both the young woman or man than is the first marriage. Wife kidnapping takes conflict avoidance one step further, by marriage to a woman who is more removed from the patrilocal group. Flight is a well-known strategy for conflict evasion among pastoralists in general and is essential to the Fulbe way of life as well.

☐ *Establishing Kinship as a Technique of Conflict Avoidance or Conflict Resolution in the Context of Military Conflict*

The role of women has also been key to conflict avoidance in other ways. The exchange of women between lineages creates a bond that often results in other integrative events. Sahelian history abounds with stories of warring or disputing clans that resolved to end their conflict by exchanging women in marriage. The story of Cheickh Ahmadou Diobbo of Macina, Mali, is an excellent example. As Diobbo consolidated his empire, he married a cousin's daughter, thereby making it more difficult for extended conflicts to occur. As it turned out, however, conflict was merely postponed. His nephew, Gueladio Hamodeejo, eventually chose avoidance and migrated with a large community to what is present day western Niger.

Another example of the force of kinship networks as a mediator of conflict is the history of Mollo Egue, or Alpha Mollo, of the Fouladou area of Senegal (Upper Casamance). Of servile origin, Alpha Mollo led a resistance movement against the Mandingue rulers of that area in the late nineteenth century. Fierce combat lasted for five years. Once the wars were over, Alpha Mollo and his son, Moussa Mollo, welcomed thousands of casted Fulbe who had migrated from Macina in support of his fight against the Mandingue. He consolidated his power by exacting allegiance from this "imported" population of Fulbe, and the *jiyaabe* (captives) soon grossly outnumbered the *riimbe* (nobles). As these newcomers married women from local communities, the numbers of *jiyaabe* created a political opening for this class, who gradually became chiefs of the majority of the villages in the area. In contrast, many of the *riimbe* left for areas less densely populated where they would not find themselves under the administration of their former subjects. Those who remained were glad to leave administration to the more sedentary captives as they returned to a more pastoral lifestyle. By siding with the historical oppressor of the Fulbe of Fouladou, Alpha Mollo and Moussa Mollo were able to call upon a broad support base.

As women's place in Africa's development is discussed and debated, it is important to understand the particular role that women played, or were obliged to assume, in the social, as well as physical, reproduction of various African societies. Further, to better assess traditional conflict management strategies, these strategies need to be analyzed in the context of options that currently exist, have been lost, or can plausibly be reworked. It is of utmost importance to understand dynamics that are no longer available and why, and to investigate what might possibly serve African societies today as replacements or alternative processes for conflict management.

In Fulbe society, marriages were often arranged between different Fulbe groups to signal that conflict should be avoided because kinship had been established between the two groups. The marriage of a noble to a woman of a Fulbe "stranger" group signaled to the other men in the society that this was an acceptable behavior. When one Fulbe group moved into territory customarily controlled by another group, marriage of men in the indigenous group to women in the incoming group signaled that cohabitation of the two groups was a social and political goal and that some form of shared access to other resources would take place. To some extent, such marriages signaled the relative parity of the two groups. Marriage functioned also as a symbol of equality, even when military means were used to force the way of the incoming group. Particularly in Fulbe society, which is by and large endogamous, the act of marriage between two such groups signifies that there is an accepted commonality of status perceived between the two groups.

Examples can be drawn from the numerous cases of Islamicized Fulbe groups invading the territory of less Islamicized groups and taking wives from the latter group. Very often the less Islamicized were the more nomadic of the two, living in dispersed camps, while the incoming group had formed a more centralized society. Historically, it has been the action of conquest that foreshadows the state formation, with greater centralization of power, more hierarchization, and more complex state functions. Acquisition of women from the conquered group contributed to the accomplishment of these political tasks, as politically subjugated pastoralist groups found themselves in a quasi-client position. The fact of kinship served to soften the blow of lost independence. In fact, in some cases, it enhanced living conditions as military protection expanded the potential area for pasture. Clear examples can be found in the relationship of pastoralist Fulbe to the incoming Torobe Fulbe during the jihad of Ousman dan Fodio in northern Nigeria. By calling upon maximal and clan affiliations, Dan Fodio established fealty among the many herding communities living in the Katsina, Sokoto, and Kano areas. A sort of Fulbe nationalism occurred, and intermarriage among once-dispersed Fulbe groups contributed to the concentration of power that made Dan Fodio's conquest a success.

Resource access. Conflict negotiation occurred throughout Sahelian history between pastoral Fulbe and the Pulaar-speaking (Hal-Pulaar) state. An important example is the transition from the Deniyankoobe non-Islamic Fulbe state to the Tukulor Muslim state in the seventeenth century, in what is now the Fleuve region of Senegal. The Deniyankoobe were aligned with the Mali empire, and at some point in their history paid tribute to that Malinke state. With the advent of the Atlantic slave trade, a condition of anarchy gradually developed, and many Fulbe, including the class commonly known as Tukulor (Hal-Pulaaren), were sold into slavery. This led to a rise of power of the Muslim Tukulor cleric class, who, in a search for compromise and in order to stabilize social conditions at the time, declared that it was unlawful to sell other Hal-Pulaaren into slavery. By limiting the source of slaves to non-Pulaar speakers, they protected their interests and the stability of their society. Land use systems were also developed that allowed sedentary Hal-Pulaaren to settle near the river, while pastoralist Fulbe Hal-Pulaaren transhumed in the *dieri* (dune grasslands some distance from the Senegal River), but were allowed to transit the farm plots of settled Hal-Pulaaren such as the Tukulor, through established passageways to the river for water access. Again, intermarriage also played a role. Up to today there are kin networks between the Tukulor and the Fulbe pastoralists that mirror resource access needs between the *dieri* and the *waalo,* the alluvial area that borders the Senegal River.

The power of the Tukulor state was based on relations of force as much as it was on religious ideology. It challenged the authority of the Deniyankoobe state. It was the possibility of military intervention that discouraged people from breaking the new edict against participating in the slave trade of Hal-Pulaaren. On the other hand, the object of this edict was to consolidate the Hal-Pulaaren state, to avoid infighting, and to maintain its labor force. Since farming on alluvial plains was the major economic activity of the Hal-Pulaaren state, protecting the labor force was important. In this case, therefore, confrontation and synthesis were two strategies the Tukulor state employed to avoid anarchy and political disintegration as the Atlantic slave trade increased in volume and importance.

In the area now defined as Guinea-Bissau, Upper and Lower Casamance, and The Gambia, there were several Hal-Pulaar states, including the Gabu state in what is now Guinea-Bissau and the Fouladou states (see discussion of Alpha Mollo, above) of current Upper Casamance. In both of these cases, conflict was managed through the allocation of pasture zones for the various Fulbe lineages transhuming in those areas. Conflict was also mediated, as in the cases noted above, by the intermarriage of more sedentary Fulbe nobles with pastoralist families.

When short-term conflict such as theft or damage to livestock occurred, the owners expected payment in kind, and such payment normally avoided greater conflict or the expansion of the arena of conflict. This still occurs as the most popular redress to loss of livestock, both among Fulbe and between Fulbe and others. The fact that there are apparently so few variations on how theft of animals is dealt with is perhaps a measure of the importance of animals to the Fulbe. Negotiation is not an option when it relates to the herd of the pastoralist. There must be compensation or further, more serious conflict evolves. Throughout western and central Africa today, it is known that Fulani herders will respond with violence if their animals are killed or stolen and no compensation is provided.

One way in which pasture use has been regulated is through the use of traditional wells as markers of pasture privilege. In Niger and other parts of the Sahel, the presence of a traditional well installed by the patrilineage using the surrounding pastures was an indication of priority over use of those pastures. Access was to be requested by other Fulbe communities passing through. This also affected the extent to which cattle from different herds did or did not cohabit, an important husbandry factor.

Within the pastoral Fulbe family, requests for gifts of livestock in order to start a herd are customarily directed toward a mother's brother or a friend of the same age grade. These traditions serve to lessen the inherent conflict between father and son or sons. Since the first son inherits the entire herd at his father's discretion (usually while his father is living), gifts from the father to other sons can be the source of much conflict (see Dupire 1969).

□ *Joking Relationships (Mutual Assistance Relationships) Among Fulbe*

Mutual assistance relationships, called "joking relationships," exist throughout West Africa between ethnic groups and between clans. Among Fulbe, joking relationships signal a past relationship between the two clans that had special significance in antiquity. This relationship is held in such high esteem that even in current times, under some conditions, an individual from one clan cannot refuse a request for help from another of a clan with whom it has the privilege and responsibility of a joking relationship. Further, in precolonial times, when two people from clans that shared a joking relationship were in conflict, leaders sometimes preferred to banish or otherwise do away with the two in conflict rather than allow the travesty of conflict to expand.

Often relations of "*plaisanterie*" count their beginnings in the origin stories of the peoples involved. This is the case of the Fulbe in general and of the Jawaambe, a Fulbe subgroup. The Fulbe trace their origin to an ancestor named *Buutorin,* while the Jawaambe trace their ancestry back to someone called *Jandalata.* In oral tradition, this relationship is described using the images of the egret (a bird that lives symbiotically with cattle) and the *pluvier,* which lives off of the crocodile. Tradition assigns them both a Middle Eastern origin.

Ahmadou Hampaté Ba (1986) describes various examples of "joking relationships," "*rapports de plaisanterie,*" or, as it is also called in French, "*cousinage.*" He states that in general, where there are joking relationships there are sometimes sexual taboos between the two groups. In other instances, it appears that this relationship is marked by an exchange of women between linages. "Joking relationships (*dendiraaku*) is a sacred tie which allows two men, or the inhabitants of two countries, or two ethnic groups, regardless of age or social rank to tease each other without suffering consequences." *Dendiraaku* implies mutual assistance and can connote a taboo against any mutual treachery. In certain cases, each member of this relationship should not see the blood of the other. Some relations of *dendiraaku* that I have been able to identify among the Peul are between Diallo and Ba name groups, between Diao and So, and between Fuutanke and Jawaambe. Others are between Mballo and Diao, Mballo and Seydi, Mballo and Kandé, and Mballo and Diallo. The Aanabi Fulbe joke with the Seydi and Kandé (examples drawn from Guinea and from Upper Casamance, Senegal). There are also relations of *dendiraaku* between Fulbe and the members of the *nyeeno* classes (artisans) in general, and in Fouladou, between the Fulbe *riimbe* and the *matchuube*.

A similar relationship exists in Fulbe tradition between children of the same father, known as "*bibbe-baba.*" There is always potential rivalry between siblings, and there are various taboos, such as eating at the house of one's sibling. On the other hand, the term *suudu-baba* refers to people of the same patronym, that is to say, maximal lineage or clan level. In such cases, solidarity in situations of adversity is considered a sacred responsibility. People who share this relationship (such as the clan Diallo, or Barry) should also be willing to pay ransom for the other in times of war (Ba 1986, 88–89). The terms of these relationships appear to be those of "confirmation," as they confirm the terms of kinship or clan identity that define the parties involved.

Finally, another form of structured conflict management in Sahelian West Africa is the lateral correspondence of patronyms, which extends from Senegal in the west to Mali and Burkina Faso in the east. Niger and Nigeria do not participate as explicitly because Muslim family names have supplanted original ethnic names to a great extent. Nevertheless, even the Wodaabe Fulbe of Niger have a corresponding patronym among the Fulbe in Mali and Senegal. They assume the patronym of So once entering into Mali and throughout Senegal, even during short visits. This correspondence of patronyms allows for people to integrate more easily into stranger communities by directing themselves to the people of a corresponding lateral patronym. Here are some examples from Ba: Coulibaly/Fall (the former is Bambara; the latter in this context, Moor); Ba/Diakité (Diakité = Bambara); So/Sidibé (Sidibé = Khassonké/Wassoulou); Bari/Sangaré (Sangaré = Khassonké/Wassoulou); Diallo/Kann, Ka (Kann, Ka are Fulbe or Tukulor names); Traoré, Taraoré, Travelé/Diop (Traoré, etc. = Bambara; Diop = Wolof).

This latter example is certainly one of synthesis as a response to potential conflict. The process of hosting strangers over time according to customary allegiances has in fact led to a parallel correspondence of patronyms across ethnic groups and between subgroups of one ethnic group, such as the Wodaabe and the So.

External Conflicts: Fulbe and Other Societies

Potential conflicts between the Fulbe and the non-Fulbe, particularly following wars of conquest or jihads waged by the Fulbe on farming communities, were mitigated through relations of kin. On the level of nobles, Fulbe have characteristically married into the existing noble structure and co-opted it. In some cases, as in the Segou state and in the Hausa states of the nineteenth century, Fulbe agropastoralists enjoyed the support of more nomadic Fulbe for military security. In spite of this sort of network, the elite Fulbe close to the state discarded the use of Pulaar (or Fulfuulde, as it is called in the central Sudan and the Sahel) in favor of an apparent integration of Fulbe into host cultures. However, concurrently to marriages with local host elites, the same Fulbe families continued to practice cousin marriage at least as often as, if not more often than, marriage to members of the host community for over two generations (Wilson 1996; Dupire 1969; Ba 1986; Smith 1960, 81–82, 168).[1] Over time a syncretization of the two cultures emerged, and can still be observed today. The example above refers specifically to the infiltration of Fulbe nobles into the existing sedentary elite population, so that conflict was avoided by the creation of myriad kin and client relationships, going in both directions (vertically and laterally).

Kinship and historical ties functioned to create ally networks in the period of the jihad of Osman dan Fodio, thereby allowing him to stabilize the area rapidly following the period of actual fighting, which only lasted about five years. Through the application of old or putative ancestral ties, communities that were normally somewhat dispersed both socially and geographically were convinced to come together and take risks for the perceived common good.

Another example of Fulbe state relations to manage conflict is the case of officially named offices within the state apparatus for the particular responsibility of state-nomad or state-herder relations. One example can be drawn from the *laman* in the Wolof states, who resided at the political center near present-day Linguere in Senegal (Diop 1981). Located at the transition zone between the northern rainy season pastures and the southern dry season pastures of the Fulbe, the Wolof clearly understood the importance of monitoring the movement of the herders and their animals, who contributed significantly to the local economy through meat and dairy sales, taxes, and manuring contracts with farmers. Up to today, the concentrations of Fulbe in these areas attest to the protection they once enjoyed from the Wolof state through the agency of the *laman*, who represented the interests of the *bur* (king). A similar pattern existed in the Hausa states. Kirk-Greene and Hobgen (1960, 128) stated that

> the various provinces of this [Tekrur, Tukulor] empire [in northern Nigeria] were governed by [al-Haj] Omar's kinsmen, and the governor of Segou, [Sheikh] Amadou, . . . was Omar's son by a daughter of Muhammed Bello of Sokoto. Muhammed Bello, on the other hand, was himself the grandson of Ousman dan Fodio. Both Bello, who ruled Sokoto, and [Sheikh] Amadou, who ruled Macina and created the great

> transhumance system which is still used today, assured that their governments provided for stable pasturing and water access conditions for the pastoralists who lived within their states' boundaries. It was good for trade, good for farming, and provided meat and diary products for the populations of the area. As importantly, taxes were levied by both states on Fulbe cattle.

The examples given above represent processes of confirmation and synthesis: confirmation because the identity of Fulbe-ness is confirmed in the process of intermarriage, and synthesis of interest and identity is achieved through kinship (Fulbe/Fulbe or Fulbe/Hausa), rather than a confrontation that reestablishes the separate identity of each group. Confirmation can also be assigned to the relationship that the Fulbe enjoyed with the Wolof, who acknowledged their difference of ethnicity and occupation and created special administrative and political conditions for them in order to avoid nascent conflicts over land use and water access. Vestiges of these Fulbe state relations exist today, and attest to the tenacity of traditional systems of conflict management or avoidance (Schmitz 1986, 11).

Adjacent territories of the Wolof *ceddo* state and the Fulbe *deyniyankoobe* state eventually led to the development of two new residential or identity groups: the fisher people (*cubbalbe*) and the muslim cleric sedentary Pulaar speakers, known today as the *torobe,* or *tukulor.*

Among less nomadic Fulbe communities, one finds an agropastoral adaptation that can be characterized by extreme mobility of a certain age class and gender, and a sedentarized life for the remainder of the community. Young men who are not married or recently married go out on transhumance while the rest of the community remains to farm. In some cases these communities are the result of military conquests of Fulbe over less militarily organized non-Fulbe farming communities. The members of the original farming communities are integrated into the Fulbe social structure through kinship relations. These relations, whether through marriage or concubinage, have served to stabilize a society that otherwise would be prone to extreme tension and insecurity. Although first-generation slaves (*matchuube*) gained a clan patronym, they rarely gained lineage affiliation, and belonged, as it were, to the collectivity. On the other hand, persons of the former class resulting from marriages or concubinage with noble (*riimbe*) Fulbe were accorded a different status, that of *rimaibe,* and took the lineage affiliation of their fathers. This movement was always achieved through "downward" kin relations by the marriage or concubinage of women by men of higher social status. These relations mitigated against social conflict by placing kin relations and relations of obligations between the various classes in such Fulbe societies.

Gift exchange was also common in both directions, from and toward the elite class. In addition to the exchange of gifts between these classes, in former times there were various financial responsibilities between the two groups. *Riimbe* (nobles) were responsible for assuming the cost of marriages of *matchuube* of their families, and *matchuube* were responsible for paying a portion of their yearly harvest as tribute to the *riimbe* of their families.

In contemporary society, gifts are still used as leverage both from lower to upper social strata and the reverse. They may be used to offset potential conflict, and are most marked in the manipulation of political favor in many countries in the region. While traveling in northeastern Mali in the mid-1980s, I often came across communities of either Tuareg, Moors, or Fulbe who still lived in close proximity to their former captives. It was not unusual to hear of how these former nobles were being further impoverished by complying with demands for gifts from their former dependents. In fact, the Sahelian droughts of 1973–1974 and 1982–1983 brought into high relief the degree to which the fortunes of all concerned had changed. The drought was a terrible leveling force that impoverished everyone. Yet, the presence of traditional social institutions promoted solidarity and aid within and between the various classes of these societies in the name of ethnic and clan solidarity.

The potential for new kin networks among former caste persons and former nobles is difficult to assess, as societies are in rapid transition. It is possible that caste can be overlooked for ethnic solidarity, as in the case of the Tuareg rebellions in Mali and Niger. In Niger, a great percentage, if not the majority, of rebels were of the *Bella* or *Bouzou* Tuareg subgroup. This process is already occurring more slowly in Fulbe communities, where the pressure of national culture (French, English, or the sedentary national language, such as Hausa or Wolof) has created a resurgence in cultural solidarity and use of the Pulaar language. In West Africa, in general, caste is becoming less and less significant as a social and economic determinant.

By integrating the captives into the society through kinship obligations (usually through concubines, which are in certain circumstances sanctioned in Islam, sometimes called the "fifth wife"), the stability and coherence of the society was protected. By insisting on adherence to Fulbe cultural norms and through the benefit of the Fulbe worldview (which is Fulbe and "sedentary others," *habe,* or *seybe,* for example), the development of a potentially subversive underclass was avoided. In this process we can identify both confrontation and synthesis: confrontation because of the relations of force that are inherent in the captive-noble configuration, and synthesis because the cultural and economic objective was integrative.

□ *Mutual Assistance (Joking) Relationships Between Fulbe and Other Ethnic Groups*

Joking relationships are a form of managing conflict between the Fulbe and others. The origins of joking relationships are not well known among scholars, and it is no longer easy to find African oral historians who can give a clear idea of how a joking relationship came to be. A joking relationship is either a signpost for past conflicts that have been resolved or a signpost of a former dependency or tribute-paying relationship. Joking relationships exist between lineages and between ethnic groups.

In the first case, joking relationships have ritualized the acknowledgment that former enemies have become friends. Joking relationships between the Fulbe and the Tiv of the north central plateau of northern Nigeria developed as a result of land overuse. After agreeing to negotiate, the parties established joking relationships so that future generations would avoid conflict. In principle, one is supposed to be more tolerant of those with whom one has a joking relationship. Joking relationship partners have the right to insult each other playfully, and are challenged by the larger society not to react in an aggressive or revengeful manner to such exchanges.

In the second case, joking relationships recall a former favor that was done by one group for the other, such as taking in political or natural disaster refugees, or a former dependence of one group on the other for reasons such as their arrival into the home region of the other as strangers to the host. Sometimes the latter situation resulted in a tribute-paying commitment by the strangers to the host. In this context, joking is a form of acknowledging that there are no hard feelings, and that in spite of this former situation of dependence, the two groups consider themselves equals. This is true of the Fulbe and the Kanuri, the ethnic group who established the empire of Kanem Bornu on the borders of Lake Chad in the fourteenth century.

Joking relationships can exist between Fulbe people as a whole and other ethnic groups, such as described above, or between Fulbe clans (patronyms) and other ethnic groups. For example, while a generalized condition of *dendiraaku* exists between all Serer and Fulbe, it also exists specifically between Diao (a Fulbe patronym) and Serer, Camara (a Mandingue patronym), Koulibaly (a Bambara patronym), Gueye (a Wolof patronym), and Seck (a patronym belonging to both the Serer and the Wolof).

There are many traditional anecdotes describing the origins of a joking relationship between the Fulbe and the Serer. One anecdote (clearly from the Fulbe point of view) states that there were once two families who lived next to each other, a Fulbe and a Serer. One day a Fulbe child and a Serer child were sitting together in a house. A Serer man came in with a torch and, not sure which child was Serer or Fulbe, inadvertently picked up the Fulbe child and brought him home. This anecdote of course includes some joking at the expense of the Serer, who implicitly were so foolish as not to know their own child, "even with a torch." The other implication is that the

Serer knew full well that the child was Fulbe, but since the Fulbe are so beautiful, chose the Fulbe child, pretending that he did not know the difference (story from Ousmane Mballo, Dakar, 1996). Another traditional story is that the Serer and the Fulbe became joking partners while migrating with their cattle from the east, the Fulbe from Yemen, and the Serer from the land of the Hindus. Because of the long travels together in antiquity, both with their cattle herds, they developed a relation of "*plaisanterie*" (story from Malang Diao, Dakar, 1996). In interethnic "mutual assistance" relationships, such as between the Serer and the Fulbe, intermarriage is discouraged, and at the same time, spilling of blood by one of the other is considered mystically and morally dangerous.

☐ *Flight, Avoidance, Pulaaku, and Hersa: Traditional Methods of Conflict Management*

Flight is a response particularly characteristic of pastoralist populations because conflicts often had their origins in overpopulation of grazing lands. Unlike a ranching system, pastoralists traditionally do not "own" and "inherit" land in the sense that settled farming communities do. Independence of spirit is necessary to the often lonely and isolated life of a herder, who may spend weeks alone or with one or two others while pasturing cattle far from the family camp or village. Among the Fulbe, flight and avoidance are common responses to conflict. Large migrations occurred for several reasons: lack of independence, lack of pasture, and religious pressure. Examples include the flight of Gueladio Hambodeejo from Macina to current-day Niger, who left with members of his own clan, the Diallube, the Feroobe, and with their Bambara captives; the eastward movements of the Wodaabe of Senegal toward Podor in search of better pasture and freedom from the incoming French administration; the flight of jihadists from the Macina plains to the Guinea highlands; the flight of less Islamicized Fulbe in the eighteenth century from the Guinea highlands to adjacent regions (Foulacounda, Fuladou, Tambacounda, Welingara); the flight of the Fulbe from the Songhay Empire in the sixteenth century to escape the advancing Moroccan army of Pasha Djonder (battle of Tondibi in 1590), which led to installation of much of the Fulbe population in southern Senegal, Guinea (Conakry), Guinea-Bissau, and The Gambia (N'Gaide 1996, 2); flight of eloping (kidnapped) couples; and flight from war.

Franchette (1996, 5, 6, 8, 9) identifies several circumstances engendering flight as a response to conflict:

> Following conflicts with the French in 1911 (revolt of Tramant), many marabouts and their talibés fled toward Guinée Bissau, Casamance and Gambia. . . . During the nineteenth century wars between Fulbe groups in

> the Timbi, the great cattlemen left the Fouta Djallon plateau to find refuge in the plains of Gawal and Bowe, and even to Upper Casamance. . . . During religious and political conflicts at the beginning of the century in Portuguese Guinee, hundreds of Fulbe fled Gabon to follow a Torodo marabout, El Hadj Ali Thiam, who had come to the region to spread Islam. . . . [During the time of Sekou Touré] Fulbe herdsmen were heavily taxed . . . and were obliged to furnish great quantities of animals to the state. They gathered their herds together and sought to flee to Sénégal.

Other conflictual conditions provoked mobility and flight as a response: the breakup of a village from the scarcity of land, Fulbe instability, and individualism; and conflicts over chieftancies and herds, among others.

This tendency to flee or avoid conflict is expressed on the household, patrilineage, and maximal lineage levels. In fact, the tendency to avoidance and prevention is applied in minute detail by behavior in the basic tenets of Fulbe philosophy and worldview. Among the elements of Fulbe education is the concept of *pulaaku,* as it is known in the east (Niger, Cameroon, Nigeria, Chad), or *hersa,* as it is known in western Mali, Senegal, The Gambia, and Guinea-Bissau. Translated into the French as "*retenue,*" it can perhaps best be characterized in English as discretion, self-control, and reserve. This concept is a significant behavioral factor on every level of Fulbe society.[2]

In conversation, younger people in Fulbe society not only should not look elders directly in the eyes, but may arrange their seating so that they are not facing them directly (personal observations; Say and Torodi, Niger; and interviews with Ahmadou Ba Nduru, Senegal). Among the Wodaabe, women do not eat in full view of their husbands, a custom also attributed to *pulaaku. Pulaaku,* or *hersa,* also connotes self-dignity and, paramount in the Fulbe culture, honor. A loss of honor and dignity are among the most serious events that a *pullo* (singular of Fulbe) can endure. Throughout central and West Africa there are anecdotes of Fulbe who have killed people and animals or left for another country because of their perceived loss of honor. Even the use of language between age classes reflects this preoccupation. A particular way of speaking, in a soft voice and with particular vocabulary, is a characteristic of Fulbe tradition. Behavior between siblings and affines and even the distribution of meat at the time of a ceremonial feast are all governed by rules pertaining to the ideals of *pulaaku* or *hersa.* The mock or ritualized fighting in the Fulbe game of *sawro* or *sharo* idealizes this behavior. Now outlawed in many countries, *sharo* is a game wherein Fulbe youths take turns beating one another with herding sticks. Often the person who is being beaten will gaze into a mirror stoically to signify his indifference. The aim of this activity is to show perseverance and self-control; it is an exercise in the removal of one's ego from a conflict at hand.

■ Conclusion

The strategies discussed above provide more examples of *conflict prevention* than of management of a conflict that has already occurred. Most strategies are integrative as well as confrontational, allowing conflicting parties to *reconfirm* their Fulbe identities in the process of avoiding or managing conflict. Can these strategies have practical applications in the current sociopolitical context? Actually, a surprising number of the customs described here are still practiced. Conflict prevention and conflict avoidance are primary elements of Fulbe culture.

With increasing land use pressure occurring throughout the Sahelian and savanna zones as the population increases and fallow periods shorten, conflicts over land use are a potential future threat in the region. The drift of farmers into areas that were once dry season pastures and the search for lands for commercial, income-producing farm enterprises are increasingly limiting land access for herders.

The function of women crossing between lineages to secure alliances through marriage is a strategy that is still used among pastoral folk in adjacent pasturelands, although perhaps to a lesser extent. Intermarriage between ethnic groups is seen worldwide (rightly or wrongly) as a measure of the openness and integrative intentions of groups toward each other. In Senegal today, one of the complaints often levied against the Lebanese community is that they most often refuse to marry African women. Although intermarriage cannot necessarily be counted upon to avoid or alleviate conflict on a large scale, it still exists in the Sahel region, and enhances social, economic, and political relationships.

Joking and mutual assistance relationships developed during another sociocultural era in Africa. The conditions and worldviews that allowed for such systems to come into being are in a profound process of transformation. These systems may still, however, teach something about conflict management. In early 1996 the president of Senegal called for a day of reconciliation between the Lower Casamance and the rest of Senegal. For the past five years the southern region of Senegal, which has a large population of Diola people, had been marked by a separatist movement that included guerilla warfare. Eventually a peace agreement with the involved parties was established. Some months later, President Diouf called for a day commemorating the "*rapports de plaisanterie*" that existed traditionally between the Diola and the Serer people. In West Africa today, particularly in Mali, Senegal, The Gambia, Guinea-Bissau, and Guinea, such relationships are referred to on a daily basis either for comic relief or to assuage feelings during an argument.

The example of formal relationships between pastoralist groups and the state is the most provocative. To date, no Sahelian government has formalized the management and oversight of state policy regarding the protection and assurance of grazing, pasture, and water rights for pastoralists. In fact, most governments in the region have been quite conservative about voicing clear policies about transhumance as a production strategy, and the question remains whether pastoralists have any formal land tenure rights in the context of the modern state. This has caused anxiety and conflict, as can be witnessed by the Tuareg uprisings of Mali and Niger in the 1990s, and in the recurrent conflicts between Hausa farmers and Fulani herders (Nigeria and Niger), and between Wolof farmers and Fulani (Peul) herders (Senegal). Although Niger in the mid-1980s set up a commission that sponsored national conferences on pastoralist issues, and Senegal has a national committee of rural counsels that includes a national herders' association, neither of these has had a significant impact on the official land management policy of these countries.

At great social cost, conflict and civil strife dominate many pastoral areas today—in Somalia, Kenya, Ethiopia, Uganda, Sudan, Niger, and Mali, among others. Shouldered most heavily by the residents of the pastoral areas, the price of insecurity and famine is also borne by their governments and by the international community at large. "Without a recognition of the problems of pastoral areas and support for development needs, problems of insecurity are likely to increase" (Scoones 1994, 4). Sahelian countries face both internal and external pressures regarding the effective management of the natural resource base that supports rural farmers and herders. Local and national means of management of these resources for sustainable use must be revisited in any case. The example of a national secretary for these concerns is a model that has historical roots in the region (such as the *lam* of the Wolof states) and deserves serious consideration.

It may be that governments in the Sahel are relying upon traditional forms of conflict management to mediate conflict in the region. Perhaps new strategies will emerge as by-products of the move toward democratization and the development of non-governmental institutions. Our capacity to understand these movements, and the historical precedents for conflicts and for the solutions that will be offered to manage them, will depend on our ability to understand existing traditions of conflict management and prevention.

■ Notes

1. The author carried out extensive interviews in northern Nigeria among young women of the elite Hausa Fulani class in Zaria over a two-year period, from 1975 to 1977, plus interviews and field observation during visits to Mali and Niger between 1984 and 1990, as well. See the author's forthcoming article in *Nomadic*

Peoples for more discussion of this aspect of Fulbe sociopolitical behavior. See also Dupire 1969; as well as Ba 1986; and Smith 1960.

2. Examples of jihads in the region waged by Fulbe include the wars of the eighteenth century that took place in the Futa Jallon of Guinea, the jihad of Ousman dan Fodio in northern Nigeria, and the wars of Oumar Tall in Segou, present-day Mali.

5

West Coast Diplomacy Among the Akan and Their Neighbors

Edmond Kwam Kouassi

Far from being an invention of a peculiar human society, diplomacy was independently developed by most people in the world as a functional imperative. Even in a society of priests and believers, misunderstanding is bound to rise and there must be people to resolve it. Robert Smith (1977, 7) reported that "diplomacy, the fundamental means by which foreign relations are conducted and foreign policy implemented, far from being an invention of capitalism of the modern nation state, or classical Antiquity either, is found in some of the most primitive communities and seems to have been evolved independently by people in all parts of the world. The basic object of diplomacy is to enable men to live with their neighbors, a fact which requires a measure of accommodation to the interests of the others; the more detailed ends of diplomacy are equally universal."

The main objective of this study is not to prove that diplomacy existed in precolonial Africa. Consistent books, articles, and dissertations written by historians and anthropologists have positively closed the issue on this matter. A. A. Boahen (1973, 2) decisively wrote nearly a quarter of a century ago that "it is quite evident from oral traditions as well as from both European and Arabic sources that diplomacy has been known among African States from time immemorial." Evidence of diplomatic exchanges comes from relations between the medieval empires of Mali and Songhai and the sultanate of Morocco and between the Sahelian state of Kanem-Borno and the Mediterranean states of Tunis and Tripoli. Ibn Khaldum (1377/1967) and Leo Africanus (1550/1956), as well as the local histories (*tarikh*s) written in the western Sudan, document the exchanges of gifts and ambassadors and the negotiation of offensive and defensive alliances. Ibn Khaldum, for instance, chronicles the diplomatic mission headed by two Mandingo officials sent by Mansa Musa of Mali (1307–1332) to the Moroccan sultan Abu Al-Hassan and a return mission from the sultan led by Ali ben Ghanim. Again, Boahen reports that the request of the

Portuguese commander Don Diego da Azambujo for permission to build a permanent fort on the West African coast in 1482 met an answer from the representative of the king of Aguafo, the Caramansa, that was "indicative of people not uninitiated into the delicate art of diplomacy and the use of diplomatic language" (Boahen 1973). My purpose here is to analyze the structure, values, methods, personnel, results, and meaning given by West African societies in the management of their conflicts.

■ Controlled Conflict in Traditional West African Societies

In traditional Africa, wars arise from quarrels over fishing grounds, wrongs done to one community by another, and various efforts of self-defense. The wars involved the use of traditional and rudimentary weapons, such as assegais and shields, and diplomacy, including the use of marriages as a form of alliances, swearing of oaths, "drinkings of the gods," and exchanges of prisoners to ensure lasting peace. Another important feature of traditional West African conflict is its limitation in terms of loss in human resources and time. West African people generally observed the concept of limited warfare. A Yoruba proverb says that "the fact that we are quarreling does not mean that we want our opponent to die," and a Togolese principle holds that "if peace is necessary to preserve life, men have to be friends if they have to survive." Yet, men quarrel over many things—cattle, land, women, prestige, indeed over accidents—or, if men don't quarrel, they have differences of opinion about the rights and wrongs of a contract and these differences have to be settled by some rule other than that of brute force if social relations are to be maintained. Thus, although a war may be a major one, tradition requires that loss of life be minimal. This healthy situation was changed from the fifteenth century (Dike 1956, 18).

In most West African societies, war rarely entailed a complete repudiation of the restraints of peace, and the regulation of peaceful contact with outsiders was also accompanied by some regulation of their warfare (Smith 1977, 4). Formal declarations of war eliminated surprise in attack, unconditional surrender seems to have been uncommon, and annexation of foreign territory was infrequent. In the Ikwere society in Nigeria, for instance, the enemy was usually sent notice of war. One dry stick and one green stick were sent—choice of the dry stick meant war, for the dry stick was a dead stick that meant that the chooser wanted death. When the cannon became available, people sent their enemies a cannonball and a piece of yam. The choice of the cannonball, of course, meant war (Amadi 1982, 35; Jones 1963, 46–47). Outright victory in war was often followed by the establishment of "a tributary relationship which left those of the indigenous cultivators who survived in possession of their farms" (Smith 1968, 4; also Mattingly 1970, 10–63). When conflicts erupted, there were people to solve them on the basis of certain moral or legal principles, of certain ethical ideals and according to certain methods, techniques, and procedures, because "these societies have such well established and well known codes of morality and laws of convention and ritual, that even though they have no written histories, many reasonably assume that they have persisted for many generations" (Gluckman 1955, 3).

In agrarian society in general (such as Igbo society in eastern Nigeria), which has beliefs deeply rooted in moral values of the Earth deity (the goddess of land and fertility), civilization possessed a "rigid" or "constant" cosmogony centered on the earth force and the manipulation of spirit forces, which militated against the growth of militarism. Conflicts were policed by sacred laws made by a council of elders. These laws were considered necessary for the survival of everything that thrives on earth and they sought to maintain a ritual equilibrium between mankind on one hand and the ancestral spirits on the other. They are then helpful to an understanding of why these people placed emphasis on moral uprightness, peace with the gods, and peace with men.

Purity, it was believed, was essential in blocking the anger of the gods or the ruin of evil spirits. Hence, seasonal festivals including purification rites, and an onslaught of an epidemic or a bad harvest, were countered with divination and special purification rights (Kalu 1978, 43). During these periodic festivals, laws were elaborated to promote peace and prevent conflict. The laws were binding on every individual irrespective of his or her status in society. The time of the festivities was regarded as a holy season, during which people feared to quarrel or engage in any violent activity that would pollute the earth. Other laws forbade serious crimes that could threaten the stability of a community, such as homicide, kidnapping, poisoning, theft, and adultery (Mike 1937, 25). To prevent land disputes, people were prohibited from leveling mounds and cutting down trees symbolizing gods, which were used to demarcate boundaries of land holdings.

Indeed, the god was the source of moral strength in a community. Individuals were therefore required to notify and seek the consent of their priest before going to war to "ensure that they fought for a just cause" (Uchendu 1965, 98). If an outsider killed a member of the community, the council of elders was obliged to dispatch some of its members to the offender's kinsfolk asking for compensation within a specified period of time. Failure to meet their demand would lead to an intercommunity war (Jeffrey 1956, 77–78). Whenever violations of the ethical prescriptions were unclear and controversial, the council of elders adopted peaceful measures in resolving them. They might consult a diviner and traditional medicine man to seek his advice. When this was not possible, however, the elders and wise men could arrive at their own judgment, which would be pronounced by masked spirits representing the ancestors. The contending parties were obliged to accept the decisions then made in order that they might not rouse the displeasure of the venerated ancestors (Abam 1985, 71–72). If rival parties led by powerful individuals started fighting before the elders were able to resolve their disputes, the elders would dispatch their messengers bearing palm fronds, a sign of peace, to enforce a truce. When the messengers arrived, the combatants who were afraid of harming them or spilling their blood were expected to stop fighting so that the elders could fix a date for the arbitration of the dispute (Orijini 1978, 528–529).

■ Methods, Techniques, and Procedures

In traditional Africa, conflict prevention and peace preservation consisted of the use of marriage, oath swearing, and "drinking of the gods."

Marriage was not just perceived as a union between two persons or two families, but was also conceived as a promise of peace and cooperation that fostered intergroup relations, a real communion between the gods of the communities involved. Thus, through marriage, there emerged new types of peaceful relations in which peoples were committed to never, at least directly, fight each other, and to avoid war and bloodshed.

Societies that observed exogamy banned mating within the family and within the clan. This rule of banning marriage in the clan compels the man of each agnatic vengeance group to seek in other agnatic groups for their own wives and for husbands for their sisters. To marry thus requires first of all some kind of friendship with those other groups. Some African peoples say of groups other than the one to which they belong, "they are our enemies; we marry them"; but after marriage, there is a sort of friendship, though it differs from that of the main bloodline. Moreover, when a man took a wife from another group, he had interest in being friends with that group that his fellow agnates did not have, though they too regarded his in-laws as relatives. Their wives make them friendly with other groups. It is not just sentiment. A women remains attached to her own kin, and if her husband quarrels with them, she can make life pretty unpleasant for him. But her ancestors are also able to affect her and her children, and hence her husband's well-being. A man's brother-in-law, maternal uncle to his children, is required to assist them in many critical situations. He can bless his nephew and his curse is believed to be among the worst. So for the welfare of his family and the prosperity of his children, each man is led by his interest in being on good terms with his wife's kin. As the child of a woman from yet another group, he has an interest in being on good terms with his own mother's kin. Again, this interest is supported by customary rights to seek help and by danger of suffering mystic retribution if he does not conform with these customs. The fact that men of a single group of agnates have mothers from different other groups, and many wives from still other groups, strikes into the unity of each group. Some members of each warring group have an interest in bringing about a settlement of quarrels. In this respect, custom produces cohesion, through settlement of quarrels, in a wider range of social life.

Another technique in the process of conflict resolution was oath making. Ritual objects were assembled and the gods invited to witness the ceremonies and to be prepared to punish any party that might transgress the spirit of the agreement reached. Thus, oaths between two groups or communities served to eliminate conflict between them for decades or centuries. For instance, the oaths between the Andoni and Bonny peoples in 1869 have kept peace between them for more than a century.

Three other well-known and well-tried instruments were probably unique to African states, namely, the exchange of gods, the establishment of jocular relationships, and the use of clan ties. Diplomatic relationships such as practiced between the states of Dwaben and Krakye in the Volta region began with the establishment of a shrine of the Krakye god, Krakye Dente, in Dwaben. On this basis, the relations between Dwaben and Krakye have continued to the present. Indeed, "so powerful was this god that even the English had to conclude a treaty of friendship with it during the last two decades of the nineteenth century" (Boahen 1973, 9).

The establishment of jocular relations between states is another unusual practice. The intimate and friendly ties that grew up in the eighteenth century and continued to the present between the Asante and the Nzema have been symbolized by a joking relationship between the two peoples, making a particular level of relations that facilitates the management of conflict.

The Akan rulers also used their common membership in the same clan to build relationships that transcended conflict. Strong fraternal relations continue to exist among the former states of Kumawu, Agogo, Domaa, and Akwamu simply because all the rulers belong to the same clan, the Aduana, reinforcing on a historical level the fact that these states are now part of the modern polity of Ghana. Similarly, the then independent states of Kumasi, Dwaben, Bekwai, Kokofu, and Nsuta were able to come together to form the nucleus that would later grow into the famous Asante Empire primarily because their ruler came from the same Oyoko clan, cutting across state lines. Most of the stools that came to constitute the Akyem Abuakwa State—Kyebi, Kukurantumi, Kwaaben, and Osiem—were all members of the Asona clan. Common clan membership of state rulers provided fraternal ties but more importantly shared values and identities that made conflicts easier to handle.

The most common method by which the Akan sealed their treaties, alliances, and diplomatic relations was the "drinking of gods"—*nom abosom*—or swearing of oaths by the parties involved. A drink would be prepared from herbs and powders taken from the grove of the god mixed with liquor, and all members present would drink this concoction and then swear an oath to abide by the terms of the treaty on pain of being killed by the god. In 1726, the Dutch reported that "it is not only that these two districts [of Fante and Kwanu] are bound by oaths and otherwise to inform each other of such matters but they are also so closely allied that if the one is attacked the other is bound to help." In 1759, the English reported that the Fante and the Asante had "taken oath or fetish" and, in 1764, that the Wassa and the Fante had agreed to "drink fetish and be friends." Sometimes the oath was reinforced by other ties, such as the exchange of hostages. The alliance between the Agona and the Fante in 1715 was sealed by an oath, and then "as a pledge of good faith, the King of Agona had sent his son to live at Abrah," according to a Dutch report at the time. To make an alliance or a treaty irrevocable, the Akan usually swore an oath, "drank a god," or exchanged hostages and fired a gun—"Yeato tuo agu so"—at the end of the negotiations" (Boahen 1973, 9–10).

The secret was in the belief that emphasized not only the fear of death of individuals but the fear of being rejected by the ancestors and gods in the spirit world, often expressed as the fear of natural calamity likely to come from the anger of the gods. This belief system affected people's attitudes in their quarrels over fishing grounds, trade routes, and territorial boundaries (Dike 1956). Sometimes, the ability of the king to monitor political crises in his relations with chiefdoms required him to use caution in the exercise of authority in order to prevent the escalation of conflicts.

■ Armistice, Arbitration, and Authority

Despite the preventive effects of management and measures, war did occur. Customary ways were provided to end it. According to Talbot (1969, 25), when one of the parties wished to make peace during the war, it sent some friends from a neutral town or one of its own men draped in palm leaves, holding an alligator pepper in his hand, to the enemy. If the proposal was accepted, a meeting would be arranged that war ended as soon as the warring villages received a flag of truce from the council of elders or from a prominent chief willing to mediate.

However, when efforts made by the council of elders to resolve the conflict among the same community group were frustrated by the recalcitrance of a faction, the council, which could no longer tolerate the threat to its authority, compelled the factional group to travel elsewhere to set up a new establishment (Nicolson 1954, 15). The group was chased out of the community. Here, ostracism differs from similar situations called "split" or "secession" in that in the latter cases, the persecuted, discontented, or simply dissatisfied group decided to go by itself, left the community, and found a new establishment elsewhere.

Within a village, differences between persons are discussed by the elders of the village and an agreement is generally easily reached by kinship and common interests. Disputes between members of nearby villages, between which there are many social contracts and ties, can also be settled by agreement, but less easily and with more likelihood of resort to force. However, between sections on opposite sides of a tribe there are fewer chances of settlement.

In West Africa, people worship the earth, and in this worship groups who are otherwise in hostile relations annually unite in celebration, because people live, work, dance, breed, and die on the earth in the company of other people. They obtain their rights to earth by virtue of membership of groups and they can maintain themselves only by virtue of this membership. To live on the earth they require friendship with other people over a certain area. The earth, undivided as the basis of society, thus comes to symbolize not individual prosperity, fertility, and good fortune, but the general prosperity, fertility, and good fortune on which individual life depends. With this concept or vision of general prosperity are associated peace and the recognition of a moral order over a range of land.

Apart from the important role performed by the council of elders in the process of internal or interneighboring community conflict resolution, the employment of accredited agents to represent and negotiate on behalf of a state or society seems to be a nearly constant practice in West African tradition (Smith 1968, 11). Specifically, Boahen (1973, 8) reported, "it seems clear that the Akan resorted to all the known methods of diplomacy. The first and obvious one was the dispatch of diplomatic missions or ambassadors to conduct negotiations which would lead to the formation of alliances or the conclusion of treaties of amity."

A number of different, special rules also existed. Arbitrators are ritual experts who are called "men of the earth." They have no forceful powers of coercion. They cannot command men to do something and expect to be obeyed, but they are political as well as ritual functionaries. If a fight broke out, the "man of the earth" can restore peace by running between the combatants and hoeing up the earth. Inside a community, the slayer of a man is defiled with blood and can neither eat nor drink until the "man of the earth" has let the blood of the dead man out of his body. If the slayer resides near the home of the man he killed, he will live in sanctuary with the "man of the earth" to avoid death at the hands of his victim's kin. The "man of the earth" will then negotiate between the two families or groups and try to induce the deceased's kin to accept compensation. This they are bound in honor to refuse, but they will eventually yield when the "man of the earth" threatens to curse them.

In precolonial Ibibio society, there were also persons known as messengers or errand men; linguists or priests sometimes played this role, especially if language difficulty was likely to arise. The person who was assigned this duty may have been chosen because he had skills in oratory, persuasion, language, literacy, technology, and social management, or because of his ability to deliver messages with dispatch, or just because he had a respectable name and was highly regarded in the society.

Within the context of peaceful settlement of conflicts, there is generally among the Ouatchi an exceptional character. In Togo and parts of Ghana, this person was called *du nku,* in Benin *agbadjigbeto* or "the community eye," and in other communities the same character exists under different names. *Du* contains the notion of community. While it fits the hamlet or village, town or city, it also fits the extension of the same notion to the state and can refer to a whole continent as in the expression *Africa dua* (the African continent), *America dua* (the American continent), or *Yovode dua* (the European continent). Consequently, *du nku* is that exceptional character who can be encountered in the village, in the town, in the nation, as well as in the world, meaning the world conceived as a synthesis of many nations (*Xixedua*). *Du* can subsidiarily convey the notion of an indicative sign, of a coded message that has to be decoded to draw the underlying meaning from it. Such is the case of *Fadu,* indicating the quality of calmness.

The second term, *nku,* means "the eye," the perception with all its qualities. *Du nku* is therefore the city man who emerges because of his exceptional qualities, and is perceived as such by others. Thus, *du nku* holds two poles: the emergence of the individual and its perception by the others. In order to emerge, *du nku* must have exceptional qualities that distinguish him from the others and inspire trust. These qualities include *amenkuta* (personality), *ametohe* (exceptional character), *ngonola* (the one who is at the community's service), *du mega* (great experience and credibility), and *dunya gblola* (the spokesman, but who also remains faithful to the given or spoken word). Because of the deep knowledge he has of his environment, *du nku* is the conciliator, the adviser (Asafo or Asafotse Adonudoto), the confidant.

The qualities that other citizens require of their *du nku* are that he must be one who knows his environment and who, when he speaks, knows exactly what he is talking about. He is familiar with history, culture, beliefs, and with the secular power's forms of devolution. Through his behavior, he must prove that he is telling the truth and that he is conforming to the spoken word. What he says and does must be identical, which means that his behavior should become identified with the word. It is intolerable to lie. The person who is persuading embodies the true word. Because of his human qualities, *du nku* teaches by way of example. The citizen judges him through everyday concrete life. *Du nku* is the living example of the citizen whose morality resists any temptation. Living in community necessarily poses social problems, problems displayed publicly before the king of the village, or worse before a court. We are thus always relieved if we can confide in a conciliator to find an amicable arrangement for our difficulties.

Similarly, among the Akan of Ghana, it is quite evident from oral traditions that peacemaking was the responsibility of a professional class consisting of the Akyeame, the Ofenasofo (the sword bearer), and the Esen (the court crier). Each Akan king has a minimum of five Akyeame and a maximum of ten or more headed by the Akyeamehene, or king of the Akyeame. The Akyeame is the king's closest adviser on all matters of a constitutional, political, cultural, and specifically customary nature. But his greatest and probably primary role was undoubtedly the conduct of diplomacy on behalf of the king, and it was usually the Akyeame whom the king would dispatch to conduct all negotiations about war and peace, about the establishment of friendly relations with neighboring states, and the conclusion of defensive and offensive alliances (Boahen 1973).

■ Conclusion

Conflicts are a dynamic part of social life. A number of prominent scholars have highlighted the positive effect of conflict within a nation. For example, Eliot (1949, 3) suggested that both class and region, by dividing the inhabitants of a country into two kinds of groups, lead to a conflict favorable to creativeness and progress. Like any other human society, the African people had their share of conflicts during the precolonial period. All African peoples, notably in the western part of African, had such well-established and well-known codes of morals and laws, conventions, ethics, and rituals that even though they had no written histories, they persisted for long periods with a fairly efficient system of internal law and order, successfully evolving and defending themselves against attacks by others. African peoples facing wars and conflicts in precolonial times successfully developed and applied diplomatic techniques, procedures, and methods to maintain peace among themselves as they forged codes of customs, ethics, and laws to institute cohesion within their societies. The question that one may ask, therefore, is: To what extent are we able to draw useful lessons from their experiences for the benefit of Africa's current quest for regional security?

To establish the usefulness of transferring the traditional, peaceful, conflict resolution system to the contemporary system, one must first answer the question: Why did the traditional system of conflict resolution disappear? It is because the entities involved have changed in dimension and scope. During the precolonial times, there existed small communities that practiced this system within their limited boundaries. Today's society has become very complex; the old communities that used to enjoy their own independence are now forced to be part of more or less artificial national contexts longing for national identity. These new states in turn join larger regroupings such as the Economic and Monetary Union of West Africa (UEMOA), the Economic Community of West African States (ECOWAS), the Organization of African Unity (OAU), and others.

Under such circumstances, the transfer of a traditional institution like *du nku* to the contemporary context could be envisaged at several levels. In the context of a nation hypothetically consisting of various ethnic groups, tribes, or nations, the crucial issue to be addressed on the way to national construction is the need to compensate for the lack or the absence of a real transmission belt between the ruler and the ruled, and a correspondence between the ruler and the rules. Members of parliament, in their capacity as representatives of the nation, are supposed to play these roles. But in fact they do not, because most of the time they are elected on an ethnic basis and consequently embody only a section of the population whose interests they struggle to defend. Furthermore, in most African countries, tribunals are nonexistent or poorly operational.

This leaves a role that *du nku* can usefully play by expressing the needs and aspirations of both the population as a whole and those citizens who have no access to the public authorities in order to get hearing. The role of *du nku* is to serve as a moderation between the ruled and the rulers in order to anticipate and settle conflicts.

It would be good to choose a retired person known for competence and integrity. He or she should be a first-class moral authority with no political affiliation and should enjoy the confidence of the various partners among whom he or she is called upon to act as a reconciliator. His or her job would be to collect the feelings of frustration or dissatisfaction experienced by the population and suggest ways to settle conflicts and remedy administrative shortcomings. The *du nku* can play the role of go-between and could be very efficient in establishing honorable agreements. A mediator can also be chosen within the framework of professional organizations structured into specialized activity sectors and union and religious organizations. There should be a moderator for each socioeconomic sector in conformity with the structure of the government whose ministries reflect the various activity sectors. At the ministerial and interministerial levels, one could envisage a board of mediators whose mission could consist of producing a synthesis report on the social and professional problems of the country. An annual report should be submitted to the prime minister, to the speaker of the house, to the president of the socioeconomic council, and to the president of the republic in his capacity as supreme arbitrator.

It is possible to institute *du nku* at the level of state relations. In this case a structure could be established that goes from the tribes to the major national communities. Each state could identify its own *du nku.* In the case of regional organizations like ECOWAS and the Front Line States, a board of *du nku*s could be put in charge of promoting honorable agreements in order to solve conflicts in the region.

A collective effort should be made in each country to identify citizens that are morally recommendable people who, in addition, could remain neutral and indifferent regardless of the demands that would be made on them from various sources. The African Human Rights Observatory should be charged with listing such resource persons who could generate confidence in the parties involved in various conflicts.

Conflicts and wars break out most of the time because the people who initiate them believe that they are strong as individuals, ethnic groups, village communities, countries, and so on, but mainly because they count on potential allies in case of complication. The international *du nku* must be trusted by as many people as possible so as to shake, through persuasion, the foundations of all alliances that constitute a permanent threat to peace. Internationally known and respected African personalities such as General loumani Toure of Mali, Wole Soyinka of Nigeria, Olusengun Obasanjo of Nigeria, Nelson Mandela of South Africa, and Julius Nyerere of Tanzania, among others, have already been playing this role. The concept of *du nku* and the philosophy sustaining it could be used as a key element in defining or elaborating strategies of conflict resolution in the context of interstate relations.

6

Indigenous Processes of Conflict Resolution in Oromo Society

Hamdesa Tuso

Every society develops a worldview through which it perceives and interacts with the surrounding reality. A society's worldview is constructed through the cultural lenses that people have developed through years of socialization. The debate that has been raging for many decades with respect to the origin of war and violence in human society was long between those who believe war is the result of human aggression innate in human biology and those who argue that it is a learned behavior; it now subsides into a third school holding that social conflict is a socially learned phenomenon, just like any other complex activity, such as development of speech and construction of language (Montague 1978). Most anthropologists, following Malinowski (1948), have been focusing on structures of institutions, ideologies, and socialization processes that harness and channel aggression in culture (Bariso 1988).

The data originate from three main sources. The first source comprises interviews that I conducted during 1994–1996 among Oromos living in exile in North America, in Portland, Oregon; Seattle, Washington; and East Lansing, Michigan. The second source is information that has been borrowed from different field works on Oromo culture and society, particularly since World War II. These sources are augmented by my own reconstruction of knowledge from my memory of growing up among the Oromo. I was born and raised in an Oromo family within an Arsie Oromo community of the Rift Valley (in the Negale and Shashamene area) that practiced indigenous Oromo culture in its total orientation—material, symbolic, and ideological. Although as a lad I ran away to school as many kids of my generation did in search of the new challenges promised by the new global system on the horizon, I was able to inherit considerable knowledge both through socialization and practical observations on numerous occasions when *jarsa biya* (community elders) feverishly labored to resolve social conflict at various levels in the community. In addition, during the last two decades, I have been active among Oromos of various backgrounds (region, religion, class, etc.) in the diaspora—the first generation of Oromo to have been outside their cultural environment—in North America, Europe, and Australia. In the process, I have observed considerable efforts made by the Oromo community leadership in the diaspora to employ Oromo methods of conflict resolution in dealing with social conflict among Oromos at various social levels: interpersonal, organizational, ideological, and political.

■ Emerging Dynamics in Oromo Society

Our exploration with respect to the traditional processes of conflict resolution in Oromo society should be viewed in the context of certain dynamics that have had profound influence on Oromo society during the past few decades.

First, the Oromo society and culture have undergone much stress during the twentieth century, primarily as the result of conquest, colonization, and partition. In contrast to the European colonization of most of African societies, the Oromo society was conquered and colonized by the Abyssinians (Amharas and Tigreans) during the late nineteenth and early twentieth centuries. From King Sahle Sellassie (1813–1848) to Emperors Menelik II (1867–1913) and Haile Sellassie (1930–1936; 1941–1974), the founders of the modern Ethiopian empire unscrupulously plundered the Oromo population and recklessly sacked Cushitic cultures, including that of the Oromos, in the manner comparable to their European colonial counterparts (Zahar 1974). Unique cultures were decimated and local leadership was destroyed (Levine 1972).

During this period, the conquerors and the conquered interacted on negative terms. The Habesha culture was imposed on the Oromo society, creating two antagonistic societies within the imperial social order. The Habesha society was considered God's "chosen" people, while the Oromo society was considered subhuman. Until 1974, the Oromos were referred to as "Gallas"—meaning "uncivilized, savage, and cruel" in Amharic—both in the state official communication as well as in Habesha social circles. Its culture was referred to as *aramane* (pagan) and viewed as inferior and only suitable for destruction. Accordingly, the Habeshas developed mythical portraits—a common phenomenon that emanates from the interrelations between the colonizer and the colonized (Memmi 1968)—with respect to the Oromo society as early as the sixteenth century (Abir 1980, 144). The overall policies of suppressing Oromo culture and language sharpened during the reign of Emperor Haile Sellassie. The new policy directives called for the expansion of (Orthodox) Christianity, the predominance of Amharic culture and language throughout the empire, and the formulation of quick and effective mechanisms of Amharanizing the majority Oromos before they could develop their own consciousness and cause problems.

New religions, primarily Christianity and Islam, penetrated the Oromo society during the same period. Orthodox Christianity was imposed on the Oromos by the colonial rulers, and in reaction many, particularly in the southern and eastern regions, accepted Islam during the 1940s, essentially as a protest against the oppressive Abyssinian system (Trimingham 1965; Baxter 1983). In some areas, Catholic and Protestant Christianity had been introduced as the result of Western Christian missionary efforts (Mazrui 1990; Nyang 1994).

In Ethiopia, this was the period when the imperial state bureaucracy system penetrated every facet of the social fabric of the peoples in the periphery, including the Oromos, as modernity, though limited, was introduced into Ethiopia by Emperor Haile Sellassie. In essence, modernity was coded in the context of Amhara-Tigray culture and language. This policy further intensified the friction between the urban *naftagnas* (colonial settlers) and the Oromo rural dwellers. The tensions emanating from these discriminatory imperial policies created divisions within the Oromo society itself, between the illiterate masses and the educated few. Educated Oromos, in order to succeed in the Habesha-dominated imperial system, were pressured to learn Amharic, to marry Amhara women or men, to change their names from Oromo to Amharic, and to behave as though they were Amharas (Shack 1976; Tuso 1982). The Oromo masses in general came to view the Habeshas as enemies.

Oromo society was separated and organized under various forms as a result of natural and political barriers that had been put in place during the last centuries. The natural barriers include rivers, valleys, mountain gorges, and sheer distance. As the population increased and spread itself in all directions in search of resources, including a sizable migration south into northeast Kenya, its members mingled with other ethnic groups, and separation from the Oromo traditional cultural centers increased. Some adopted the cultures and values of their new neighbors, while others, in due course, regionalized and localized their traditions and cultural practices (LeVine 1972, 78–86, 149, 158). Lack of literacy and modern means of communication and transportation, along with the lack of freedom to plan and manage its own national affairs, has weakened Oromo culture and the language. The European missionary endeavor to introduce literacy into the Oromo society in the Oromo language during the nineteenth century and during the subsequent decades was repeatedly thwarted by the successive Abyssinian rulers (Hassan 1981; Tuso 1920). Having no heritage of literacy has had considerable negative impacts on Oromo society. Among the great handicaps such societies face is that their histories depend mostly on oral traditions and guesses. Worst of all, as in the case of most subjugated people, they are defined by others. Thus, naturally, the origin of the Oromo people has been a source of controversy. Some have suggested that they migrated to Ethiopia from somewhere outside, perhaps through the Indian Ocean during the periods prior to the sixteenth century (LeVine 1961, 78–86). However, more recent scholarship based on linguistic and oral history has established that the Horn of Africa, between the Bale plateau and the Rift Valley, has been their home for their known history (Levine 1972, 78; Lewis 1966; Laitin and Samatar 1987, 5–10).

Increasingly, stress has been exerted by the successive Addis Ababa regimes on the Oromo people. There is great fear that if the Oromos gained their democratic rights, they might call for the independence of Oromia, with other regions to follow, to threaten the very survival of Ethiopia as a viable political entity. Perhaps as the result of the psychology of rising expectations, the Oromo people are experiencing dramatically increased consciousness, and consequently Oromo nationalism is currently at its zenith after the overthrow of the Mengistu regime in 1991. Culture and language have been the two rallying factors, which is a common phenomenon in the rise of nationalism. Under the general rubric of Oromo culture, there has been a rise of great interest in the Oromo indigenous methods of conflict resolution.[1]

One of the most numerous indigenous peoples on the African continent, the Oromos belong to the general family of Cushitic peoples indigenous to northeast Africa (Ethiopia, Kenya, and Somalia) along with the Somalis and Afars (Baxter 1983, 7; Laitin and Samatar 1987, 4–7). Out of the approximately 52 million Ethiopians, about 25–28 million are estimated to be Oromos, spread through the highlands of Ethiopia including Addis Ababa itself and south across the lowlands of Kenya.

As with other Cushitic groups in the Horn of Africa, the Oromo social system is genealogically based. The society is divided into major autonomous branches: Boran, Guji, Arsie, the Harar confederation (including primarily Ittu and Afran Kallo), Tulama, Matcha (including Wollega and Illibabor), and Abichu-Raya (the two groups in Wollo and Tigray). Each branch comprises four levels from the largest (clan) to the smallest (family), sometimes with variations. These units are: *gossa* (clan), *balbala* (subclan), *anna* (extended family), and *worra* (family). Like the Somalis, the next largest Cushitic group, the Oromos use the clan system as well as the eldership system in the coordination of the social affairs of the nation.

Within their diversity, Oromos share certain basic characteristics: common ancestry, common threads of culture, a common mother tongue, a common psychological makeup, a common institutional memory (the Gada system), and common colonial experience (Baxter 1983, 1996).

The Oromo have a strong and well-defined belief system, based on seven interrelated concepts: (1) *Waaqa;* (2) *Ayaana;* (3) *Setana;* (4) *Chubu;*

(5) *Ballessa;* (6) *Kayyo;* (7) *Qittee.* Oromos believe that *Waaqa* is the universal God, who created everything. There are different versions with respect to his past dealings with human beings on earth, one of which tells that he was troubled by the evil deeds of human beings, escaped to the sky, and currently resides there. Historically, the Oromos also worship other objects such as rivers, animals, and trees. They, however, do not consider these objects as Waaqa, the creator; rather they worship them in their effort to solicit the intermediary services of these elements in their pursuit of mercy and reconciliation with Waaqa and blessings from him (Bariso 1988). *Ayaana* is the process of creation through which Waaqa made all things. It is the grace by which Waaqa expresses himself (Megerssa 1994).

The Oromos believe in the existence of the evil spirit whom they refer to as *Setana.* According to the Oromo notion of sin, Setana constantly tempts people to do wrong things, and one has to watch against being trapped by Setana. *Chubu* refers to one's conscious acts to harm other people, constituting sin against society and Waaqa. It upsets the internal consistency of society and impairs harmonious relationships between humans and Waaqa, *laffa* (the earth), and other elements in the ecosystem. Disharmony as the result of social conflict must be repaired through *jarsumma* (reconciliation/peacemaking.) *Ballessa* refers to the transgression caused when someone harms someone else, usually through omission. *Kayyo* is a broad concept that describes a person's fullest life or lack of it. In the Oromo worldview, everyone should behave in such a way to have *Kayyo qajella* (good *kayyo.*) This requires that one worship Waaqa through gifts, treat fellow human beings fairly, and revere the ecosystem (Hinnant 1977, 36–38).

Qittee expresses the Oromo notion of equality among persons. Legesse (1987, 12) suggests that the Oromo notion of *qittee* (egalitarianism) has shaped the very syntactical construction of the Oromo language.

The system of value is reflected in the language and conduct of the people and in their day-to-day activities. It is no accident that Oromo language does not have complicated pronouns of power. You (*ati*) is a perfectly serviceable multipurpose pronoun whether one is referring to a child or an adult, a man or a woman, a junior or a senior individual. Contrast this, if you will, with the complicated ways of saying "you" in authoritarian societies such as the Ethiopian Amharas.

Believing all people are created equal and therefore deserve equal treatment in most aspects relating to life and basic rights, Oromos spend an unusual amount of time and energy in peacemaking among themselves.

Social scientists have observed that in some societies (e.g., the Amharas of Ethiopia), social conflict is a way of life, while in others (e.g., the Semai in Malaysia), it is nonexistent or minimal (Levine 1972; Dentan 1968; Robarchek 1994). In some societies, violent conflict is allowed under limited circumstances and strictly stipulated guidelines. The Oromos' societal experience relative to social conflict and peacemaking fits this third category. Oromos wage wars, but under strict circumstances and for limited purposes, to meet their basic needs: self-defense; new resources (e.g., new territories for grazing); and for fulfillment of personal aspirations (to become a hero). Internally, social conflict also takes place at various levels, but Oromo show their attachment to internal social harmony and peaceful coexistence with their neighbors through elaborate principles and processes to manage it.

The Oromos work very hard to manage conflict on three different levels: to prevent social conflict from occurring; if it occurs, to prevent it from escalating; and if it escalates, to make peace between the conflicting parties through the intervention of the *jarsa biya* (elders of the community). The ideological themes underpinning the processes of conflict resolution are *effort* (society has to work at it until the conflict is fully resolved and total reconciliation is consummated because there is no conflict that cannot be resolved); *truth* (*dhuga bassu*) (conflict is resolved by unearthing the truth about the causes of the conflict); *justice* (the goals of peacemaking have to include the consummation of justice); *punishment* (*guma*) (payment for the wrong committed is not usually excessive since the Oromos do not have jails or the death penalty); and *reconciliation* (an act that is believed to be necessary to keep harmony between the creator and the creatures—humans and nature). These then govern construction of political structures (the Gada system), religious customs (the Kallu system), social structures (the eldership, or *jarsa biya,* system), and the elaborate processes of reconciliation (*arara*), systems that the Oromos developed to manage conflicts in a way that transcends divisions along regional, clan (*gossa*), and subclan (*balbala*) lines.

■ The Gada System

The Gada system may be the most studied indigenous African institution. The first writer on the Gada system on record is a sixteenth-century Abyssinian ecclesiastic by the name of Bahrey (1954). Other travelers, diplomats, and social scientists studied the Gada system during the nineteenth and twentieth centuries, many of them considering it uniquely democratic. For example, W. Plowden (1868), who traveled in the region in the nineteenth century, stated that among republican systems, Gada is superior. Atsime Giorgis (1988), another Abyssinian writer at the end of the nineteenth century, wrote that the Gada system unites and mobilizes all members of Oromo society into a formidable and invincible force. Paul Baxter (1978, 151), a contemporary British anthropologist, wrote, "They [Oromos] have especially captured the imagination of travelers and ethnographers because of their ancient, enduring and complex system of age-grading, Gada, which, it has been consistently reported, has also served as the basis of a uniquely democratic political system." Asmarom Legesse (1973), an Eritrean anthropologist who is considered to have written the most definitive interpretation of the Gada system, observed:

> The gada system is an institution that appears so exaggerated that it is readily dismissed by laymen and scholars alike as a sociological anomaly. Anomalous though it may be, it is one of the most astonishing and instructive turns the evolution of human society has taken. . . . Gada seems to be one of the universals that binds the entire nation into a coherent system and gives people a common political basis for understanding each other. It constitutes a shared political idiom.

This, then, is the philosophical vantage point from which we view the character of Oromo democracy. What is astonishing about this cultural tradition is how far the Oromos have gone to ensure that power does not fall into the hands of war chiefs and despots. They achieve this goal by creating a system of checks and balances that is at least as complex as the systems we find in the Western societies.

In the Gada system, men are organized along two sets of five categories. The first set is a chronologically based age-grade designation. In this set each male goes through five grades of eight years each where he performs a set of duties and responsibilities prior to moving to the next period. Ideally, a male enters into this generation-grade system on the day he is born and stays in the system through his life, completing the cycle when his active duties are completed at age forty-eight. After that, he retires from active duties but remains an elder statesman who counsels and makes peace within the society. However, Oromo society being a polygamous society, children are born at different parental age periods, which creates major gaps in the age-grade system. The two major purposes in this differentiation in the generation-grade system are to provide the necessary human power for the society all the time and also to prevent sons and fathers from entering into the ruling period at the same time. Each eight-year period in the cycle has a name for the generation grade: (1) *Iti Mako* (8–16 years); (2) *Daballe* (16–24 years); (3) *Folle* (24–32 years); (4) *Qondala* (32–40 years); (5) *Luba* (40–48 years).

The second critical component in the Gada institution is the *luba* system. The equivalent concept for *luba* in the English language is "party." Men are organized into five *luba* (party) sets. The *luba* system is known by other names, such as *misenssa* and *gogsa,* among Oromos. Scholars have used the term "classes" or "age-sets." Thus, each male is born into a party and each party goes through the five periods (generation set system) as described above. Table 6.1 illustrates the relationships between these two sets (the generation-grade set and the *luba* set [party] and the summary of roles and responsibilities performed. Thus Gada, as a system, is conceived as a unity of interacting parts. The system organizes the social order by dividing all men into groups and providing a blueprint that specifies an arrangement of strategies (grades); the relationships among different grades; rights, rules of behavior, and the tasks to be performed in each grade; and the process by which groups (parties) move from grade to grade (Waldansso 1980).

Table 6.1 Duties of Each Grade

Iti Mako (usual age: 8–16 years)
- Looking after livestock
- Messengers and errand runners

Daballe (usual age: 16–24 years)
- Herding
- Care of livestock
- Look for new trade opportunities

Folle (usual age: 24–32 years)
- Warriors; use physical strength to protect Oromo nation
- Live separate from other Oromo peoples

Qondala (usual age: 32–40 years)
- Reserve army
- Learn the laws and principles of administration
- Marry
- Select their officials

Luba (usual age: 40–48 years)
- Ruling grade
- Handle judicial matters
- Diplomats, arbitrators, and councilors

The result is a hierarchical system of authority or legitimate power (Lasswell and Kaplan 1950). Authority is transferred to a new generation grade every eight years; authority is held in balance, and corruption and nepotism are prevented through the institution of succession; the party in power for eight years assumes responsibility in military, economics, politics, rituals, and peace and reconciliation; the leadership of the ruling party is chosen through open and fair elections; the system has pluralistic characteristics; the system prohibits the political leadership from amassing wealth while in office; and there is a mechanism to recall officers in case of incompetence or corruption. The nature of the system forces every party to enter new generation grades every eight years when the party acting as luba (the ruling party) retires at the end of the forty-year cycle. Thus, for example, sons and fathers cannot be in the same or even successive ruling generation grade (Legesse 1987; Manglapus 1987, 134–137).

The Gada system of conflict management moves through thirteen identifiable steps on its way to managing and resolving conflict and arriving at *arara* (reconciliation) so that harmonious relations can be restored among conflicting parties, God the Creator, the community, and the surrounding world. These steps are in regard to the most dramatic and emotional of any kind of social conflict, violence leading to loss of life.

As soon as the community learns that there has been violence that has caused the death of an Oromo, male or female, it is shaken by the news and becomes mobilized. The kin (up to the clan level) both of the person who committed the crime and of the dead person want to avoid the escalation of the conflict into a cycle of violence. Whether accidental or intentional, the death of an Oromo is treated by both kin groups with the same level of anxiety and vigilance. Of course, if it is learned early on that the death was accidental, tensions are lessened since Oromos are usually willing to look at such accidents as the will of Waaqa and are much more disposed to give the reconciliation process the matter of due course. If, however, the killing is shown to be an intentional act, then the pressure to mobilize the resources for the purpose of revenge would be enormous and, indeed, could escalate so much that the conflict could get out of hand.

Thus, the community members, being cognizant of this enormous danger, move with great speed, essentially to achieve three critical goals at this stage: to mobilize the community leadership for immediate intervention; to warn the killer's kin that they should conform to the Oromo traditional law of collective responsibility in the case of death caused by a kinsman, considering every kinsman of the killer to be a party to the killing and therefore liable for revenge by the kin of the victim; and finally to avoid spilling more blood. The Oromo believe that spilling Oromo blood would poison the total environment, risking health to all the communities concerned; in Oromo mythology for example, if a person touches or steps upon spilled blood, even when he or she has no part in the incident, he or she, in due course, would develop leprosy or a similar disease (Hinnant 1977).

Thus it becomes important to recruit *jarsa biya* (elders) of the killer's kin groups to assure the kin of the dead person that they are working on the case in compliance with the law (*sera*) and custom (*adda*), that they will soon begin criminal procedures (*gumma*), and that they are eager to work earnestly on reconciliation (*arara*).

In step two of the process, the appropriate *jarsa biya* are selected. The qualification of *jarsa biya* are many, and steps required for the selection of the elders to serve at this level of societal responsibility are rigorous. At the philosophical level, they must have a commitment to the Oromo societal ideology, which encompasses the five major themes of effort, truth, justice, punishment, and reconciliation. The key qualifications for eldership in such matters include thorough knowledge of both law and custom; intellectual ability to grasp issues and interpret them according to the *sera* and *adda;* skills in managing group dynamics including communication; absolute integrity of character; commitment to the Oromo ideology relative to the cause of truth, justice, and reconciliation; and earned trust from one's peers and the community.

The process of selecting the *jarsa biya* may be initiated at different levels. Usually members of the family of the person who committed the crime approach the elders of their community and ask for assistance. In cases where family leadership does not exist, the elders of the clan or subclan may come forward with the initiatives in selecting the *jarsa biya.* Usually two elders are selected from each side and one person from each representing the Gada institution. The persons representing the Gada institution physically sit between the elders representing the parties at conflict. The *jarsa biya* meet to develop a common understanding of the crisis at hand and the strategy to take. They use a legal inquiry procedure known as *qorra,* in which they are allowed to ask any question with respect to the law and custom relating to the case at hand, sifting information and establishing basic facts. Once consensus is reached as to the nature of the problem, they send a message to the other party that the kin of the defendant wish to settle the matter in accordance with the *sera* and *adda* and respectfully request to meet with the *jarsa biya* from the other side as soon as possible.

In a case where no one has admitted to the act, if the family of the dead person knows the killer or suspects someone, a member will approach the kin and clan to begin the process of charging the suspected person. In such cases, the process of identifying the *jarsa biyas* and developing strategy could be laborious and time-consuming, but once agreements have been reached on the selection of the elders, the next steps are the same.

In step three, the selected elders and the representatives of the Gada institution meet by themselves for the first time to exchange ideas and work out procedures and to select a *haiyu* (judge) from among themselves. For a person to be selected *haiyu,* one needs to have qualities as a member of the *jarsa biya,* plus a superior ability to use proverbs and metaphors, leadership ability to steer the discussion and keep tempers cool, and a record of success in making peace in the community. Once the *jarsa biya* and the Gada representatives meet, they usually go to the clan (*gossa*) of the dead person to ask that the matter be given to the *jarsa biya* and the Gada representatives and to give permission for the use of three critical places by the family and clan of the person who committed the crime: residence (that means they do not have to flee from their homes), river, and the market. In the meantime, they assist the family in burying the dead and stay with the family during the entire period of mourning, ranging from one to four weeks. These activities and gestures are designed to ensure de-escalation of the conflict by both demonstrating sympathy and exercising surveillance, so that no one would take the matter in one's own hands and seek revenge.

In step four, the *jarsa biya* deliberate on the nature of the conflict, the law that was broken and the customs that have been violated, and the laws and customs that could be applied in resolving the case. Essentially, they begin to move from the stage of diagnosis to that of finding a formula for resolution.

In step five, the elders meet separately with conflicting parties. This is a very critical strategy for the purpose of controlling the tempers of the parties and the process, consistent with the Oromo philosophy of forestalling escalation and maintaining civility. They listen carefully to the concerned parties and make inquiries. If need be, they may break to caucus (*maqqo*) and discuss it privately.

After meeting with the parties, step six is to meet with the witnesses. The presiding elders instruct the witnesses to tell the whole truth and examine the responses point by point as they interrogate the witnesses.

In step seven, the elders then recess again to debate among themselves on the issues that remain unresolved. If there is still uncertainty or if they feel that the defendant is not telling the truth, the elders (with the plaintiff, in accordance with Oromo tradition) will require the entire family, subclan, and clan of the defendant to swear in accordance with the Oromo law and customs that every person in the community has been socialized through family, civic, and religious teachings to the tell the truth and do justice, to keep harmony in the society and the environment; they are placed before their social responsibility, failure in which would lead to the loss of blessings from Waaqa. If the family and clan believe that their member has been accused unfairly or he or she is telling the whole truth, they defend him or her. After all, to defend a family and clan member against any unfair treatment and false accusations is part of their moral and social obligation.

Everyone looks forward to the verdict (*murtte*)—step eight— that will produce *arara* between the parties and restoration of peace and harmony among the spirits of the people, the deity, and the ecosystem. To the elders who have accepted the responsibility of peacemaking and to the presiding *haiyu* this is a very critical moment too, for their task is not only to declare their findings but to do so in such a manner as to bring the expected peace and reconciliation. The presiding *haiyu* will cite an Oromo prayer to Waaqa that their efforts will bear fruit and ask that the spirit move the parties to accept the *murtte* and move forward in peace and reconciliation. He then provides a brief summary as to the reasons why they had come together, the work the elders have done, and their readiness to declare a *murtte* and facilitate peacemaking and reconciliation between the parties at conflict. Then the elders will begin *qorra* (legal inquiry) into the issues, the laws and customs, investigations, and the process of reaching the *murtte* (verdict).

Once the process of *qorra* is completed, the *haiyu* will begin carefully declaring the *murtte* followed by the appropriate course of action in response to the findings. If, for example, murder was involved, there will be a determination of the blood payment price (*gumma*). Usually in such a case, the family members of the dead person, with assistance of the kin and clan wise men, will put forward the demands for the *gumma.* However, the guilty party may petition for lenience, and the elders usually support moderation in such matters and may lean toward recommending more symbolic gestures in paying the *gumma* rather than profit making. All of these things are sorted out ahead of time (perhaps in step seven).

In step nine, the *haiyu* representing the elders will proceed and implore the guilty party to accept *balessa* (wrongdoing). In this process, they repeat their findings and remind the party to consider the *sera* and *adda.* The guilty party usually accepts such murtte rather readily, as his relatives and wise people from his community will urge him to do.

Once the guilty party accepts his wrongdoing, the elders will turn their attention to the grieved party, in step ten, and implore him to accept the *dhuga* (truth), to forgive, and to be reconciled. Since the aggrieved party has been represented in the composition of the *jarsa biya* by the elders he and his party selected, and since it is in everyone's vital interest to complete this process and move toward reconciliation, he too usually readily accepts the essence of the *murtte,* including the acceptance of the *dhuga* decided by the elders.

Step eleven is the administration of penalty. In the Oromo traditional system, human life is considered precious, and the penalties (*guma*) for committing a crime against another Oromo are designed to reinforce this social value. They are intended to serve as a deterrent. This is shown by the amount of cattle one is required to pay and the quality of the animals designated as fitting for such purpose. Symbolically, the amount is usually referred to as *kuma toko* (one thousand) cattle; however, in reality, it may be about a hundred. Only cows and horses are acceptable, not other animals such as donkeys, mules, or goats. Cows and horses are the most loved and respected in Oromo society, and one hundred is a sizable number for an average person in that economy. In step eleven, the task is to announce the penalty to the parties in public, and agree on the nature, amount, and time of its payment.

The twelfth step in the long and arduous process of conflict resolution in the Oromo cultural system is a legal as well as a religious service for the conflicting parties and for the entire community. It is aimed at reconciliation between the parties and between the community and the divine, the earth and the entire psychological and spiritual ecology. It is aimed at cleansing the anger and ill feelings from everyone concerned. At the spiritual level, Oromos believe that receiving continued blessings from Waaqa is dependent upon their forgiving, forgetting, and totally reconciling, making sure that family and clan members will not inherit bitterness and animosity as the result of the conflict.

Thus the conflicting parties and members of their respective communities gather for the ceremony of *arara.* Some kind of drink is prepared for the occasion—*bulbulla* (honey mixed with water) or *dadhi* (soured *bulbulla*) or coffee. The participants share the drink as the elders conduct the ceremony. A variant of the blessing offered on such occasions, as captured by Hinnant (1977, 37), from his work among the Gugi Oromos, contains the central themes of blessings delivered at such ceremonies:

> *biyya arrara* (let the country be reconciled)
> *guda arrara* (let the big, senior, powerful be reconciled)
> *dikka arrara* (let the little, junior, weak be reconciled)
> *loni arrara* (let the cattle be reconciled)
> *nu arrara* (let us be reconciled)
> *nu nagaes* (let us be at peace)
> *nu itit* (let us be thick like yogurt)

The last step is bonding. The activities the conflicting parties undertake during the postreconciliation ceremony are also very critical. For example, if the conflict has involved the loss of human life, family members usually will take further steps to overcome the memory of bitterness and animosity resulting from the conflict. Such actions may involve marriage arrangements or *gudifachaa* (child adoption) between the family members. Another type of activity involves providing lifelong services to a family member whose livelihood has been affected seriously as the consequence of the death of a person in the conflict. For example, if a mother has lost her son, depriving her of the natural help she would normally receive from him, the person and the family responsible for the death will provide lifelong assistance on the farm and other areas of her needs.

The processes discussed thus far are dominated by men. However, Oromos have developed a complex system relating to the role of women in conflict resolution. In the Oromo social system, women are the only group that are protected from physical attack by any party in any conflict. They are sacred humans. Thus, women play important roles as messengers of peace; they organize themselves and physically intervene between the conflicting parties in case of violence; they mobilize the community to respond to the situation of conflict quickly and appropriately; and they serve a moral voice in times of social turmoil.

Oromo Process of Conflict Resolution: Change and Continuity

Do Oromos currently use this system in all regions? And do Oromos use the same system in resolving interregional conflicts (e.g., Arsie vs. Shoa or Guji vs. Borana)? Both questions deserve in-depth research studies and intensive fieldwork. However, the available information shows that the Oromo people in general have retained and practiced these processes, with local variations, in different regions, and have used these processes, with some variations, in responding to interregional conflicts. (Legesse 1973 on Borana; Knutson 1967 on Shoa; Hinnant 1977 and Bariso 1988 on Guji; Tuso forthcoming on Arsie; and Bartel 1983 on Wollega).

Variations can occur at several levels. First, there are cases where Oromos in different regions have extended some type of allegiance and Oromohood to other groups. Second, during the last three years, in the face of intensified political, economic, cultural, and linguistic oppression from the authorities of the Ethiopian empire, Oromo political, intellectual, and community leadership at all levels have embraced traditional methods of conflict resolution in their effort to build solidarity for the purpose of empowering the Oromo so that they may be able to restore their basic rights in the fundamental affairs affecting their daily lives. For example, the Maetcha Tulema Association, the first pan-Oromo organization since the Oromos became colonized, which emerged during the mid-1960s, laid its foundation by entering into a covenant, in accordance with Oromo tradition, with the community leadership from various regions to work together as Oromos, irrespective of the diversities the Oromo people have inherited along the way (Zoga 1993).

Third, perhaps the most dramatic development in the restoration of Oromo cultural traditions in modern times took place in 1991 immediately after the fall of the Dergue (military junta). For the first time since the colonization of the Oromo people, Oromo elders across the entire population within the Ethiopian empire-state formed, almost instantly, a pan-Oromo association of elders. Two elders were selected by the grass roots from each eleven main Oromo regions. Then two elders were selected from each of the fifty-two *Woredas* (subdistricts) of Oromia. The purpose of the elders' association was to bring together the then-five Oromo liberation fronts to avoid bloodshed by Oromos against Oromos in the unstable new political order and to make peace and build trust among Oromos wherever they reside within Ethiopia. They succeeded so well that the new regime eventually banned the newly formed Oromo elders' association, just like all the previous Addis Ababa regimes that had manifested perennial fear and hatred against the Oromos and persecuted the leadership of the elders.

Other examples indicate the Oromos have used the same model of conflict resolution in situations of interethnic conflict. Hinnant (1972, 154–155), from his fieldwork among Oromo Gujis, reports an incident where the Oromos and Sidamas, after fighting for three to four days, sent elder women with messages calling for a truce to the conflict and initiating peacemaking. The conflicting parties met in the presence of those women and made peace. My own informants indicate that the Arsie Oromos use similar patterns of peacemaking after their engagement in violent conflict with their neighbors such as the Sidamas and the Alabas. Bariso (1988, 27–28), an Oromo anthropologist from Guji, reports similar incidents, including a covenant between Gujis and Gedeos (Darasa) not to wage war against each other. A widely reported tradition throughout Oromo history points to a rich legacy of *gudifacha* (adoption) of their victims of war on an equal footing with respect to rights and responsibilities accorded an Oromo citizen (Bariso 1988, 32-33; Hinnant 1977, 112). Historically, Oromos have made peace with their enemies and extended friendship and treated them as neighbors. For example, after they drove the followers of Imam Ahmed Al-Ghazi (Gran) all the way to the city of Harar, where the Adares built a wall around the city as protection against the Oromo cavalry, the Oromos still extended friendship and developed successful cultural and commercial ties with them. Oromos encircled the Amharas in Shoa, and even penetrated the heart of the Abyssinian kingdom during the seventeenth and eighteenth centuries, but never imposed dominance over any of them (Hassan 1983, 147–220; Waldron 1983).

■ Conclusion

This chapter has presented the Oromo processes of conflict resolution in the context of Oromo national historical experience. Oromo systems of conflict resolution are rooted in a worldview that encompasses religion, individual basic rights, human equality, social ethics, and peaceful coexistence with non-Oromo neighbors as well as with the ecosystem. Oromo national ethos can be characterized as egalitarian collectivism. National institutions—political (Gada), religious (Kallu), and social (eldership)—were designed to prevent conflict from happening. Checks and balances were created within the Gada system and between the Gada and Kallu institutions so that no person or group could abuse power. If prevention fails and social conflict occurs, mechanisms are put in place to keep it from escalating and to resolve it based on a search for the truth (*dhuga*) and a verdict (*murtte*) of justice. The system attaches collective responsibility to the crimes committed by an individual member. The ultimate goal in Oromo processes of conflict resolution is to effect conflict transformation through reconciliation (*arara*) between the conflicting parties and the respective community members, the creator, and other creatures, and to restore harmony (*nagaaa*).

As Oromo society has gone through dramatic social changes, particularly during the last two centuries, many of its traditional institutions have been affected negatively. Both the Gada system and the Kallu institution have been undermined by the impact of external social forces (colonization and the introduction of new religions). Yet, its processes of conflict resolution have survived, and provide comparative models of conflict resolution.

■ Notes

1. Two important points need to be included in here. First, during the last century, the successive Addis Ababa regimes have partitioned and rearranged the Oromo territories under different imperial provincial systems. In some instances, new provinces were created bearing the names of the land rather than the Oromo branches. A case in point is the division of the Arsie republic into three units during the early 1960s. A new province, Bale, was created; the Arsie Oromos in the Rift Valley were assigned to Shoa Province; and a small territory was retained as the Arsie Province. As a consequence of this history of a system of division (at least in part), by the end of the Dergue rule, there were eleven Oromo regions. Second, the educated Oromos straddle between the two major systems of references. On one hand, they relate to each other at the national level (the Oromo nation); on the other hand, they also relate to the local social structures as described in this section. I formulated these observations after extensive discussion with my informants.

7

Reaching Out: A Dinka Principle of Conflict Management

Francis M. Deng

In answer to a question about the fundamental principles and attributes that he considered essential to an effective discharge of his duties as a leader, Babo Nimir (initially named Osman), paramount chief of the large conglomeration of Missiriya Arab tribes of southern Kordofan in western Sudan, recalled advice given him by an elder when he assumed his leadership position at the early age of fourteen, advice that he said he followed throughout his leadership (Deng 1982, 36–37):

> Mukhtar . . . a friend of my father . . . caught me by the hand and said, "Come with me, Osman, let me give you a piece of advice. When you become a man and take charge of your job and the cases come in front of you, if the people in conflict are a Kamili and a Feyrani, take the side of the Feyrani; do not take the side of the Kamili. If a Feyrani is in conflict with a Mazghani, be on the side of the Mazghani. And if a Mazghani is in conflict with an Omrani, be with the Omrani." His point was that you always take the position of the person farthest from you. That was the advice of Mukhtar. In my own feelings and in the way I spoke, I followed his advice, but without contravening justice. One must not allow it to cause injustice. But as a general principle, I would always place a great deal of pressure on the side of my relatives.

Of his neighbor and friend, Chief Deng Majok, paramount chief of the Ngok Dinka of southern Kordofan, it has been observed (Deng 1986, 120): "It was Deng Majok who made [his clan] Pajok equal to the rest of the tribe. . . . If he found a man from Pajok clan holding somebody else's right, he would take it from him and give it to the person entitled." And in the words of another observer, "As a leader, Deng did not have a brother, he did not have a father, and he did not have a mother. All the people were the same in his eyes." It is widely acknowledged that "Deng Majok literally lived up to the traditional wisdom that the best way to unite people and protect one's own interests and those of one's close relatives is to safeguard the interests of the stranger and more distant persons first, in order to win them over to your side."

This can indeed be stated as a general principle of dispute resolution in customary law. As noted about judicial procedure among the Dinka (Deng 1971, 168):

> Interested evidence, but not evidence of an interested party, can only widen the gap between the interest groups involved. An interested person may speak, although he may decide not to. Should he speak, he is usually expected to emphasize the wrong of the side in which he is interested. This attitude is especially important among the judges and since the process of litigation involves the gathering and the evaluation of evidence simultaneously, it must be demonstrated throughout the proceedings. Of course, a person to whom the judges and especially the pivotal judges are known to be related, or in whom they are at least interested, has a higher expectation of winning the case. A tactful judge or elder can best favor his relative by condemning him. Unless the wrong is too apparent, such an attitude often encourages the court to find in favor of the relative. Even when the wrong is apparent, the indignation of both the wronged person and the court is mitigated by the alignment of the chief with them against his own relative.

When I made reference to this principle in a recent conference on ethnic conflict, one participant cited a proverb from Ghana to the opposite effect, that by reaching out to an opposing group, a leader risks losing his political base. This reaction totally misses the point. Reaching out is intended as a bridging function that benefits not only the more distant party, but in fact is intended primarily as a means of protecting the party closest to the leader.

Chief Babo Nimir told of a peace conference between his tribe and the Rezeigat, another Arab tribe in the western province of Darfur. A Missiriya man had killed a man from Rezeigat. According to the Missiriya custom, blood wealth was thirty head of cattle, while among the Rezeigat, it was one hundred. Negotiations on the price were deadlocked. "We spent that whole day without result." Babo Nimir reports (Deng 1982, 21): "We spent the night. The following morning, we withdrew and reviewed our position. I was the one who spoke with the Mamour. I said, 'Here we are, stuck at 30. Our position, I believe, is wrong. We are basing our argument on our own custom within our tribe. Conflicts within one tribe are not the same as conflicts between separate tribes.'" His position moderated the demands of the Rezeigat and a compromise was reached at 70 cows, with one bull for the burial cloth, setting a precedent at 71 cows.

Reaching out must be from a position of strength, magnanimity, and generosity rather than from weakness, whether in terms of right and wrong or of wits. You have to have a cause that you concede, a leverage on the people you are pulling along, and a credible expectation that if your concessions are not heeded, you can threaten the opponent with worse consequences. Peace conferences among tribes are in many ways an ambivalent blend of fighting with words, backed by discreet expectations of force, while striving to bridge and restore harmony and relationship. In these words, for instance, the singer brags about the combative qualities of their leader, Chief Deng Majok, in intertribal assemblies where disputes between the tribes were settled (Deng 1973, 151–152):

> The Assembly of tribes met at Tongliet
> Deng de Kwol was our warrior
> Our Deng, [son of] Kwol, the Decorated One
> We gave Deng a helmet and a club
> He fought with the Chiefs of Bahr el Ghazal
> So that we acquired some prisoners.

This ambivalence is also reflected in the way Chief Deng Majok was viewed as staunchly pro-Arab and yet perceived as a strong defender against the Arabs. Chief Babo Nimir, who had been a strong ally of Deng Majok in his contentious struggle for succession to his father's position against the more favored half brother, Deng Abot, observed (Deng 1982, 59): "When he became Chief, we found what we hoped for in him. By God, we in our area had not the slightest doubt that no man who went before Deng Majok would ever leave feeling injustice. Deng would give him full justice. He would give a man what we were sure the man would not find with Deng Abot or with Akonon or with similar people. With Deng Majok, we felt assured of the protection our people would get whenever they went there." On the other hand, a Dinka elder from the South, lamenting Deng Majok's death, and his protective role on the South-North border in confrontation with the Arabs, described the response in the South to the news of Deng's death (Deng 1986, 269): "One felt that the world was destroyed. And that is what it is: the world is not only spoiled; it will continue to be spoiled. Nobody seems to be able to bring it back under control. If Deng Kwol were alive, he would have checked the Baggara Arabs. . . . Deng would tear the Arabs apart with his teeth. And indeed, we and the Arabs have always been cannibalistic with one another. People run away from a person when he is brave and strong or when he has some supernatural powers. The power of Deng Kwol was unique."

While the principle of reaching out is applicable to the management of conflict in all situations of human interaction, it is particularly pertinent to bridging the role of leaders of groups in conflict. Chief Babo Nimir noted (Deng 1982, 28):

> The cordiality of relations between tribes begins with relations between their respective leaders. Between the Missiriya Homr and the Rezeigat, relations were initially so bad that when our respective people met, they would immediately fight with clubs. Then Nazir Ibrahim [Mousa Madibbo], who was my elder, and I established a good personal relationship. We met here in Khartoum. After that . . . a deep friendship was established between us. Our people followed our example and established very cordial relations among themselves. The Homr and the Rezeigat began to graze together in peace. None of them ever hurt the other again. They became brothers.

About Babo Nimir's relationship with Deng Majok, a Dinka chief observed (Deng 1986, 85), "The genuine friendship that can exist between two sons of chiefs I saw for the first time between Deng Majok and Babo Nimir. Their relations were excellent." Babo himself, commenting on the interconnection between his friendship with Deng Majok and the relations between their respective tribes, said (Deng 1982, 60–61), "As for my relationship with Deng Majok: by God, no other relationship can exceed it except perhaps with my own brother, Ali. We were absolutely together. This brought the Arabs and the Dinka close together. Our relationship with Deng made the Dinka and the Arabs become closely tied with one another."

Social anthropologists and legal scholars of African traditional societies have generally emphasized the importance these societies attach to the values of unity and harmony and the conciliation in conflict management or resolution. Only when an issue in dispute has been thoroughly discussed, analyzed, and evaluated, and a conclusion is reached that the parties to the dispute recognize as a fair and just settlement can a conflict be said to have been resolved. As the noted legal anthropologist Max Gluckman (1965a, 9) observed decades ago, "Many writers have discussed the process of law in tribal societies in such phrases as restoring the social balance or equilibrium, securing the agreement of both parties to a compromise judgement and, above all, reconciling the parties. This is the main aim of Barotse judges in all cases that arise between kin, for it is a dominant value of the society that villages should not break up and that kin should remain united." It is important to emphasize the family, lineage, clan, or communal orientation of the African value system and the degree to which most problems are in some fashion "family affairs." Managing such conflicts must of necessity lay stress on conciliation, which contrasts with the adversary procedures of modern state adjudication. The pioneering Nigerian jurist, T. O. Elias (1956, 268), drawing a distinction between Western and African traditional law, observed that "whereas African law strives consciously to reconcile the disputants in a lawsuit, English law often tends to limit itself to the bare resolution of the conflict by stopping at the mere apportionment of blame as between the disputants." Dispute settlement in the traditional

African legal system "was, therefore, an agreement intended to restore and preserve the social balance and differed materially in principle from a judgement in European courts which is a judgement by decree intended to enforce the legal rights of one party to the complete and permanent exclusion of the other, whatever the effect on the social equilibrium may be."

Building largely on the relationship between the Ngok Dinka and the Missiriya Arabs, in the broader framework of Arab-African conflict in the Sudan, this chapter tries to substantiate two overlapping themes. The first is the overarching principle of reaching out, particularly as applied to the role of leadership in managing intercommunal conflicts. Second, it will show how the principles of cooperative coexistence that had evolved between the two groups over centuries have now been interfered with by the intervention of the state, which does not observe these conventional norms, but, far from it, has become partial, a development that has upset the traditional balance of power that had sustained the cooperative approach.

■ A Microcosm of Arab-African Relations

Sudan has been at war with itself since 1955, with a decade of precarious peace from 1972 to 1983. The war has largely been between successive governments in Khartoum, dominated by the Arab-Muslim North, and rebel movements in the more indigenously African South, whose modern leadership is predominantly Christian. During the first phase of the war, from 1955 to 1972, the objective of the southern liberation struggle was secession from the North, although the then Southern Sudan Liberation Movement, with its military wing, the Anyanya, settled in 1972 for regional autonomy. With the resumption of hostilities in 1983, provoked by the government's abrogation of the peace accord, the Sudan People's Liberation Movement and its military wing, the Sudan People's Liberation Army (SPLM/SPLA), although Southern-based, embraced elements from the North, especially in the non-Arab regions of the Nuba and the Ingassana bordering the South. Commensurately, the SPLM/SPLA postulated the liberation of the whole country from Arab-Islamic domination, the goal being to create a "new Sudan" that is free from any discrimination based on race, ethnicity, religion, culture, or gender. The feasibility of this project, at least in the short run, has been questioned, and there is indeed reason to wonder whether it was ever seriously intended or presented only as a ploy to widen support and minimize resistance from national, regional, and international forces opposed to secession, which remained a secret objective. The goal of creating a new Sudan has become even more remote as the Islamic fundamentalists who seized power through a military coup on June 30, 1989, have tightened their Arab-Islamic grip on the country. As a result, the SPLM/SPLA has reactivated the southern call for self-determination, not only for the South, but also for the marginalized regions of the North.

While the North-South relations appear to be deadlocked in a zero-sum conflict of identities, the experience of relations between local communities that have coexisted for centuries tend to suggest that under appropriate conditions cooperation across racial, ethnic, tribal, religious, or language lines is possible in the mutual interest of both sides. The case of the Ngok Dinka and the Homr Arabs is a good example.

The Ngok and the Homr live on the volatile borders between the Arab Muslim North and the African South, an area in which the pastoral warrior Arab and Nilotic tribes interact and often clash over pastures and sources of water. Even prior to the colonial intervention, Ngok leaders entered into a friendship pact with their Arab counterparts that fundamentally altered the nature of their relationship, provided their people with significant protection against slave raiders, and fostered cordial ties that transcended racial and religious differences between their respective peoples. This history is frequently recalled both to explain the deterioration that has taken place in recent years and to uphold standards that are not only desirable but achievable, and indeed were once achieved. The problem then becomes not so much the inability of local communities to coexist, but the penetration of the state on divisive identity lines and the imbalances in the power equations that it introduces into the relationship.

□ *The Ngok Dinka at the Borders*

Despite centuries of contact with Arab tribes and the adoption, adaptation, and assimilation of certain northern cultural traits, the Ngok have remained distinctly Dinka and in some respects more so than their compatriots further south. Placed at the point of contact with the outside world and confronting a forceful, assimilationist civilization that claimed universality, their instinct for cultural self-preservation appears to have been commensurate with the threats of inequitable integration. Paul Howell (1951, 248), a British anthropologist-administrator who served in the area, noted, "To the casual observer . . . the Ngork [*sic*] Dinka may appear deeply affected by Arab influences. Closer observations show that the so-called process of 'Arabization' is only skin deep. . . . [Ninety-nine] percent of the Ngork, despite generations of contact with the Arab, are quite unaffected by any form of Islamic traits and are as completely Dinka as their Dinka neighbors to the South."

The pre-condominium relations between the North and the South were characterized by slave raids that peaked during the Turko-Egyptian and the Mahdist eras of the nineteenth century. These hostilities in the Ngok-Homr context were later ameliorated by a pact of friendship, indeed of kinship between their respective leaders. Ibrahim al-Hussein, an Arab elder, recounted the story of a friendship pact between leaders of antagonistic racial, ethnic, and religious groups (Deng 1995, 258):

> We are relatives of Arob, the son of Biong from the days of our ancestor Azoza. It was a friendship witnessed by Biong (Arob's father) himself; it was also witnessed by our ancestor, Mugaddam, the uncle of Azoza.
>
> This is how the friendship began. Azoza was traveling with his cattle. He entered Dinkaland. There was a man by the name of Dut, "the Buffalo," from Anyiel sub-tribe. He was a very strong man. When Azoza entered Dinkaland, Dut captured Arab cattle. Arob Biong had spiritual powers which had totally dominated Dinkaland. Even Dut was frightened of him. Arob sent for Azoza [to discuss the issue of their looted cattle].
>
> Azoza went to his brothers and they all came in front of Arob, the son of Biong. They said, "We no longer want the cattle; we have abandoned them. What we want is friendship and brotherhood. We want that the path between us be clear and that we live together as cousins." From that moment, brotherhood was created.

Because of the importance associated with blood as a symbol of lineage-oriented ethnic identity and kinship, the two leaders conducted a ritual of blood fusion to consolidate their relationship. As Ibrahim al-Hussein recounted (Deng 1995, 258), "Arob, the son of Biong, spilt his blood and my grandfather licked it; and Azoza spilt his blood and Arob, the son of Biong, licked it. They became relatives. Drums were beaten to celebrate the occasion." Even then, relations remained ambivalent, combining friendship with some Arab leaders and hostility with others. With the advent of the Mahdiya revolution, the Arabs themselves were divided between those who supported it and those who resisted. Famine also intervened, forcing some of the Arabs to flee for both safety and relief into Ngokland. Chief Arob welcomed them and gave them land on which to settle and cultivate. This was indeed one of the outcomes of the friendship pact between him and Azoza.

The response of the Ngok Dinka to the Mahdiya was cross-cultural and interracially astute. Naturally, the Mahdi, being a Muslim and an Arab, was viewed as closer to Homr than to the Dinka. And since the Homr leaders had become relatives of the Dinka leaders, they became intermediaries between the Mahdists and the Dinka when cooperative and part of the Muslim-Arab camp when hostile. Arob's Arab relatives, who were of course cooperative, brokered a contact between him and the Mahdi. According to the Arab elder, Ibrahim al-Hussein (Deng 1995, 260), "Our ancestors took Arob to the Mahdi. He went to declare his allegiance [to the Mahdi]. . . . The Mahdi said, 'From this day your name will be Abdel Ra'uf, instead of Arob.' He initiated him with prayers and gave him a sword. Arob then returned home." Here, we clearly see the emergence of religious intolerance. To be accepted and respected, Arob had to be converted to Islam and have his name changed, something his Arab-Muslim neighbors had not expected or asked of him in their previous interaction and relationship.

Arob's supposed initiation into Islam is a good example of how the Dinka have responded in the past to the Arab-Islamic culture, adopting certain traits, but integrating and assimilating them into their own cultural and religious belief system. Arob's alleged conversion to Islam is hardly ever mentioned in the oral history of the Dinka except for the assertion that he had gone to *Jenna,* the Arabic word for heaven or paradise. Certainly, his supposed adoption of the Islamic name Abdel Ra'uf is totally unheard of among the Dinka. That they prayed with the Mahdi is acknowledged, but with qualifications that indicate pragmatism. As their heads were bent to the ground in prayer, Arob's companion, Chief Allor Ajing, whispered to him (Deng 1995, 261), "Arob, son of Biong, do you see God?" Arob whispered back, "No, Allor, I do not see God, but let us leave matters as they are."

Arob's objective in visiting the Mahdi was to complain against ongoing slave raids by Arab factions that remained hostile to the Dinka. The outcome of the meeting was that the Mahdi assured him that henceforth Arab-Muslims would no longer raid Arob's people for slaves. The Mahdi then gave Arob insignia of his power, including a spear and a sword, and implored him to govern in accordance with the ideals of Islam, such as the rich assuming responsibility for the poor, values that were in full harmony with Dinka culture and practice.

With the advent of colonial rule, Ngok leaders sought protection for their people from the central government to the North by affiliating themselves into Kordofan, one of the northern provinces. By virtue of their early contact and agreement with the government in the North, Ngok leadership was viewed by the southern Dinka as providing a protective shield in their adversarial relations with the Arabs, mostly through diplomatic representation and management or resolution of conflicts on their highly explosive borders with the Arabs.

The administrative status of the Ngok in Kordofan was, however, recognized as an anomaly by the British. Howell (1951, 240) saw the Ngok as

> something of a problem. Situated as they are between the Baggara Arabs of the North and the main body of the Nilotic peoples in the South, they are in a peculiar position and the problem is whether they should be included in a Rural District Council in which Arabs must always predominate or whether they should be joined to kindred tribes further South. Should tribal and racial boundaries remain intact or should territorial associations be created in which tribe or race is of no consequence? There

are purely practical arguments in favor of both such lines of political development.

K. D. D. Henderson, another British administrator who had served in the area, in a written response to questionaires for Deng (1986), also commented on the anomaly of the Ngok situation on the North-South border:

> Tidy-minded persons—British and Sudanese alike—were always suggesting that the Ngok be transferred to Southern administration. I resisted this partly because it would have been impossible to draw a fair boundary between them and the Homr, but chiefly because their presence in Kordofan provided an invaluable buffer-state and meeting ground and gave the Northern administration knowledge of and sympathy with the Nilotics. Further West, the Malwal and the Rezeigat were perfectly at loggerheads. To the East, the transfer of the Rueng to the Upper Nile Province had given rise to endless friction. But the relationship of the Ngok was excellent with the Homr on one side and the Twij on the other. Arabs with a grievance against the Twij or the Hijeir [Rek], and vice versa, always approached Kwal (*sic*) [the Ngok chief] in the first instance to act as an intermediary.

Later the administration changed its position and decided in favor of the Ngok joining the South, but Kwol refused (Deng 1980, 39–40, 74–75; 1986, 49–50; 1992b, 53).

In 1951, the British again gave the Ngok the option of joining Bahr el-Ghazal or Upper Nile in anticipation of Sudan's independence. The governor of Bahr el-Ghazal, Richard Owen, who had been district commissioner of western Kordofan, influenced the Dinka chiefs of Bahr el-Ghazal to persuade Deng Majok to join the South.

The Arab elder, Ibrahim el Hussein, a descendant of the Arab leader Azoza, with whom Deng Majok's grandfather, Arob Biong, had entered into a pact of friendship, gave this account of the consultations that ensued on the issue (Deng 1986, 224):

> Deng consulted with us. He got on his horse. And with him were all the omdas and a number of sheikhs. . . . He said to us, "I went to see the governor, the Englishman. And he said to me, 'The English are about to leave. Their period of rule in the Sudan is coming to an end.' And he said to me, 'Join the South.' I said to him, 'Why should I join the South?' And he said, 'Listen to my advice; join the South.' . . . I told him I was going to consult with my people. So I have come to seek your views. What is your opinion?"

The Arabs were apparently stunned by what Deng Majok had told them, according to El Hussein's recollection (Deng 1986, 224–225): "Our fathers, who were elderly people, did not even understand what he was saying. 'Son Deng,' they said, 'what sort of a thing are you saying?' I said, 'Listen Deng, go and tell that Englishman who asked you to join the South that he found you a northerner. The English found us as brothers from a long way back. We were brothers when the Turkish government came. The Mahdiya also found us brothers. And when the English came, they found us sitting together on one rug. The South is not for you; it is not for you.' We said a great deal to him."

Deng Majok responded positively to their plea: "In front of all the people assembled he said, 'Very well! That was what I wanted. We are not going to the South. That is my opinion.'"

In the opinion of the Dinka, Deng's decision to remain in the North was not a rejection of the South but indeed a means of ensuring the protection of his people, including the southern tribes, against their Arab neighbors. According to one elder, Deng argued (Deng 1986, 226–227; Henderson 1965, 164n): "Should we join the South now, the black people will be harassed and reduced to a small entity. It is our path which stretches the height of the black people. And it is our path which guides the black people. And one day, should tragedy befall this country, the survival of the black people will start here at Abyei. . . . Should we [be forced to] abandon this land with all its blessings, our descendants will one day blame us."

□ *Crisis at the Crossroads*

With independence, the Missiriya Rural Council was established as a vehicle for local administration. The Dinka found themselves to be a negligible minority. With the British gone as neutral moderators, both the local and the central governments became identified with the Arab-Muslim racial, cultural, and religious identity that favored the Homr over the Dinka. Even worse, the dominant Umma Party, led by the Mahdi family, derived its political base from the Arab tribes of the West, and Babo Nimir, the paramount chief of the Missiriya Arabs, consolidated his own connection with the center by marrying into that family. In a variety of ways, the Dinka felt increasingly disadvantaged and subordinated.

Nonetheless, as a result of tensions among the Arab chiefs and in particular between Babo Nimir and the chiefs of the other tribes under his paramount chieftaincy, these chiefs conspired to have Deng Majok elected as the president of the Council. While this enhanced his image as a symbol of unity, it antagonized his friend Babo Nimir, who had indeed tried and failed to have the Ngok incorporated into his all-embracing paramountcy. As a consequence, relations between the two men deteriorated drastically and, over time, closest friends across the racial and religious divide became foes. Deng Majok became increasingly aware of the gulf between him and his northern partners. Even though some supported him because of their internal differences, he now realized that he was a Dinka and they were all Arabs.

It was during the first South-North civil war of 1955–1972 that Ngok identity as southerners and the ambivalence of being Dinka among Arabs became most pronounced. For a considerable part of the war, Ngok area remained sheltered from the war and, to a large extent, was the only secure area in the southern cultural-ethnic-geographic complex. However, as the war continued to intensify, the Ngok began to sympathize and identify more and more with the South, and some of their young men began to join the military wing of the southern movement—the Anya-Nya—and even assumed leading positions in the struggle.

During the mid-1960s, rumors began to reach Abyei that the southern rebels might attack under the command of one of Deng Majok's sons. This naturally heightened the anxiety of the Arabs. One incident after another fueled the fire that ignited the 1965 Ngok-Homr hostilities in which several hundred people, and many estimate over a thousand, lost their lives. As it was during the dry season, when the Arabs were on their seasonal migration southward, the war was fought on Ngok soil and the Arabs initially suffered heavy casualties. But, with superior arms, they retaliated with a vengeance that devastated the Dinka.

A peace conference was held later with the help of prominent tribal leaders as *ajaweed* mediators. In the conference, Deng Majok maintained his firm identification with Kordofan and therefore the North rather than with the South, even though his sympathy for the rebel movement and the southern cause in general was by then relatively well established and known. His unequivocal claim to be a northerner must therefore be understood as a shrewd political move. After long deliberations, a peace agreement was eventually concluded, which stipulated the termination of acts of violence; restriction on display of arms, guarantee of the safety of members of each group in the territory of the other; return of all property captured during the fighting, preparation of an inventory of persons and property lost during the hostilities; the administration of oath-taking by each group according to its beliefs, the Muslims on the Koran and Dinka on the Sacred Spears; and cooperation with the local authorities in the maintenance of peace and security (Deng 1986, 229–230). It was also agreed that no *dia,* the customary blood wealth of cattle, would be paid for those who had been killed on both sides. All that was forgiven as part of the peace and reconciliation agreement, a unique arrangement in the history of tribal warfare and a peace agreement that would later haunt Ngok-Homr relations.

Deng Majok's absolute consistency and therefore credibility on the issue of his loyalty to northern identity in the North-South cleavage, while winning the Arabs, was a more complex strategy than they realized. Of course, he fully identified with the southern cause, but he chose to play his role in the most constructive way within his control. He wanted to avoid identifying the central government with the Homr Arabs. In his view, it was essential to the Dinka cause to force the central government into the moral position of a third party, judge or mediator, even though he realized that the shared Arab identity of the Homr and the central government favored the Arabs. It was a case of upholding virtue to moderate evil to foster objective judgment that could only work in favor of the Dinka. There is every reason therefore to believe that Deng Majok emphasized his identification with the North as a means of winning some favor from the central government and thereby ensuring a degree of justice against the Homr.

☐ *Breaking or Making the Relationship*

Since the death of Deng Majok, a number of peace initiatives have been taken on the Abyei problem. Some of these have been periodic consultations among tribal leaders; others have been attempts to address specific crises in the relationship; yet others have been peace conferences involving prominent tribal leaders as *ajaweed,* or mediators, in cooperation with government authorities. Because of lack of space, I will focus on three initiatives with which I was personally associated and which symbolize the history of dialogue between the Dinka and the Arabs. One concerns negotiating alternative approaches to the status of Abyei with the national government in the early 1970s. Another was a peace conference following violent clashes between the Arabs and the Dinka in 1977. The third involved negotiating the release of the Ngok Dinka political elite arrested en masse in the wake of the local rebellion that eventually fed into the renewal of North-South hostilities in 1983.

The 1972 Addis Ababa Agreement that ended the war in the South stipulated that the Ngok Dinka would decide by referendum whether to join the South or remain in the North. It soon became obvious to me that the government did not intend to implement that part of the agreement and the South was not prepared to go back to war over Abyei. After a close assessment of the precarious situation the Ngok were in and the possible options offered to them in regard to inclusion in the North or the South, I proposed a plan that offered a bridging approach to the Abyei problem. I made the proposal in a special report, entitled "A Proposed Plan for the Development of Abyei as a Model for National Integration," submitted to the government several months after the February 1972 Addis Ababa Agreement and following a visit to the Sudan during which I held intensive discussions with leaders in the North and the South as well as with the Ngok political elite. The strategy behind the proposed policy was to build on the conciliatory aspect of Ngok-Homr historical relations and the achieved peace and unity in South-North relations rather than place Abyei in the negative position of a disputed territory. It used the experience of reversing the southern demand for separatism into a celebration of unity and combined it with the historical role of the Ngok Dinka as an autonomous bridge between the North and the South, suggesting that introducing a micro form of autonomy to the area with a special program of accelerated development could reverse the separatist tide and consolidate the historical role of the Ngok, fostering the unity and integration of the country.

The proposal was formally endorsed as government policy. Ten well-selected local government administrators were posted to Abyei, where there had been none, and Justin Deng, a Ngok Dinka, was appointed province deputy commissioner to head the local administration. A number of Ngok Dinka policemen, schoolteachers, and other officials were also transferred to Abyei. Several tractors, a modern medical center, a junior secondary school, and a number of other reforms were introduced as initial steps in what was envisaged as a major development program in the area.

However, the educated Ngok, whose nationalist sentiments toward the South were at their peak, felt that the policy of autonomous development within Kordofan was a capitulation, a betrayal of the cause of joining the South. They also perceived the promised development as an attempt to buy their freedom and the right of self-determination.

Kordofan authorities and the Arabs, on the other hand, separated the idea of autonomy for Abyei from the notion of special status as a symbol of national unity. They attributed the first to the influence of the Ngok at the center and opposed it as separatist, anti-Arab, and pro-South. They credited the president and his minister of local government for the second and interpreted it as a declaration that the Abyei area was a common ground for the Arabs and the Dinka to interact and mutually assimilate into a model for national unity and integration. The commissioner of southern Kordofan, Mahmoud Haseeb, in a statement in which he claimed that the Abyei area was Kordofan territory, wrote (Saeed 1982, 212), "It is for this reason that Abyei has been thought of as an ideal nucleus for peaceful coexistence, and as a meeting ground where tribal hostilities and racial prejudice may be destroyed, through continuous interaction in pasture grass lands and by transactional activities in marketplaces, so that our animal wealth may be preserved from extinction."

This interpretation meant that the central government had not only ruled out the call of the Ngok to join the South, but had instead given the Arabs rights over Ngokland on equal footing with the Dinka. With this misrepresentation and manipulation of the policy, the Ngok Dinka felt as though they had suffered double jeopardy: first to have imposed on them a policy that compromised their goal of joining the South; and then to have that compromise solution misconstrued, to open the doors of their land to the Arabs on equal footing with the Dinka. What was intended as a bridging strategy that would improve the lot of the Dinka in partnership with the Arabs was subverted into a tool of even greater oppression and exploitation.

With time, the brewing tensions between the Arabs and the Dinka exploded in violence. One incident after another escalated into a bloody tribal war in May 1977, in which the security forces working in cooperation with the *marahleen,* an armed mobile force that moved with the Arab pastoralists for their protection, sided with the Arabs. Several hundred people lost their lives on both sides.

General Mohammed El Baghir, the first vice president who was also in charge of security, decided to go to the area and asked me to accompany him. First we flew to Abyei, where we met with the local security committee to assess the situation, and then called for a public meeting to listen to the people. Emotions were very high and the Dinka unconstrained in their expression of anger. The theme was the same: unprovoked aggression by the Arabs and the partiality of the security forces behind them. One spokesman went as far as saying that the government and the Arabs were one and the same thing: "We will face the Arabs knowing that you, the Government, are fighting with them against us."

The vice president listened patiently, but when it was his turn to speak, he was stern in his response, arguing that the army was, by its composition, training, and deployment, a national institution that could not be allied to any faction. He had allowed them to say what they said simply because he understood their pain and bitterness, but they must dismiss those thoughts and trust in the neutrality of the army and the government to see to it that peace was restored and justice done.

At Muglad, we met with Arab leaders and elders in the house of Chief Babo Nimir. The Arabs seemed obsessed with what they saw as the separatist trend in the Dinka area for which they held the Dinka deputy commissioner for the area responsible. Everything was misconstrued to make the policy of autonomy and development in Abyei an anti-Arab strategy.

Baghir spoke about the need for peace and security in the area and the higher goal of Arabs and Dinka living together as they had done in history. I also spoke, explaining the grievances of the Dinka to the Arabs and pleading the case for the historical role of Abyei as a bridge in North-South relations, which, I argued, could only be done on the basis of mutual accommodation and respect. I explained the genesis of the policy for the development of Abyei as a model for national unity and integration, how the project had been meant to serve the mutual interests of the Dinka and the Arabs, and how it had been grossly misunderstood as a separatist ploy that aimed not only at eventually annexing the area to the South, but also at benefiting only the Dinka with development. I urged the assembled Arabs to question themselves seriously whether they thought the Ngok Dinka could voluntarily choose to remain in the North in an unequal status with the Arabs, while their fellow Dinka in the South were masters of their own situation. If they wanted the Ngok to favor unity with the Arabs, they had to give them reason for doing so. Domination was not the answer.

Most of the Arab speakers recalled the cordial ties that had prevailed between the Missiriya and the Dinka, the good old days of Arob Biong, Kwol Arob, and Deng (Majok) Kwol, but contrasted that era with the prevailing climate of hostilities. For the deterioration in relations, they blamed the young men who, as Nazir Babo Nimir had predicted at Deng Majok's death, had been educated mostly in Christian missionary schools in the South, and favored joining the South. Babo Nimir went as far as saying that if the Dinka should insist on joining the South, the Missiriya would not want to be separated from them and would prefer to go with them to the South.

As we sat with Arab chiefs and elders in Babo's sitting room, I spoke informally of how I thought the Arabs and the Dinka were divided only by myths of identity that did not reflect the reality of their racial mix. I asked Babo Nimir, "Uncle Nazir (Chief), you have been to Saudi Arabia and other parts of the Arab world. What do the people there look like?" He said, using colloquial Arabic, "*Wallahi hommor*" ("By God, they are light-skinned!"). I said, "Well, look around and see the color of the Arabs assembled here. Where do you think this dark color came from, is it not from the people you consider racially different from you? There is more in common between you people than you realize." My comment was greeted with roaring laughter. Establishing a basis for kinship was a conciliatory gesture which they appreciated.

On my return to Khartoum, I learned that my speech in Muglad had been broadcast by Radio Omdurman. Southerners, in particular the Ngok Dinka who felt extremely embittered, were outraged by my conciliatory tone. In one gathering, a southerner was reported as having remarked on hearing me talk, "Someone should advise Mading; he is going to get himself assassinated."

As was characteristic of intertribal conflicts, the government eventually organized a peace conference with tribal chiefs from different parts of the country as mediators—*ajaweed.* It was to be held in Kadugli, the headquarters of the newly established region of southern Kordofan. Abdel Rahman Abdalla, the minister of public service and administrative reform, an intellectual and a highly experienced administrator, was asked to chair the conference. He in turn asked me to assist him.

As soon as we arrived in Kadugli, I asked the governor, Mahmoud Haseeb, about the composition of the Dinka delegation. From what he said, it was obvious that Matet Ayom, Achwil Bulabek, and Patal Biliw, very articulate and experienced elders who had been close associates of late

Deng Majok, but had become collaborators with the security forces and the Arabs, were not in the delegation. I immediately concluded that they had been excluded because of their links with the Arabs and that their exclusion was going to be a source of ongoing disunity that the Arabs would exploit and could indeed undermine Dinka-Arab reconciliation. I asked the governor whether it was too late to bring them to the talks. He said that he had just sent a helicopter to bring the deputy commissioner and that if he could send a message immediately, it might arrive before he left. I decided on a course of action that would bring them immediately while leaving open the issue of whether they could join the delegation. I would then discuss the latter issue with the Dinka delegation. My message to Justin Deng was that I wanted to interview those elders in connection with a research project I was working on. No mention was made of the peace talks.

Meanwhile, I went to see the Dinka delegation, talking first to Deng Abot, the eldest, and then to other key individuals, and finally to the entire delegation, trying to persuade them that it was strategically and tactically wrong for them to exclude those individuals. After all, they had the knowledge and the professional experience to be among their best spokesmen and, if antagonized, could be their worst enemies to the advantage of the Arabs. Deng Abot, guided by the same considerations, agreed and gave me his blessing, but he had a bad cold and was too ill to assist in persuading the others. His son, Hassan (Arob), disagreed with his father. He could not see how they could be accepted by the people as their spokesmen. Kwol Adol, Deng Majok's young son who had become the chief, agreed with Hassan. All in all, the Dinka, the most influential among whom were educated youth, alienated from and ignorant of traditional principles and strategies, did not want to have anything to do with those people, and the news that I had arranged for them to come was greeted with anger. I argued my case with equal passion and determination. One by one, the tide turned in favor of admitting the renegades back into the delegation.

Ironically, when the chairman of the conference, the governor, and I went to have introductory talks with the Arab delegation, their demand was that the three chiefs, together with Zachariah Atem, another pro-Arab renegade who had been left behind, be brought to the conference because they were their principal witnesses among the Dinka. I later learned that the Arabs had indeed planned to transport those men to Kadugli through commercial lorries. Obviously, they were not aware that I was at that very moment striving to let them attend as members of the Dinka delegation. I told the Arabs that their objective should not be to get a few Dinkas to side with them against their own people, but rather to make peace and be reconciled with the Dinka as a whole. The more united the Dinka were in their agreement with them, the more reliable the peace agreement would be. The governor supported my position and added that as the Arabs could not imagine the Dinka questioning the composition of the Arab delegation, they had no right to question the composition of the Dinka delegation. The Arabs eventually conceded.

When the renegade group arrived and I confronted them with the problem and how it had been resolved, the issue suddenly became one of how they could change their frame of mind that had been set to oppose their own people. It was quite obvious that they were tormented by the dilemma that confronted them. They seemed pleased to have been accepted back by their people, but disturbed by having to shift positions, especially against the more powerful Arab adversaries. Achwil Bulabek conveyed the personal anguish they felt when he asked me whether there was anything legally wrong with one changing one's testimony. He said the Arabs had made them take an oath to testify against the Dinka. But he intended to explain that they had done so because of anger, having been rejected by their own people. Now that they had been accepted back, he had no reason to be vindictive against his people. Was there anything wrong with that? I assured him that I saw nothing morally or legally wrong with that. Certainly, no legal action could be taken against them.

During the talks, I moved in four circles that were diametrically opposed and in which my message had to be custom tailored. There was my inner circle with the chairman of the conference and the governor of Kordofan, probably the most straightforward and the easiest, although it also involved continuous discussions and interpretation of the various moves of the different groups we had to monitor. The main challenge of my close association with both men was to make them appreciate the justice of the Dinka cause, while also mindful of Arab concerns. Since the chairman was a fair-minded person and the Dinka were obviously the underdogs, that task was not at all difficult. And yet, his sympathy for the Dinka was rather exceptional among northern authorities. The governor, too, was sympathetic to the Dinka cause, but hostile to Dinka leadership and bent on winning and maintaining Arab political support; he was therefore quite torn and ambivalent, but with a pro-Arab profile.

There were the two opposing delegations with whom I tried to keep equally close contact so as not to be accused of bias for the Dinka. Nevertheless, the Arabs assumed that as a Dinka I naturally had the interest of my people foremost at heart. They were of course right, but what they did not realize was that I was also trying hard to reach out and look at the situation from their point of view and arguing their case with the Dinka where I thought it justified. This, the Dinka delegation resented. On the other hand, whenever the Arabs took an unreasonable stand, I found myself free to argue with them, which reinforced their suspicion of a pro-Dinka bias.

At one point, the Dinka walked out of the talks and it fell mostly on me to try to persuade them to return. At another point, the Arabs, invoking the 1965 precedent referred to earlier between the Ngok Dinka and the Missiriya Arabs, argued against the payment of the conventional blood wealth, *dia*. In their view, the precedent required that everything be forgiven and forgotten. They offered instead a ridiculously small sum of fifteen hundred Sudanese pounds per person for what they called an appeasement fee. Since many more Dinkas than Arabs had been killed, this outraged the Dinka. I was equally outraged. For the first time, I threatened to pull out of the mediation role. With pressure from the chairman, the commissioner, and the *ajaweed* (the tribal mediators), the Arabs eventually agreed to increase the amount considerably, estimated in cattle terms at fifteen head per person, as opposed to the usual thirty head for *dia*.

It was suggested by the *ajaweed* that in the future, the parties should revert back to the conventional payment of the *dia*. The Dinka refused and insisted that if the payment of *dia* was dispensed with on that occasion because of the alleged precedent, then that practice should be maintained in future cases. The obvious implication was that the Dinka intended to avenge and expected to inflict more casualties on the Arabs than they would suffer. In a heated, almost violent confrontation with the Dinka delegation, I tried to impress upon them that it was self-defeating to convey that impression, not only because it revealed an aggressive intent, but also because it alerts the Arabs to be prepared. In any case, it was grossly naive to assume that the Arabs would suffer more casualties in the future, since past experience showed the contrary and since the Arabs were far better armed than the Dinka. At one point, a hot-headed young man said to me, "Why do you always have to step between us and the Arabs? Why don't you allow us to confront one another?" At the same time, one Arab remarked in the conference that if it were not because of their respect for the government, they would have demanded that "that Dinka" be removed from the podium of chairmanship.

Almost equally problematic was my relationship with the *ajaweed,* the tribal mediators. Seeing me move between the parties and maintaining a close association with the chairman and the governor, these mediators seemed to feel that their role was being usurped. They even complained to the chairman that they felt redundant and threatened to withdraw from the conference. The chairman, the governor, and I applied our greatest powers of persuasion to restore their confidence in the process.

All in all, the process was an extremely frustrating uphill struggle, day and night, for two weeks, several days beyond the allotted time. But in the end, it was an astonishing success. In addition to the reconciliation of the parties, clear principles were agreed upon for regulating the movements of the Arabs into Dinkaland in their seasonal search for pastures and water. Procedures for preventing, managing, and resolving future conflicts, including periodic peace conferences, were also established. Elements of the original policy for the administration and development of the Abyei area were reiterated and reaffirmed.

□ *Encroachment on National Security*

Despite some improvement in the Ngok-Homr relations as a result of the Kadugli Accord, the issue of the Ngok status between the North and the South continued to be a source of tension in the relations between the Ngok and the administration of Kordofan. The situation in the South was also brewing with tension. A local rebellion led by Michael Miokol Deng, one of the sons of Deng Majok, had broken out and was threatening to spread to the South and trigger a resumption of hostilities. The Ngok Dinka and in particular the family of the late Deng Majok were being held responsible for the mounting insecurity in the South.

After joining the rebels, Michael became not only the leader of the Ngok group but also one of the leaders of the rapidly growing guerrilla force in the Dinka region of Bahr el-Ghazal. By now, the Ngok movement had established itself as the Abyei Liberation Front (Johnson and Prunier 1993). Soon, the name of Michael became synonymous with the gradual, but inexorable, resumption of hostilities in the South. The national dimension of the mounting crises heightened when on January 18, 1983, the rebels attacked a station on the only railroad linking the North and the South "killing twelve Northern Sudanese merchants." (Niblock 1987, 288) The chain of violence that subsequently spread over the South-North borders, perpetrated by Anya-Nya II, was blamed on the Ngok Dinka, under the supposed leadership of Deng Majok's sons, of whom Michael had become the hero or the villain, depending on the point of view involved.

The national security authorities reacted swiftly. Massive arrests of Ngok leaders, including tribal chiefs and intellectuals (North- and South-educated, Muslims and Christians alike), several of them sons of Deng Majok (among them Zachariah Bol, who had been deputy speaker in the southern regional assembly and minister of health in the southern regional government, and Kwol Adol, the young, newly appointed chief), took place across the country, some in Abyei itself.

Even as the authorities were playing down the rebellion in the South, the situation in that part of the country was rapidly deteriorating under the impending threat of redivision of the southern region and the overall interference of the center in regional affairs. About the same time Abyei leaders were arrested, a number of prominent southerners, among them the speaker and deputy speaker of the regional assembly and several former ministers, were also arrested on the grounds that they were planning a rebellion in the South. The resumption of a full-fledged civil war seemed imminent.

I had just returned from Canada, where I was ambassador, to attend the national congress of the ruling Sudan Socialist Union, in which the governors of Kordofan and the southern regions voiced condemnation of the Ngok Dinka and the Deng Majok family. After informal consultations with a wide variety of individuals, I decided to embark on a mediation effort between the Ngok leadership and the authorities of Kordofan, led by Fadhalla Hamad, the deputy governor, as the newly elected governor was on a visit to the United States. I first explored the idea with the first vice president, General Omar Mohamed El Tayeb, who was also the chief of national security, whose initial response was supportive, but said that he would have to seek the president's approval. After a long wait, a green light from the president and the vice president commenced a process that was to last several months. As national security became a factor, the objective was now to reconcile the national security authorities and the rulers of Kordofan on the one hand and the detained leaders of Abyei and their followers on the other hand.

Ironically, there was also a strong opposition to the initiative among the Dinka. Several subtribal chiefs and elders sent me verbal messages, urging me to keep out of the situation, allegedly because they were afraid for my own security. Several family members argued that any mediation might result in a compromise on principles and should be avoided. There was, however, significant support for my plans. In Khartoum itself, views were sharply divided. I disregarded the opposition and moved ahead with the plans.

The authorities of Kordofan with the support of the national security leaders at first wanted the family of Deng Majok to secure the surrender of Michael, which, I persuaded them, could not be done. I explained to the authorities that their best option was to cultivate the cooperation of those who were still within the system in order to consolidate peace and security in the area. That could be their most effective weapon against the rebels, including Michael himself.

Even as I was making progress in my consultations with the authorities, they continued to make statements that, at least on the face, seemed to undermine my efforts. After visiting the South, General El Tayeb again put the responsibility for the rebellion on the Ngok and went as far as declaring to the nation through the media of public information that the detainees would be charged and tried for treason. Even at this late hour, the national security authorities were either unaware of the seriousness of the situation in the South or were deliberately playing it down for security reasons and using the Ngok Dinka as the scapegoat, especially as they were seen as not posing a serious threat to the system. They seemed to believe that by acknowledging a Ngok rebellion and then crushing it, the incident could provide an effective deterrent to the more potentially dangerous rebellion brewing in other areas of the South.

In a statement to the Arabic daily *Al-Ayam* of March 21, 1983, El Tayeb offered this report about the security situation in the South:

> Rumors typically rely on some degree of truth around which they can build a coherent fiction. I do not deny that there are groups of rebels engaged in skirmishes with our Armed Forces, but I am not unduly apprehensive about our situation. After all, at one time, the entire South was in rebellion and our Armed Forces were fighting to maintain the unity and integrity of the nation. At present, we are fighting isolated groups which are small in numbers. In fact, from our tour throughout the southern provinces, we witnessed a high degree of peace and stability in the provinces of Equatoria region, and parts of Upper Nile. . . . However, I cannot deny that skirmishes continue between the two sides. . . . The Armed Forces cannot adopt the tactics of the rebels, such as hiding in the bush, ambushing non-combatants, and plundering and confiscating peoples' property.
>
> This does not mean, by any measure, that the rebels have the upper hand. I want to assure you that they represent only a minority of the local population—many of whom come from Abyei and want to secede from Kordofan. I met with 9 sub-tribal chiefs [Omdas] from the area and of those 9, 7 were opposed to secession. The two that favored seceding from Kordofan were followers of Deng Majok and his sons, extremists like Dr. Zachariah and Michael, who is in the bush. When they realized that we [the central government] paid them little attention, they formed a group of about 39 people and began to collect weapons from outside sources. It was not long before they began their campaign of plundering the area. In fact, they were responsible for the incident at Ariath.
>
> At present, we have Dr. Zachariah in custody and will charge him before a court of law because he, more than anyone else, was behind what happened. One of the reasons for this is that Dr. Zachariah's position as regional minister under the last government enabled him to relocate most of the residents of Abyei to Bahr al-Ghazal. Recently I learned of a bizarre development, that he and his supporters sent 25,000 Sudanese pounds to the relocated residents of Abyei . . . on the grounds that they were refugees. I cannot understand how a person can be a refugee in his own country. This is a very dangerous practice. Nevertheless, we in the central Government have the means and the capability with which to deal with practices that disrupt the security of the country.

Although I took the statement as part of the psychological warfare aimed at intimidating the Ngok to cease their hostilities, it clearly had an adverse effect, as it hardened the stance of the Ngok. Indeed, winning the cooperation of the detainees was to prove extremely difficult. Dr. Zachariah Bol Deng himself was ambivalent about the process, at times hopeful, but at times despondent and despairing, though still appreciative of my attempts. After the vice president's statement, he asked me to focus on getting him a good defense lawyer.

The process itself was remarkable. Every morning, the detainees were brought from prisons and detention homes around the capital for the meetings, which were held at the security headquarters under conditions of comfort and relative freedom, without any harassment, intimidation, or undue influence. But at the end of each working day, they were returned to their confinement.

During the first session with two senior security officers present, I asked the group which language we should use. Zachariah Bol immediately suggested that we should use Dinka since some of the elders did not understand Arabic. His real intentions were quite transparent to me, for he did not want the security officers to be fully in the picture. For the same reason, I immediately disagreed with him and suggested that anyone could speak any language, Dinka, English, or Arabic, but that whichever language people spoke, it should be translated so that all those present could follow. The senior officer seemed somewhat embarrassed and announced that he would leave in a few minutes. As the discussions progressed and everyone opened up, the officer not only stayed for the entire duration of the talks, but said in the end that it had been the best course in political science he had ever had.

And indeed, although the Dinka were initially suspicious about the presence of the security officers in the discussion, they took an increasing interest in their attendance and were concerned whenever the recording officer was not taking notes. They were clearly satisfied that their point of view was getting to the top through the security channels. It was obvious that they felt they were having a sympathetic hearing from the security authorities. There was of course no doubt that they objectively had a convincing case and felt assured of the third-party moderating role that the central government had always played in their relations with the Homr Arabs.

The gist of my message to the detainees was to explain the nature of the ongoing struggle over the area, the threat that Abyei's potential annexation to the South posed for the pastoral Arab tribes of Kordofan for whom the area was a source of water and pasture. I explained to them that the historical position taken by the leaders of the tribe to remain under the jurisdiction of Kordofan had been a strategic move to circumvent confrontation over the land. If the Arabs were forced by Ngok political association with the South, they could falsify history to claim the land, as they had already done, instead of the gratitude they had historically shown to Ngok leaders for being given access to water and grazing lands. And however absurd their claim to the land, they were likely to receive the support of the authorities. The message was both pessimistic and pragmatic.

On their part, the Dinka rehashed in great detail the history of mistreatment, oppression, and subjugation that they had received from the authorities of Kordofan aligning themselves with the Homr Arabs. They invoked their legal right under the Addis Ababa Agreement to determine their status between the North and the South. In candid, yet discreet language, I told them that their approach, while understandable, missed the real issue. It assumed a situation of objective justice where there was none, impartiality where the judge was inherently an interested party. The best they could expect was the old formula I had proposed, and which the president had endorsed for the autonomous development of their area within Kordofan. I therefore urged them to support the main elements of the president's policy over Abyei, which had been designed to include effective control over local affairs by the people of Abyei and the provision of services and a nationally sponsored development program in the area.

After seemingly endless discussions from early morning to late afternoon for weeks on end, an agreement was eventually reached that secured their release in a remarkable manner that appeared to transform hostility into cordiality. Before finalizing the agreement, one of them remarked that if they gave in on their political demand for the referendum on joining the South, it was because they had no alternative way of pursuing their rights. I agreed with that formulation. They all laughed at my humility. We now stood on the same ground.

The plan of action, which was agreed upon with the authorities of Kordofan and sanctioned by the central government, promised special administrative status for Abyei in Kordofan, with increased autonomy, services, and development activities. It was in essence an agreement to reactivate the implementation of the initial policy on Abyei without touching on the sensitive issue of the referendum provided for by the Addis Ababa Agreement of 1972.

The sons of Deng Majok and the Ngok leadership issued two statements. The statement of Deng Majok's sons said (Deng 1986, 266):

> We, the undersigned sons of Deng Majok, hereby reaffirm our commitment to the noble principles which our late father and our forefathers before him pursued for centuries within the framework of Kordofan to advance the cause of peace and unity as a link between the southern and the northern parts of the country.
>
> Some of us have recently felt themselves driven to the call of separating the area of Abyei from Kordofan and joining it to the southern Region in the hope of ensuring participation in the government of the country on equal footing with fellow countrymen in that region. We have now learned that one of us has even taken up arms in pursuance of this objective and with most regrettable consequences to the peace and security of our people.
>
> While we recognize the frustrations which have led to this sad development, we remain unequivocally opposed to this destructive means of attempting a solution to the problem of Abyei.
>
> We also declare that our objective in the area has always been to secure for our people the dignity of equal partnership in the government of their country. To promote this objective in line with the ideals which our forebears have always spearheaded in the area, we have resolved to work within the framework of Kordofan and in full cooperation with our brothers and sisters in that region for the common good of all our people in the region.

The declaration of the Ngok leadership was similar in essence, although it did not, understandably, attribute the bridging role of Ngok history to any individual or family (Deng 1986, 267):

> We, the assembled sons of Abyei, have been watching with profound sorrow and anguish the recent developments in our area and the general threat to the security of innocent people in the area. We are also deeply concerned that these developments have had the effect of reversing the historical image of our area as a vital link between the southern and northern parts of our country. Rather than the symbol of national unity and integration which it has been for centuries, our area is now seen as a point of confrontation and animosity and a threat to peace and unity, the most precious achievements of the May Revolution.
>
> We have always considered it absolutely essential that the call for joining the South be conducted peacefully and in accordance with the constitution and the laws of the country. While we therefore recognize the frustrations of the political tensions and conflicts which have recently prompted some people in the area to resort to violent means, we totally oppose the use of violence as a means of solving the problem of Abyei.
>
> We would also want to emphasize that we have always regarded the call for joining the South as a means and not an end in itself. The main objective has always been to secure for the people of Abyei the enjoyment of full rights of citizenship as free and equal partners in the government of their country. We therefore declare ourselves willing and ready to work within the framework of Kordofan as long as opportunities for the enjoyment of full rights of citizenship are offered to our people on equal footing with the rest of the people in the region.
>
> We have also concluded that the policies and principles declared by His Excellency the President of the Republic for the administration and development of Abyei area as a symbol of national unity and integration constitute a sound basis for the realization of the common interests in the area. We hope to achieve this in accordance with such programmes as may be agreed upon with the authorities of Kordofan in a spirit of cooperation and mutual understanding.

The agreement was celebrated in Khartoum as though it were a second Addis Ababa Accord. The luncheon I had secretly organized in anticipation of their release was attended by a hundred and fifty spontaneous guests. And for days to follow, various social functions were organized by the Dinka and the Arabs of the area together, and all were glamorously covered by the national media. In the joint press conference marking their release, the first vice president–national security chief called them the country's ambassadors for peace, a remarkable contrast to the earlier allegations of terrorism and treason.

The news was, however, ambivalently received in the South and among the "opportunists" of the Ngok Dinka who were benefiting from the hostilities as well as by the leaders of Kordofan, in particular the governor El Fatah Bushara, who had been away when the agreement was negotiated and concluded. Whether because he had not been part of it or because he was trying to gain political advantage with the Arabs in his region, Governor Bushara seemed almost antagonistic to the accord. In reaction to his attitude, I confronted him in front of his ministers and assembly members, arguing that he, as the head of the regional government, had more to be appreciative of than the national leadership, that he should be grateful to those who had made it possible, and that his attitude was a clear demonstration of what the Ngok Dinka objected to in the government of Kordofan.

The governor seemed startled by my attack and, from that moment on, tried to win my understanding of his delicate position. He explained that the people we considered opportunists were his political allies and that together with the Arabs, they had enabled him to win the elections. Indeed, the political faction with which we identified had not voted for him. Since he found the climate in Khartoum favorable to the Deng family, he wanted to assure the other side that they were not alone in the cold and that they still had his support. That way, he could then work to build bridges in order to consolidate on the regional level what we had achieved on the national level. Together, we held a meeting with the Ngok leaders and the public in which he tried to moderate his position and win approval of his idea to move the whole process to the region and broaden support for the reconciliation.

The Arabs and their Dinka allies in the area immediately sent a delegation to Khartoum, their objective being to oppose the agreement. Against the advice of many, I decided to visit the delegation. My discussions with them were more a courtesy report and an explanation of what I had tried to do than an exchange of views, even though some of them spoke reservedly, but courteously. After consultations with the national security authorities, the groups all agreed to go back to Kordofan and broaden the reconciliation process in the region. I decided that it was time for me to go back to my post abroad. News that reached me later indicated that the process continued to expand and widen its circle among both the Dinka and the Arabs.

The understanding that was reached in April 1983 between the authorities of Kordofan and elements from the Ngok Dinka brought back only a small patch of calm in what had become a sea of turbulence that would soon engulf the whole South in a second wave of civil war. Even as our success was being celebrated, President Nimeiri suddenly announced the division of the South into three regions. Shortly afterwards, the Bor and Fashalla crises that triggered the full rebellion of the units that would form the nucleus of the SPLM/SPLA under the leadership of John Garang de Mabior took place. The South was back in arms.

The history of Ngok Dinka–Homr Arab relations has been an ongoing dialogue, pioneered and spearheaded by their respective leaders. What complicates this process today is that it is no longer being pursued in an autonomous political context in which the leaders exercise independent judgment in regulating the relations between their peoples as neighbors with a mutual interest in coexisting peacefully. Over the centuries, the Homr Arabs and the Ngok Dinka had developed norms for coexisting in relative peace and for resolving their differences whenever they came into conflict. Left alone with the traditional balance of power or with a constructive third-party mediation, as was the case under the British, they would most likely have endeavored to reconcile their differences and build on their conventional wisdom in preventing, managing, or resolving their conflicts. With the force of the independent government intervening in favor of one party, the balance of power tilted and the incentive for mutual coexistence in peace and harmony eroded. The Arabs began to see advantage in adversity, since they often ended up on the winning side, and to make demands on the Dinka in areas of vital interest to them, such as access to land and water, which they would previously have had to request or negotiate deferentially in accordance with the established conventions of Dinka-Arab relations.

■ Underlying Cultural Values

Since my own studies and experiences with conflicts have focused on the Sudan and, in that context, on the Nilotics, particularly the Dinka, the largest ethnic group in the country, I have chosen to illustrate my argument with their indigenous value system. Among the central themes of the indigenous value system that the people themselves highlight and that have engaged anthropological attention are the pursuit of permanent identity and influence through procreation and the ancestral lineage system, communal unity and harmony as expressed in idealized concepts of human relations, and principles of individual and collective dignity and integrity. Together, these values constitute the cultural orientation that makes the Dinka, with their Nilotic kindred, among the least affected by the processes of modernization or development in Africa.

□ Dynamics of the Value System

The system functions through a dialectic process that involves the autonomy of the individual and the family unit on the one hand and the expansion of group identities on the other hand. Ironically the two are harmonized through the exogamous marriage system that forbids intermarriage among agnatic blood relatives, thereby extending family circles beyond the existing group, although marriage outside the largest territorially defined tribal group is discouraged. Friendship pacts are also among the well-established institutions of expanding relationships. The institution of age sets is yet another important complement to blood relationships.

Dispute resolution processes in the Nilotic culture are both broad based and leadership oriented. But, to appreciate the broad-based participatory nature of the process, it is important to see leadership in the Nilotic context not as a form of "government" but as a popularly representative institution and therefore people oriented. Despite Nilotic egalitarianism and individual sense of pride and independence, leadership is of critical importance to their value system, but more in a consensual rather than an authoritarian sense. Traditionally, a chief is not a ruler in the western sense, but a spiritual leader whose power rests on divine enlightenment and wisdom. In order to reconcile his people, the chief should be a model of virtue, righteousness, and, in Dinka terms, "a man with a cool heart" who must depend on persuasion and consensus building rather than on coercion and dictation. Godfrey Lienhardt (1963, 828) wrote:

> I suppose anyone would agree that one of the most decisive marks of a society we should call in a spiritual sense "civilized" is a highly developed sense and practice of justice, and here, the Nilotics, with their intense respect for the personal independence and dignity of themselves and of others, may be superior to societies more civilized in the material sense. . . . The Dinka and Nuer are a warlike people, and have never been slow to assert their rights as they see them by physical force. Yet, if one sees Dinka trying to resolve a dispute, according to their own customary law, there is often a reasonableness and a gentleness in their demeanor, a courtesy and a quietness in the speech of those elder men superior in status and wisdom, an attempt to get at the whole truth of the situation before them.

Edward Evans-Pritchard (1940a, 164), the renowned British anthropologist, observed of the Nuer settlement of disputes: "The five important elements in a settlement of this kind by direct negotiation through a chief seem to be (1) the desire of the disputants to settle their dispute, (2) the sanctity of the chief's person and his traditional role of mediator, (3) full and free discussion leading to a high measure of agreement between all present, (4) the feeling that a man can give way to the chief and elders without loss of dignity where he would not have given way to his opponent, and (5) recognition by the losing party of the justice of the other side's case."

The chief's mediation between individuals and groups, using largely persuasive strategies, was a feature of this all-embracing responsibility toward the dual worlds of man and spirits, but in terms of political and governmental power, not less significant. As one chief pointed out, to the Dinka, the power of persuasion is more durable than the power of the arm. "The Dinka used to say that a man defeated by strength of power comes back. . . . But a man who is defeated with words does not return" (Deng 1995, 195).

Despite the emphasis the chiefs and the elders place on persuasion, Nilotic society was quite violent not only in its confrontation with outside aggressors but also within itself. It can indeed be argued that the emphasis placed on the ideals of peace, unity, mediation, and persuasion emanates from the pervasiveness of violence. Internal violence can in turn be attributed to generational distribution of roles and functions and the sense of dignity young members of the warrior age sets acquire from their identity and status as warriors, defenders of the society from aggression (Evans-Pritchard 1940a, 253, 258; Burton 1980). Young men are organized into age sets in their midteens, when they undergo an initiation involving a physical ordeal from which they graduate as "gentlemen" with gifts of spears and bulls, "personality oxen," as symbols of their identity as warriors and herders. Boys start to train for the warring and herding roles from an early age through a wide variety of games and sports. In this, they are supported and encouraged by corresponding women's age sets, which correlate with men's, and by the society as a whole, including the elders, who view them with great favor and admiration. In fulfillment of their esteemed role, young warriors exaggerate aggressiveness and disposition to warfare so much that the slightest provocation, whether through the violation of territorial integrity of grazing lands or sources of water, or something as trivial as a slanderous song by an adversary, would provoke hostilities. Once a tribal war has broken out, however, all generations of men fit to fight and women following them to render support will join in.

The role differentiation between the leaders and elders as peacemakers and the youth as warriors was dramatized in an incident recounted by the leading Arab chief, Babo Nimir. Members of his lineage Kalabna had attacked the Ngok section of Abyor. Chief Deng Majok of the Ngok Dinka went to the scene of the impending battle and spoke to the aggressors (Deng 1982, 58–59): "You Kalabna, here you are holding the leadership, and you also want to show your manhood by fighting. Do you want to keep them both, leadership and manhood? No, you'd better take one and leave the other. Either you hold to your manhood and surrender your leadership, or you keep your leadership and surrender your manhood. But to keep them both cannot be." They were pleased by his words, and said, "It will be according to your word. We shall abandon manhood; leadership is enough for us."

The Dinka place great emphasis on the concept of "the word," by which they imply a normative code of cultural values. "This thing called the word is what is keeping the world in order," said one chief (Deng 1980, 165). "What we refuse to hear is what destroys the world and what we hear is what keeps the world in order." Dinka notion of knowledge, "*Nginy e wel,*" is "knowing the words." And by that they mean more than an accumulation of information. Knowing the words means knowing the moral code, being able to articulate its principles well and doing so to promote the ideals of harmonizing human relations in accordance with its norms. Knowing the words is more than knowing to talk well, "*nginy e jam.*" A person who talks well, "*raan ngic jam,*" is one who can manipulate words for good or evil. It is cleverness capable of being used constructively or selfishly. The amoral cleverness of the type exhibited in the tales of the fox is believed to eventually turn against its user. Knowledge of the words is ultimately wisdom not only in its abstract sense but also as applied to the practical objective of mediating and harmonizing relationships.

It is clearly paradoxical, but perhaps logical, that a society in which violence was so pervasive would be almost equally preoccupied with persuasive strategies of peacemaking through the power of "the word." To quote from Chief Arol Kachwol (Deng 1980, 511), "Man is one single word *with* God."

□ *Cross-Cultural Applicability*

While the values outlined in the foregoing section presuppose cultural homogeneity, they are also universally elastic in their applicability. Dinka religious beliefs make them respect in a profound sense what they perceive as God's creation, and the human being of any race, culture, or creed comes high on the list of God's creatures. Indeed, the list includes inanimate beings, seen as also God's creatures. As one chief put it,

> A man created by God . . . cannot be considered a fool. He is a human being, a part of the human race. Even the tree which cannot speak has the nature of a human being. It is a human being to God, the person who created it. Do not despise it; it is a human being. Our brothers, the Arabs, said that we should be treated that way because we were in their eyes like fools. . . . A human being who speaks with his mouth cannot be such a fool. Whatever way he lives, he remains a human being. And whatever he does must be thought about as the behavior of a human being. If you see a man walking on his two legs, do not despise him. . . . Bring him close to you and treat him like a human being. That is how you will secure your own life. But if you push him onto the ground and do not give him what he needs, things will spoil and even your big share, which you guard with care, will be destroyed. (Deng 1978)

Despite the extremism now exhibited by both sides, judging from the history of relations between the Ngok Dinka and the Homr Arabs and also from the interlude of peace following the Addis Ababa Agreement in 1972, racial, ethnic, and religious relations in the Sudan have not always been zero-sum. Indeed, perceptions of history shift from harmony to conflict, depending on the state of the relationship at any given time. It can also be argued that the relatively peaceful coexistence that had historically characterized the relationship of the Homr and the Ngok has been disrupted by the divisive penetration of the state.

■ Conclusion: State and Community

The experience of the Ngok-Homr relations shows that in the modern state context, it is difficult if not impossible for intercommunal dialogue or negotiations to be conducted independently of external, usually state, involvement of one kind or another and in varying degrees of intervention. By definition, internal conflict management or resolution efforts must be seen within a framework of interlocking layers of domestic jurisdiction, ultimately dominated by state power and sovereignty. This interconnection in part explains the complex mixture of successes and failures in many situations at all levels from local and national. Success emanates from realization of the mutual need for one another, acceptance of fundamental values and rules to govern the relationship, and the overall sense that there is more to gain than lose in ending the hostilities. In an autonomous context, this was reaffirmed, sanctioned, and consolidated by the recognition that there were no alternatives to what the system provided. On the other hand, much of the failure in the cases with which I was involved resulted from a negation of the bases for reconciliation due to the interconnectedness of diverse contexts and the impact of dependency on the part of one of the parties on external actors to change the balance of power, thereby undermining the mutual interest involved in the original framework of the agreement. Often, the dynamics are such that the external actor has more power and a greater leverage and therefore is more attractive as an ally. And if the external authority or actor is less interested in peace because he is more remote and therefore less harmed by conflict, or has other objectives that are fundamentally incompatible with those of one or both of the parties concerned, then destabilizing the situation becomes a strategy for weakening the adversary. This is particularly true of those situations where there is no agreement on a fundamental national or subnational framework for forging a common identity and a collective sense of purpose.

It must not, however, be assumed that the next layer up is always a source of complication and inevitable failure of agreements. On the contrary, a higher authority can be a source of impartiality and just solutions. Failure to reach a solution within the family can be remedied by a clan head or subtribal chief. Ultimately, in serious conflicts, resort can be had to the highest authority in the tribe, the paramount chief. In relations between tribes, the government, both local and central, can be an arbiter for fairness and cooperation. In the layers of interaction and potential or actual conflicts, the higher controlling authority can therefore be a source of aggravation or a force for peace and reconciliation.

In most cases, success or failure seems to depend on the degree to which there is an accepted framework of values and rules governing relations and established methods of resolving any conflicts that might arise. Within the family and the tribe this is clearly the case. In the relations between neighboring Arab and Dinka tribes, this is less the case, but customary norms have evolved that have created a code of conduct that, left to themselves, the neighboring tribes would be more inclined to observe. In the larger provincial and national contexts, however, the nation has not yet developed a consolidated framework for regulating relations among groups or for resolving conflicts in mutually accepted ways that are respected as legitimate, reliable, and sustainable.

The fact that Sudan has been engulfed in a civil war since independence with only a pause resulting from the subsequently abrogated Addis Ababa Agreement (1972–1983) underscores the lack of an agreed upon framework. This is further demonstrated by the fact that to this day, the Sudanese have not yet agreed on a permanent constitution. They have intermittently been governed by the transitional constitution bequeathed to them by the British, which has been abolished by military coups and restored, albeit with amendments, by democratic governments several times. It is now replaced by the current military regime with an Islamic agenda that has drawn the line even more sharply and made the prospects of national consensus, peace, and unity even more remote.

The parameters of the required dialogue are already evident in what I have characterized as a national identity crisis. This has now culminated in a dualism reflecting radical models on both sides, one Arab-Islamic and the other African-secular, with support cutting across the North-South divide. There are two principal dimensions to the crisis that potentially lend themselves to a productive dialogue. One has to do with the configuration of Sudanese identity in the light of historical processes that have left the peoples with layers of civilizations, racial characteristics, and cultural traditions; the other concerns the repercussions for unity in a pluralistic modern nation-state in which power, national resources, and services are inequitably distributed on racial, ethnic, cultural, religious, and correlative regional bases, and in which the identities that give the country its geopolitical significance are now in conflicting competition.

Conflict of identities manifests itself in two corresponding sets of discrepancies. One is the gap between self-perceptions of identity, what people claim to be, and the reality of what they are as determined by such visible factors as color of skin, physical features, and certain cultural patterns of behavior. The other is the gap between how individual groups perceive

themselves or are objectively perceived and how the national framework is defined.

These discrepancies lead to contrasting policy implications. One set of implications argues that the gap between self-perceptions and discernible realities of identity is unfounded and fictitious. By discrediting the divisive, subjective myths of identity, the common elements can be brought to the fore as grounds for unity. Adjusting self-perceptions to harmonize with objective realities should contribute to bridging the gap between exclusive group identities and the national identity, since the differences would then be minimized or reduced. While adjusting perceptions to eliminate discrepancies is an important conceptual step, it must be supplemented or complemented by an adjustment in the distribution of power and resources to remove the problematic disparities between groups, whether ethnically or regionally determined, provided that the national identity framework permits no divisive cleavages.

The contrasting set of implications argues that self-perceptions, whether well founded or not, must be accepted as they are and not scrutinized in the interest of a postulated framework of unity that does not in fact exist. If unity despite diversity is desirable, the argument goes, then the gap between the exclusive identities and the national framework, which is a reflection of the power dynamics of the country, far from being eliminated, should be recognized and managed through various forms of diversified unity and equity. To the extent that a formula for unity in diversity and an equitable system of sharing power and national resources can be developed and agreed upon, this line of approach may succeed in preserving some form of national unity. But under those circumstances, disparities that can nurture divisiveness and intensify the call for secession are likely to persist.

In evaluating these options and in particular the prospect of partitioning the country, the ambiguities of the country's racial, ethnic, and cultural configuration pose an ongoing challenge to both the North and the South. Even without the South, the North will continue to reckon with the question of whether it is Arab, African, or a peculiar combination, and what the policy implications of such characterization are, or should be. Future developments are bound to reveal greater acknowledgment of the African dimension, especially with a proud self-assertiveness of the African element in the South. By the same token, the South will continue to have racial, ethnic, and cultural kinship ties with the North, whether or not these ties are acknowledged in the short run. This line of analysis would argue for maintaining a framework of some form of unity, capable of being reinforced and consolidated over time. It also implies that even in the event of a partition, the North and the South will continue to be bound together by historical affinities of race, ethnicity, and culture in much the same way Egypt and the northern Sudan are bound together.

PART 2

Other Traditional Approaches to Reconciliation

8

Rituals of Forgiveness and Processes of Empowerment in Lebanon

Laurie E. King-Irani

Awakening from the long nightmare of civil war, Lebanese from all confessional communities are only now beginning to assess their considerable losses, whether physical, psychological, or political, as they attempt to make sense of their current circumstances and prepare to rebuild the future. Many are discovering that the war damage inflicted upon Lebanon's physical infrastructure was scant compared to the emotional, moral, and spiritual devastation visited upon the Lebanese people, individually and collectively, between 1975 and 1990. The Lebanese are now passing through an ambiguous and potentially dangerous period that is, in some respects, more enervating than the terrifying years of shelling, sniping, kidnapping, and assassination. After sixteen years of bitter, protracted, and ravaging conflict, every individual in Lebanon is, literally or figuratively, a displaced person. The roles, statuses, relationships, values, and expectations of the prewar period have been irrevocably altered, if not altogether erased, by the long war. Nearly a decade after the cessation of hostilities, in everyday conversations, most Lebanese voice the opinion that the postwar situation is highly unstable because the war did not end through a gradual resolution worked out by Lebanese themselves, but rather, ceased as a result of external political pressures. The scale and duration of Lebanon's violent conflict engendered deep feelings of bitterness, fear, anger, powerlessness, frustration, confusion, and despair. If the Lebanese fail to confront and transcend these legacies of victimization, they will never be free from the desires for vengeance that still lurk beneath the surfaces of daily life.

■ The Power of Ritual

Just as the repair and renovation of Lebanon's physical infrastructure will require considerable economic and political power, the rebuilding of the

Lebanese individual, and thus Lebanese civil society, calls for spiritual, emotional, and moral powers, transformative powers that cannot be legislated, imposed, or coerced from outside or from above, but which must arise from within the individual and society. Power, in this sense, refers not to the decisive, coercive might of weaponry and threats, but instead describes a constructive human potential for collective action. In the words of the political philosopher Hannah Arendt (1958, 201), true power has nothing to do with guns, muscles, threats, or dictators:

> While strength is the natural quality of an individual seen in isolation, power springs up between people when they act together and vanishes the moment they disperse. Because of this particularity, which power shares with all potentialities that can only be actualized but never fully materialized, power is to an astonishing degree independent of material factors, either of numbers or means.

These transformative social and personal powers cannot survive in an atmosphere of fear, mistrust, and dishonesty; their actualization requires that people bravely acknowledge disturbing and painful aspects of themselves and their society, share their experiences and truth with others, devise ways of reconciling diverse perspectives and needs, come to terms with the deep wounds of the past, and accept the risks of building and negotiating a new and demanding national life. For some, this may be more difficult than the war itself. But if the long nightmare of the war is to come to a decisive psychological end, not just a temporary military halt, acknowledgment of one's own and others' truths is fundamental. In the words of the German poet Rainer Maria Rilke, writing of the effects of World War I on Germany, "If a way to the better there be / it exacts a full look at the worst." Or, to cite a poet and visionary more familiar to Lebanon, Gibran Khalil Gibran, "Your pain is nothing but the breaking of the shell / that encloses your understanding."

Some of the transformative powers necessary for the healing of victimized individuals and societies may be found in rituals. Van Gennep long ago perceived and systematically described the transformative aspects of a particular category of ritual, rites of passage, that are usually divided into three stages: separation, marginalization, and aggregation (reincorporation). Such rituals readjust individuals and communities to changing aspects of their life-worlds, thereby enabling them to complete difficult and troubling transitions as individuals and as members of a society.

Noting the crippling lack of rites of passage in modern society, the British sociologist Anthony Giddens (1991, 204) observed that rituals are as crucial for individuals' emotional well-being as they are for communal harmony and social integration:

> Without ordered ritual and collective involvement, individuals are left without structured ways of coping with tensions and anxieties. . . . Communal rites provide a focus of group solidarity at major transitions as well as allocating definite tasks for those involved. . . . Rites de passage place those concerned in touch with wider cosmic forces, relating individual life to more encompassing existential issues. Traditional ritual . . . connected individual action to moral frameworks and to elemental questions about human existence. The loss of ritual is also the loss of such frameworks.

Conflict resolution can draw upon some of the rich possibilities inherent in ritual to mediate and resolve protracted disputes. Rituals may be particularly useful in treating the deeply entrenched ethnic and religious conflicts that are currently erupting all over the world. Clearly, there is some deep and primal motivating force driving these conflicts that cannot be addressed or treated by conventional means of diplomacy. This motivating force springs from unacknowledged, unforgiven, and thus unresolved psychic injuries that have transformed neighbors, colleagues, friends, and strangers into victims and victimizers trapped in a vicious, unending circle of vengeance and countervengeance. As ethnoreligious conflicts continue to break out in Africa, Central Asia, and the Indian subcontinent, it becomes increasingly imperative to find ways to treat and transcend these dangerous situations. Rituals of reconciliation may hold some of the answers.

■ The Rites of Peace

One approach to conflict resolution that was never formally attempted on a national level in Lebanon is that of the indigenous Lebanese ritual of *sulha* ("peacemaking" or "reconciliation"), which is an integral part of ancient communal traditions, whether Muslim, Christian, Jewish, or Druze, throughout the Arab world. The *sulha* ritual stresses the close link between the psychological and political dimensions of communal life through its recognition that injuries between individuals and groups will fester and expand if not acknowledged, repaired, forgiven, and transcended. *Sulha* recognizes not only the deep and complex psychological needs of the conflicting parties but also the serious social and political consequences of their injuries.

The *sulha* ritual has its roots in village life, where it serves as an institutionalized mechanism for the management and resolution of disputes between different families, clans, and tribes (Rothenberger 1978; Wittie 1980).[1] Although *sulha* is still in use among Shi'i, Sunni, and Maronite communities in rural Lebanon, notably the Bekaa Valley, the Hermel area, and the Akkar region, it is rarely employed by urban communities, nor is it a component of Lebanon's formal legal system. The Lebanese judiciary has never officially recognized *sulha,* nor has the ritual been incorporated into the state's legal code, as the *'ashira* tribal law of the Jordanian Bedouins has been incorporated into Jordan's legal system. However, since the Lebanese judiciary, like every other branch of the state government, was and remains greatly weakened by the long war, communities throughout Lebanon, whether Muslim or Christian, urban or rural, have relied on various alternative dispute resolution mechanisms such as *sulha* over the last two decades to settle differences and prevent disputes from escalating to dangerous levels.

The *sulha* ritual is employed primarily to repair a breach in relations among members of a face-to-face community following a violation of rights or norms. The violation may be simple, such as the theft of an object or a slight injury, or it may be more serious, such as a crime of honor involving the perception of immodest behavior of or insult toward a woman, which is felt to cause injury to the honor and reputation of the woman's male relatives. The most serious violation, of course, is intentional or involuntary manslaughter, which, in a tribal context, demands revenge (*intiqaam* or *th'r*) or the payment of a blood price (*'aql*) to reestablish balanced relations and psychological satisfaction. Murder poses the greatest danger to communal harmony and stability: if the families of the murderer and the victim do not reach a mutually acceptable reconciliation, the entire community, and even neighboring communities, may be drawn into a destructive cycle of vengeance and countervengeance that can last for generations.

The typical *sulha* ritual consists of three stages. In the initial stage, respected mediators (*muslih*s) chosen from among the leaders of the community are tasked with fact-finding concerning the violation. They listen impartially to the disputing parties (or individuals designated to represent them), conduct their own research into the matter, and consult other *muslih*s from nearby communities for advice and guidance. The goal of this stage is to acknowledge that a violation was committed, to ascertain precisely what happened, and to determine how and why it happened in order to assign blame according to the evidence presented and discovered. By listening actively and respectfully to the testimonies of all the parties involved, the *muslih*s also allow all those concerned to vent their anger, grief, and anxieties, thus enabling them to experience an emotional catharsis while providing them with a formal validation of their feelings. An important aspect of the initial stage is to determine what sort of agreement will be required to bring the dispute to a halt. The task of the *muslih*s is not to judge, punish, or condemn the offending party, but rather to preserve the good names of both the families involved and to reaffirm the need for ongoing relationships within the community (Rothenberger 1978, 164). The *sulha* ritual is not a zero-sum game.

Following a public acknowledgment of the reality of the injury or violation and the assignment of blame, the second stage of the *sulha* is pardon between the disputing parties. This stage of the ritual, which is usually held in the home of the injured party, is supervised by the *muslih*s, who try to ensure that the dignity and honor of all the disputants are restored and upheld, stressing that extenuating circumstances, such as the youth of one party or the incapacity of another, must be taken into account in explaining and pardoning what happened. The second stage usually ends with a speech by a member of the guilty party's family extolling the honor, generosity, and nobility of the injured party's family. Forgiveness usually is sealed with the presentation of a gift or a cash payment of compensation to the injured party.

The final stage of the *sulha* ritual is a public, formalized demonstration of reconciliation between the disputants. This is expressed verbally and symbolically. In the last stage of a *sulha* ritual between a Christian and a Muslim family, an elderly Christian man named Yussuf, the injured party, told the injurer, a young Muslim man named Ahmed, and his family that

> anger is a powerful force, and we have all been angry. And even though I will always have to walk with this stick due to my injury, the deed has been done—God help us all. There is no reason or usefulness in my thinking . . . to continue the bad blood between us. Our families have always met our obligations and kept our word, debt and honor, and have given our support to one another. God is my witness. And so I, and my sons and my brothers, and my cousins—all of my family, accept your gift and your apology. Let us talk no more of this incident (Wittie 1980, 58).

In cases of serious injury or murder, the use of symbolic behavior in the last stage of the *sulha* ritual dramatically reaffirms and underlines the sincerity of the intention to forgive and be reconciled. For instance, in one murder case in a rural Shi'i community in Lebanon, a young man guilty of murder was brought to the home of the murder victim with a red cloth tied around his neck symbolizing the spilt blood of the victim. The murderer was left to the mercy of the murdered man's family, who has the right, according to tribal custom, to kill him in retribution for the loss of their loved one. Instead, they exhibited the highly valued trait of *hilm* (magnanimity) by releasing the murderer, unharmed, to his family. In this case, the young man's punishment was to be exiled (*manboudh*) from his village for life. In the previously cited case, the injurer, Ahmad, who had shot Yussuf in the foot in a youthful temper tantrum, willingly submitted himself to a ritual shaving by the injured party. By allowing Yussuf to use a sharp razor on his face, Ahmad symbolically expressed his admission of guilt and allowed

Yussuf to ritually express his acceptance of Ahmad's apology. In the act of shaving Ahmad's face, Yussuf cleansed the younger man and his entire family of the stain of their guilt, thus enabling the two families to begin a "new page" in the history of their relations in the village (Wittie 1980, 58).

The *sulha* ritual follows the three stages of rites of passage described by van Gennep. In the initial stages of the *sulha* ritual, the offended are separated from the rest of society by the mutual pain of the injury between them. Then, with the assistance of *muslih*s, they are transformed from hostile victims and victimizers into coexisting fellow men and women through the mediation of symbolic words and actions during a period of marginality and intense emotional experience. In the final stage of the *sulha* ritual, the parties to the conflict are reincorporated into their society, now divested of their burdens of blood and vengeance and free to start their communal life anew. Ideally, the *sulha* ritual emphasizes the necessity of assigning blame, reaffirming predominant social norms and values, accepting responsibility for wrongs committed, and healing through atonement and compensation for injuries, all of which stress the importance of preventing one limited conflict from escalating into unlimited internecine violence and destruction. As a ritual of reconciliation and a method of conflict resolution, this indigenous Arab rite of passage has much to offer Lebanese individuals and groups interested in conflict resolution, coming to terms with the past, and rebuilding postwar Lebanese society. A modified form of the *sulha* ritual may also have much to offer other societies whose members are trapped in unending cycles of violence and vengeance.

■ Empowerment Through Ritual

The key transformation accomplished by the *sulha* ritual is the transition from the social status and emotional perspective of victim or victimizer to the status and perspective of fellow inhabitants of a particular sociotemporal setting. A defining characteristic of victimhood is that the victim is passive and acted upon by forces beyond his or her control. Victims and victimizers are trapped by a limited and limiting past that overshadows the present while devouring all future possibilities. In other words, victims and victimizers are people devoid of constructive power and hope.

Through the transformative powers of the *sulha* ritual, individuals and groups leave behind their roles as victims and victimizers rendered powerless by the compulsive need for revenge. No longer passive objects of injury and injustice, no longer at the mercy of the drive for vengeance and countervengeance, they acquire an awareness of alternative possibilities. Several recent studies of the psychological dimensions of forgiveness and reconciliation (Flanigan 1992; Jenco 1995; Weschler 1990; McGary and

Lawson 1992) emphasize that individuals who have experienced reconciliation are transformed as a result. Flanigan (1992, 173) describes this phenomenon most succinctly: "The entire process of forgiving is a process of conversion from being an object of another person's passions and actions to being a person who acts upon his or her own injury." Hannah Arendt referred to forgiveness as "a power, a human power," likening it to a miracle in its unpredictability and classifying it, along with promising, in the category of key human actions that enable human beings to continue to interact in spite of all the ambiguities, suffering, regrets, and vulnerabilities of their condition. Similarly, Donald W. Shriver, Jr. (1991, 193), notes the close relationship between forgiveness and the enhancement of personal and communal power: "The power to forgive remains one of the awesome powers of human beings. . . . The power to forgive, like the power to enter into new social covenants, is an essential power for social change . . . [it] is a human action which belongs to the array of powers of those who exercise and increase their personal powers for the building and maintenance of societies."

Emerging from a deeply injurious war in which every confessional group, at one time or another, assumed the roles of both victim and victimizer, Lebanese intercommunal relations would undoubtedly benefit from the transformative powers inherent in the *sulha* ritual. But might Lebanese individuals also thereby benefit from a transformation of their ideas, beliefs, and behaviors concerning power? Are prevailing Lebanese conceptions about power conducive to or obstructive of peace, justice, and security in the postwar context? These questions demand a fuller analysis of Lebanon's prewar and postwar political culture than this chapter can provide. However, some initial observations concerning Lebanese psychocultural phenomena indicate that prevailing Lebanese concepts of and behaviors toward power are dysfunctional.

The Lebanese system of confessional power sharing, *ta'ifiyya,* is both an expression and a cause of dysfunctional attitudes concerning power. As noted by Daoud Khairallah (1994, 260–269), confessional power sharing is, in fact, disempowering from the perspective of the Lebanese *individual:*

> Under the prevailing system [i.e., *ta'ifiyya*], an individual's political entitlement, as well as his rights and obligations with respect to inheritance and personal status, are decided at birth. . . .Through his family and sectarian upbringing, the individual inherits all the historical experiences, generated fears, and biases harbored by his or her sect. The aspirations of the sect become the goals of its members. . . . Political life is perceived as a "zero-sum" game in which the gains of one sect mean losses for another. Instead of representing the united national will, the state is merely a fragile shell for containing the struggle between sects. . . . Confessionalism . . . denies people the right to participate in the process of choosing

> laws and institutions that govern very important aspects of their lives . . . [and] denies them the ability to develop as moral and social beings.

Because of this confessionally based system, the individual in Lebanon is first and foremost a Maronite, a Shi'i, or a Sunni, and only afterwards a Lebanese citizen. By emphasizing the group over the individual (thereby minimizing the individual's choice, power, and sense of responsibility), and by privileging the sect over the state (thus contributing to the fragmentation of the polity), *ta'ifiyya* cannot but set the stage for future violent conflicts in Lebanon.

The prevailing emotions of fear, anger, bitterness, mistrust, and despair in postwar Lebanon are not simply the results of the war; they were also some of the motivating causes of the sixteen years of conflict. Even before 1975, the Lebanese were thinking and acting as potential or actual victims. Clearly, many of the eighteen different sects officially recognized by the Lebanese government had valid historical, political, and economic reasons to worry about scarcity of power, security, and resources. Lebanon is unique in being a state comprised solely of minorities (Harff 1993). If a minority is a group that lacks power, it is only a short leap to the conclusion that a minority group is always a potential victim group. Members of minority communities are often mistrustful, quick to take offense, pessimistic, and ready to defend even minimum interests with maximum force. After all, any incident could well be a life or death matter for a group continuously threatened with marginalization, exploitation, or even extermination.

In Lebanon, the entire population, being a mosaic of contending minorities, was thinking and feeling like victims even before war broke out on April 13, 1975. It is no wonder, then, that the war was so violent, so bitter, and so protracted. As Theodor Hanf (1993, 1–2) describes the nature of the conflict in his monumental study of the war in Lebanon, "It was a macabre game of musical chairs in which no one wanted to be the only one left standing. . . . The fear of being the ultimate loser is the motivating force in [Lebanese] politics."

Lebanon's system of confessional power sharing has had a detrimental effect on conceptions, attitudes, and behaviors associated with personal power. In Lebanon, power is not vested in the individual; rather, individuals can attain power only through their community, or, more specifically, through the leader (*za'im*) of their community, who usually wields absolute power (backed up by credible threats of force) in the context of his confessional group. The concentration of power in the hands of a few individuals in Lebanon's political system has increased the sense of powerlessness and dependency that is already so prevalent among the members of each of the country's contending minority communities. If two communal leaders become embroiled in a personal conflict, the strife can quickly spread to their supporters in each respective community. The good of the wider, national community is thus thoughtlessly sacrificed for the political or economic interests of corrupt and grasping leaders who often have more in common with each other than they do with the communities they ostensibly represent. Indeed, few Lebanese political leaders display sincere concern for the entire Lebanese nation, preferring, instead, to focus only on those regions and populations associated with their own hold on power and prestige, even if this entails manipulating and provoking interconfessional conflict. Salibi (1988, 184–190) observed that this tendency was one of the factors that plunged Lebanon into its long and bitter civil war:

> To boost their threatened traditional power, in the rural areas as well as in the cities, leaders . . . played unscrupulously on the ever-present confessional or tribal rancors and suspicions among their followers . . . as social tensions began to develop in the country in the wake of its uneven social and economic development. . . . In the rural and tribal areas, the leaders had no interest in seeing their constituencies develop, fearing that this would rob them of the mainstay of their power: the blind tribal allegiance of their followers. Development would make the blind see, and this, from the point of view of the tribal leadership, was politically undesirable.

Unfortunately, Salibi's indictment of prewar Lebanese political leaders remains a valid description of the postwar political situation. Although the militias that terrorized and devastated Lebanon for sixteen years have been disarmed and disbanded, most of the militia leaders have taken up key positions in the resurrected Lebanese government. Having conveniently pardoned themselves for their wartime atrocities by way of an official decree, these leaders now psychologically punish the thousands of Lebanese citizens victimized by their militia organizations during the war by ostentatiously living the "high life," wearing expensive clothes, living in exquisite villas, and causing traffic jams so that their convoys of Range Rovers and Mercedes can take them to and from parliament. Hence, the war's victimizers have been rewarded and most of the victims continue to be victimized.

To restore a just social order in the wake of Lebanon's wartime atrocities, violations, and suffering entails restoring a sense of morality based on universal principles, not a Machiavellian moral code based on fickle political expediency. It is the individual, not the group, who is the ultimate locus of morality. Only individuals can sense, think, judge, decide, choose, and act. Individuals, not groups, possess free will, the sine qua non of morality. If individuals are oppressed, morality will, as a consequence, be suppressed. As one political philsopher (Kymlicka 1992, 242–244) notes,

> Groups have no moral claim to well-being independently of their members. Groups just are not the right sort of beings to have moral status. They don't feel pain or pleasure. It is individual, sentient beings . . . who suffer or flourish, and so it is their welfare that is the subject matter of morality. The claim that individuals, not communities, are the ultimate bearers of moral value is simply a recognition of the separateness of consciousness.

Several scholars of Middle Eastern society and politics (Makiya 1993; Said 1995) have recently broached the sensitive and controversial issues of leadership, justice, democratization, and the exercise of political power in the post–Cold War Arab world. They have concluded that there is an urgent need for individual citizens throughout the Arab world to take more interest in and responsibility for the pressing issues of their societies, to speak out and become involved in the resolution of problems, the expansion of social and economic justice, and the making of policy, and to question the relevance and the efficacy of traditional models of leadership based on power hoarding and coercion, models that spring from a long history of victimization, uncertainty, mistrust, and vulnerability in this region of the world. But no Lebanese individual will be able to join with other Lebanese individuals to raise such questions and call for such reforms so long as individuals feel powerless, frightened, frustrated, and despondent. Individually and collectively, Lebanese individuals will have to first undergo a significant psychological transformation, a process of empowerment, before they will be capable of transforming their wounded society.

A similar process can be noted among Palestinian citizens of Israel in Nazareth. In the early 1990s, when I conducted research there, the people of Nazareth were confronting crises of leadership, a power vacuum in society, and a need for introspection stemming from the profound ideological and political changes that followed the collapse of the Soviet Union and the conclusion of the Gulf War. One of my informants, Walid, a lawyer who devoted time to defending juvenile political detainees held in military prisons throughout the West Bank, observed that the crisis of leadership was not only the fault of the leaders. "If we are to build an independent Palestinian society and government worthy of all of our suffering and sacrifices," he told me, "then it won't be enough to get rid of Israeli rule or bring new leaders. What's really important is that each one must make his own personal, psychological *intifada* (*kul wahid lazim ya'mal intifada nefsiyya dakhaliyya*); we are not used to having and exercising power ourselves—it's always been imposed from above, so we have to shake off our mentality of powerlessness." This process of shaking off (the actual meaning of the Arabic word *intifada*) an inherited legacy of powerlessness and victimization would require Palestinians, individually and collectively, to come to terms with themselves, their leaders, their enemies, and their history in order to heal, grow, and move forward to a new and more constructive stage of their history.

If conflicts are to be truly resolved, and not simply "managed," in both Lebanon and Palestine, the psychological dimensions of protracted disputes must be fully acknowledged and sensitively addressed. Traditional rituals of political and personal transformation, such as *sulha,* may be useful in this effort. The transformation of traditional Arab models of power, by means of a traditional Arab transformative rite of passage, could be instrumental in the healing of individuals, societies, and polities.

One way of realizing psychological and political transformation and healing in postwar Lebanon is the adaptation of the *sulha* ritual for use in conflict resolution workshops undertaken by respected Lebanese nongovernmental organizations. Given the Lebanese government's seeming neglect of the requirements of national reconciliation, as well as the Lebanese judiciary's current weaknesses in the wake of the long war, nongovenmental organizations (NGOs) representing Lebanese of all confessional backgrounds are better positioned than the state to initiate the challenging process of national reconciliation between the victims and victimizers of the Lebanese civil war. Lebanese NGOs, which provided so many necessary services in the course of the conflict, have more legitimacy and credibility than the state government, some of the key ministries of which are staffed by known war criminals. Furthermore, Lebanese NGOs, being rooted in local communities, have a better grasp on the actual capabilities, priorities, and needs of the Lebanese public than does the government.

A 1994 conference on "Acknowledgment, Forgiveness, and Reconciliation: Alternative Approaches to Conflict Resolution in Post-War Lebanon," during which the need for national reconciliation was passionately discussed, could serve as a model for workshops employing a modified form of the *sulha* ritual to facilitate the acknowledgment of injuries suffered, the forgiveness and apologies for violations committed, and the needed reconciliation between representatives of different Lebanese sects and factions. Such a modified *sulha* ritual might also serve the same function in Lebanon as did the truth and justice commissions that aided processes of healing and reconciliation in South Africa, Chile, and Argentina after those two countries emerged from the shadows of apartheid and military dictatorship.

■ Conclusion

The choice before the people of Lebanon, and indeed, of the entire Arab world, is the potentially revolutionary choice between power hoarding and power sharing, between continued victimization or empowerment. Since power sharing will never succeed in a society crippled by hatred, mistrust, prejudices, and all the other poisonous residues of a long history of victimization, the ultimate goal of empowering individuals and establishing a more just social and political order can only be hastened and facilitated through processes of acknowledgment, forgiveness, and reconciliation. Rituals of reconciliation and forgiveness are increasingly needed in our overcrowded, resource-strapped, and highly armed world. As Shriver notes (1991), "A political form of forgiveness may not guarantee that we humans can survive our sins against each other, but without it, we might not have survived this long, and we need it, as our capacity to harm each other grows more than ever."

Notes

1. I also rely upon information collected during an August 16,1995, interview with Ghassan Mokheiber, a Lebanese attorney and human rights activist who conducted field research on *sulha* in the Hermel region of Lebanon in the early 1990s.

9

Contrasts in Conflict Management in Cleveland and Palestine

Mohammed Abu-Nimer

Western and non-Western (sometimes called traditional) approaches to conflict management start with different assumptions, proceed by different methods, and achieve different results. These, and cases that illustrate them, need to be juxtaposed in order to make these differences clear. Otherwise the similarities, which also exist, would make it seem that all approaches, methods, and results are the same. This chapter therefore examines two different sets of assumptions, serving as the bases for two different cases, to produce different outcomes.

■ Western Conflict Resolution

Underlying the newly emerging field of conflict resolution in the United States are a number of fundamental assumptions:

1. Conflict resolution processes can benefit both parties and have the potential to satisfy their wishes, desires, and needs, particularly those of the underdog. By establishing a conflict resolution mechanism, the community can improve its internal economic and social relationships.
2. Bargaining and negotiation can produce a collaborative decision-making process to reach consensus over an action plan.
3. Legality is the main basis of intervention in a dispute. Government and police officials perceive the law as a rule to be preserved and used for achieving their goals. Outcomes of the process have to follow legal procedures.
4. Since Western society is based on individualism, people who are not related directly to the conflict have minimal involvement in the

process and outcome. Social pressure does not operate as a factor that increases parties' commitment to the settlement.

5. Since Western society calculates every step and behavior according to rational measures, there are always five to twelve fixed and predetermined steps for handling disputes, providing mediators with rules and guidelines for behavior. These involve the "professional behavior" and the "business image" that give the mediator credibility (public policy, community, interpersonal, or international).
6. Facing and confronting a conflict is a basic assumption in the Western conflict resolution approach. Conflict is the source of growth, not necessarily a negative to be avoided.
7. The direct method of interaction and communication, face-to-face negotiation and bargaining, is the best approach for dealing with disputes.
8. The focus on issues and substantive points is the main concern of the conflict resolver.
9. Individualization of the conflict resolution processes focuses on the individual's desires, needs, and identity.

□ *Case 1: The Cleveland Roundtable Racial Unity Program*[1]

Although blacks had contributed to the community of Cleveland since the 1800s, and civil rights laws had already influenced many other cities, in Cleveland in the mid-1980s, it was clear that the changes of the past twenty-five years had not been reaching the general population. According to the July 1987 edition of *Black Enterprise,* Cleveland was ranked thirty-second in the nation in black economic development. Census Bureau and other statistical reports showed Cleveland had a black median income that was only 56 percent of whites with comparable education and training. Cleveland had one of the highest unemployment rates in the country and a disproportionate number of those unemployed were black. Surveys done by Cleveland organizations also showed few blacks sitting on boards or rising to high management positions. In the preceding years, reported incidents of racial and religious intimidation had increased substantially.

The Greater Cleveland Roundtable was established in 1980 to encourage revitalization of the metropolitan area. It was an urban coalition of the CEOs of major Cleveland/Cuyahoga County corporations, senior local political officials, clergy, and major civic leaders. The group was about two-thirds white and people of other color, and one-third black. The organization's mandate was "to foster racial harmony, cooperation and the empowerment of all segments of Cleveland's diverse population in a unified effort to improve the quality of life enjoyed by every resident."

In 1986, a series of shootings in residential neighborhoods in the

Cleveland area took place. Racial tension and strife began to increase markedly after the shootings. Section 8 housing was being located in traditionally white, low- and middle-income neighborhoods, and minorities were moving into these communities. Discomfort was high and the rumors and agitation that often accompany such changes were on the rise.

The Roundtable recognized the need for averting further strife and tension and easing the current situation. Local programs, funded by philanthropic organizations and businesses, were addressing some problems, but there was no effort to coordinate activities. In the early fall of 1986, an ad hoc group of fourteen community members formed to look at the issues.

The racially mixed ad hoc group met every two weeks for a period of four months. It consisted of a city councilman, a representative of Case Western Reserve University, a member of the City of Cleveland Community Relations Board, a police representative, and members of the clergy and civic and neighborhood groups. By early 1987, they recognized that the discussion needed to be more inclusive. The roundtable, with the help of racial and organizational development consultants and the ad hoc group, identified forty groups that it felt should be represented in efforts to address discrimination in Cleveland. In 1987, the Race Relations Forum was established, with the Greater Cleveland Roundtable as a major sponsor.

The group met every three weeks for approximately five months using consensus-based decisionmaking and facilitators to manage meetings. Members reported to their individual community organizations between meetings and solicited their input to be taken back to the forum members. Ten committees were formed to work on specific problems and issues. The forum develop a list of twelve initiatives to be addressed and developed a report entitled "Facing Reality: Progress Through Racial Unity in Greater Cleveland." The forum continues to meet quarterly to monitor the progress of the initiatives.

The overall outcome was a more comprehensive way of looking at discrimination and factors that lead to it. In its concluding report the forum reached unanimous agreement that piecemeal, band-aid approaches cannot solve long-standing problems. The forum's report was meant to serve as a catalyst for continued collective action. The specific outcomes were grouped in four categories that included the twelve initiatives:

1. A hotline to be designated the "Cool Line," which would respond to calls regarding housing discrimination, racial violence incidents, racial or religious harassment, neighborhood or school tensions, rumor control, and hate group activities.
2. "Turning Point 88," a community-based organization, designed to develop programs to reduce racial tension in neighborhoods and

provide leadership training for neighborhoods. Neighborhood leaders would be trained to reduce racist attitudes and problems in schools, housing, and other areas.

3. Race relations training, which was developed for and targeted specifically to police, business, clergy, and civic agencies. A resource center was set up to coordinate training and collection of training materials in the Greater Cleveland area.
4. A committee on "Bias in media research," which would produce a report on bias in the print, electronic, and advertising media. Media were involved in the study and both positive and negative examples were to be gathered. The goal was to achieve more unbiased reporting and develop criteria for how the media can best serve a multiracial community.

Nine months elapsed from the first meetings of the ad hoc group to the final report of the Forum, which was presented on the one-year anniversary of the shootings that prompted the process.

The process cost was $50,000 and was paid for through operating funds of the Greater Cleveland Roundtable and contributions from the Cleveland and the George Gund Foundations.

The intervention in this conflict was designed and led by existing institutions and organizations that aimed to reduce racial tension and improve quality of life for all citizens, particularly those who belonged to the black minority. These agencies included local politicians, governmental officers, and community leaders. The decisionmaking process implemented by the third party was based on reaching consensus among the ad hoc group members. The third-party structure reflects the balance of power among the parties (whites, blacks, and people of other color).

The set of outcomes reflects a preventive approach to conflict, an approach that addresses the conflicts and attempts to deal with their consequences. The specific outcomes generated mainly responded to one cause of the dispute, lack of tolerance among community members. It did not and could not solve the roots of the problem, unequal economic opportunities for blacks and whites in Cleveland. However, the initiatives reflect an agreement among the parties on the need for a collaborative approach to the problem.

■ Non-Western Conflict Resolution

Basic features characterize the non-Western process as exemplified in this case by practices in the Middle East:

1. Conflict resolution does not particularly seek to change the status quo or power relationships but seeks to restore social order and disrupted balance of power.
2. Groups and collectivities (family and extended family, community) are important actors.
3. The initiation and implementation of the intervention are based on the social norms and customs of the society.
4. Negotiation and bargaining to reach a settlement are based on the preservation of social values, norms, and customs. Negotiators refer to these values as a method of pressuring the other side.
5. Future relationships are crucial elements in settling a dispute and determine the intervention procedures, nature, size, and settlement.
6. The core assumption of intervention is a combination of rational calculations and consideration of social values and norms.
7. Even if a dispute is over scarce resources (such as money, or debts, or land), values such as "honor," "shame," "dignity," "social status," and "religious beliefs" are at stake.
8. Conflict is negative, threatening, and disruptive to the normative order and should be settled soon or avoided.
9. Priority is given to people and relationships over task and structure.
10. The dispute is best resolved without face-to-face bargaining or negotiation, which can be perceived as a further antagonistic or as a humiliating act for the victim's party.
11. Presenting the story produced by the parties in the negotiation process is the most crucial part of the interaction; it reflects the parties' social status and power. Therefore, each side's storytelling is conducted several times during the intervention.

□ *Case 2: Village Conflict Among Palestinians in Israel*

There are about 14,000 people in this village, with 60 percent Druze, 23 percent Christians, and 17 percent Muslims. In the region, the Druze are a minority and the Muslims a majority. The balance of power had changed in this village beginning in 1956, when young Druze males began being required to join the Israeli army. This factor divided the village politically into two divisions, those who supported the Israeli government policies and those who opposed the government policies, especially on the Palestinian-Israeli issue.

As a result of the intensive confiscation of lands, this village, like other Arab villages in Israel, no longer depends on peasantry. Army service is the essential source of income for the Druze. The Christians mainly have small businesses and administrative and educational positions in the village. Muslims work outside the village in the Israeli construction factories.

The social structure of the three communities in the village is based on clan units. However, the Druze stress community interests and religious identity more than the other two communities. Muslims and Christians are less unified on the basis of their religious affiliation. They identify themselves with the broader national Palestinian identity in Israel and in the Arab world.

The relationship between the three religious groups had been peaceful and respectful since the establishment of Israel in 1948. This was reflected in mutual visits among the leaders of the communities, particularly during weddings, funerals, and other social events. Younger generations attend integrated schools and they usually were not separated except for religion classes.

In January 1979, a group of Druze youths threw stones at the wedding party of a Christian leader's son. Two days later, some of the Christian clans' heads visited the houses of the suspected Druze youths. They complained about the disturbance at the wedding. The youths were warned by their fathers not to repeat this shameful behavior, which, as Christian leaders argued, could destroy the good relationship between the two communities.

One month later a violent confrontation at midnight resulted in the hospitalization of two Druze young men. Christians in the neighborhood claimed that the Druze group was screaming and disturbing the people when some Christians tried to convince them to leave the area. The following day some of the Christian clans' leaders visited families of the injured youths. They offered a settlement and tried to prevent any further violence. The Druze families refused and argued that they would talk only when their sons were released from the hospital.

The following day, as a result of a rumor that the two injured Druze died, approximately two thousand Druze attacked the Christian neighborhood. They destroyed furniture in some houses, injured several Christians, and caused damage to stores owned by Christians. As a result, many Christian families took shelter in surrounding villages.

A few hours after this attack started, many delegates from other Muslim villages in the area entered the village and stopped the Druze youths who were still threatening the Christian neighborhoods. The Israeli police patrols left the village and did not return until the morning of the next day.

Through the following week, Christian-owned stores were closed and Christian students did not attend the schools. Their neighborhood was paralyzed. This situation disrupted all aspects of village life. Meanwhile, the

Druze leaders of the attack were discussing in open meetings (at the Druze religious center) political, economic, and social sanctions against the Christians. Respectable Druze leaders did not attend these meetings. Some of them even expressed their rejection of sanctions (the recent and former mayors and some other clans' heads).

The dispute involved the security of the whole region and has some special characteristics. Neither the local mediators nor the Islamic minority of the village were able to settle the conflict or intervene effectively. Since the dispute had no explicit economic or tangible resource in question, the parties did not consider the Israeli court system.[2] Honor, shame, respect, and dignity of both communities were the values underlying the conflict. There was an asymmetric power relation between the parties.

A few days later, many outsider delegations were visiting Druze leaders' houses in an attempt to settle the dispute. Some of these delegations intervened because Christian leaders asked them to and others volunteered.

A formal third-party group of twenty-five regional leaders, led by a committee of seven members, took the responsibility of mediating this dispute. The following characteristics of this group reflect their source of credibility and legitimacy and some of their strategies:

- Outsiders: all of the group members were outsiders. They did not have any direct clan relationship with the disputants.
- Age: the average age was fifty years old. This is a very important source of respect in traditional Arab society.
- Mayors: several were mayors of big villages in the region.
- Religion: they belonged to all religious groups.
- Historical knowledge: members of the group knew very well the history of this village, the history of mediation and intervention in the region, and the customs and norms of the three religious communities.
- Political power: a few members of the Israeli parliament were also members of this group. These members were elected to the parliament by the Arab minority only. Also there were among the group some Druze who held high military positions.
- Members of this committee did not have power to place any type of economic or political sanctions upon the parties.
- Some members of the third-party group had either a direct or indirect political interest in the dispute. However the majority were outside traditional and religious leaders.

The seven-member committee visited several Druze houses, especially the leaders' houses (mayors, heads of clans, and religious leaders), and also the Christian leaders' houses and observed the damages caused by the mass attack. They then conducted separate consultations with the parties, followed by negotiation and bargaining to reach the settlement: (1) the Druze would allow the Christians to return to their houses; (2) Druze families would not receive money for their injured youths, but the Christian families ought to apologize directly to the youths; (3) Druze leaders would guarantee to prevent any further attacks on Christian neighbors; (4) economic sanctions should be suspended immediately; and (5) Druze students would stop disturbing Christian students in the schools.

The social values and norms used by the intervenors included (1) shame and honor of the parties, (2) unity of the village, family, and region, (3) the sake of the next generation, (4) religious values of tolerance and respect of elders, (5) a history of peaceful and respectful relationships in the village in the past, and (6) the fact that they all subscribe to the Arab tradition of forgiveness and dignity.

Only the first condition of settlement brought the parties together face-to-face. After the Christian families fulfilled the conditions of the agreement, the Druze families permitted the return of all Christian families. But the economic and social sanctions continued for a year. They were suspended as a result of internal arguments within the Druze community. The argument emerged again when leaders of the mass attack opened several new stores and groceries near Christian stores. This act revealed some of these leaders' intentions, which caused people to be less enthusiastic about continuation of the sanctions.

After only one year, the dispute became a part of the village's history that young students and children were advised to avoid mentioning (since it was a shameful and a dangerous event).

Thus, conflict resolution in this context was conducted through existing traditional social institutions, operated by the local social and political leaders. It was not based on a legal framework, although this alternative existed since Israeli law is used at every other level. In this case, none of the parties called on the formal legal option.

The management of the dispute in this case illustrates the use of dispute resolution processes to restore social order and the power relation between the parties. There was no substantial plan, action, or even recognition of the need to change this power disparity between the parties, even though both parties recognized the power disparity as one of the major causes of the conflict.

■ Comparison of the Dispute Resolution Process in Both Contexts[3]

An initial comparison on several levels between the intervention in the Middle Eastern dispute and the American community dispute and the summary of assumptions on Western conflict resolution processes of intervention suggest the following differences:

☐ *The Process*

1. In the Middle Eastern case immediate intervention takes place even without the request of the parties. In the Western context third-party intervention in such community conflicts does not occur immediately.
2. In the Middle Eastern case the negotiations are conducted in a public forum. In the Western context the negotiation is conducted in a private and formal setting.
3. In the Middle Eastern case the mediators often go between the parties. In the Western context mediation and intervention are usually conducted face-to-face.
4. If the settlement includes material compensation, in the Middle Eastern case the third party is responsible for delivering and arranging the payments in a social public ritual. In the Western context compensation is directly delivered by the parties or through a legal format.
5. In the Middle Eastern case the process was based on the third-party authority as arbitrators and mediators (all mediators and arbitrators in community conflicts were males). However, the decision was made after the negotiation processes between the parties had been completed. In the American case the process was based on collaborative decisionmaking.
6. To be effective and accepted by the parties, the process in the Middle Eastern case has to respond to the values and norms of the society, values such as honor, shame, dignity, religious and patriarchal identity. Such Middle Eastern values and norms are totally different from the Western values and norms that underlie the Western process of conflict resolution.

☐ *Nature of the Third Party*

1. In the Middle Eastern case third parties have high community status and considerable power. In the Western context third parties (mediators particularly) are always strangers to the dispute and tend to be low-power court officials or community volunteers.
2. Mediators in Middle Eastern settings bring considerable knowledge of events, the character of the dispute and disputants. The Western mediators lack this knowledge and must struggle to develop a coherent account of the dispute and assist the parties based on their statements in the sessions.

3. In the Middle Eastern case mediators are often directive, advocates for a settlement that accords with notions of justice that are accepted in their societies. Western mediators are more concerned with achieving lasting settlement and less concerned with forcing societal norms.
4. The broader community in the Middle Eastern case often places pressure upon disputants to settle and abide by the settlement. In the Western case such pressure, if it exists, comes from the court.
5. In the Middle Eastern case the third party's credibility to intervene is based on kinship connections, political position, religious merit, previous experience, and knowledge of customs and community. In the Western case the credibility emerges from training and experience of mediation.
6. In the Middle Eastern context the mediators are involved in the dispute emotionally, in actual kinship relation, or have a general interest in the settlement. The Western mediators should be most successful in detaching themselves from the dispute's values and be committed to the values of the process (negotiation and compromise).
7. Mediators in the Western dispute resolution have no substantial power or authority over the disputants except their control of the process; therefore the cost and benefits of the agreement are the main motivation for the parties to continue in the bargaining. In the Middle Eastern case, mediators are very powerful and highly respected among the disputants, therefore the disputants will try to maintain good relations with the mediators.
8. In the Middle Eastern case the solution of the dispute will be in the hands of the mediators. That is why the disputants accept the mediators' role. In the Western context parties control the solution of the conflict even if they invited the mediators.

■ Settlement/Implementation of Agreement

One major difference in the contexts of the two disputes is the expectation of the cultural dominance of Western judicial form and the power of judicial institutions in the Western case. Such notions were very clear in the outcomes of the Cleveland Roundtable process, which involved legal and government official representatives. Thus, third-party (mediators particularly) techniques symbolically resemble the judicial forms, such as: (1) the mediator functions as a judge who claims authority; (2) the use of official documents; (3) the procedures of signing and funding; and (4) the construction of the agreement is based on a contract concept. It is semilegal.

In the Middle Eastern case the mediation is flexible, open, and shaped by the culture and the institutions of the society. Western mediation is shaped by legal ideology and the powerful image of judicial dispute resolution.

In general, in the non-Western context the third party advocates fairness and customs reflecting community judgments about appropriate behavior. In the Middle Eastern case, instead of signing papers, the parties meet for final arrangements in a crowded public setting, which functions as a strong social commitment to the agreement. In the Cleveland case, most of the outcomes were designed to educate the community in how to deal with racial differences. The outcomes aim to increase the level of tolerance among the community leaders with a hope that these leaders will influence their grassroots constituencies. There was an attempt to deal with the influence of the media as an important factor in managing and preventing future racial conflicts in the Cleveland area. Finally, the outcome of the process clearly indicated that the process cannot solve a root cause of the conflict, the unequal economic opportunity among residents of the area.

In the Middle Eastern case, too, none of the outcomes of the process address the roots of the conflict: economic opportunities in the village, ethnic and religious stereotypes, and prejudice. In addition, the process did not handle the social and educational consequences of the dispute; there was no public program or initiative to educate community members on the need to be more tolerant and respectful of the different ethnic and religious groups in the area. The outcome/settlement does not deal with the future implications of the dispute or the relationship between the parties. On the contrary, it relates to the dispute as a crisis situation on an immediate basis as if no conflict exists between the two groups.

■ Conclusion

What principles can be exchanged between the two approaches? Based on the previously described features of the two intervention strategies and the short comparison, there are some principles that can be exchanged and perhaps adopted by both sides:

1. The Middle Eastern approach can benefit from adopting the new emerging cooperative and collaborative techniques of a problem-solving approach. The collaborative, participatory process of decisionmaking is crucial to reaching a lasting agreement.

The intervention in the Middle Eastern context is based on a hierarchical system of mediators and procedures. One of the main problems in the Middle Eastern case is that the asymmetric power relations of the disputants determine the settlement and intervention processes. This problem is not solved yet in Western conflict resolution approaches, but there are several approaches that suggest interesting solutions for such limitations, such as Burton's analytical problem-solving process (1990); Kelman's approach to problem-solving workshops (1997); and a group of scholars who propose empowerment as a cure for asymmetric power relationships (Susskind 1981; Laue and Cormick 1978).

2. Western conflict resolution approaches can adopt the involvement of the community and society in placing pressure on the disputants to reach an agreement rather than using violent methods. Such a strategy can be adopted in the Western approach instead of alienating community members from processes and agreements that do not relate to their immediate interests (or to create more involvement and interest of the society in settling the conflict).

3. It will be very difficult and sometimes inappropriate to change the focus of disputants in the Middle Eastern context from values and principles to interests, but in some cases, such a change of focus might assist in solving disputes, especially those that are based on scarcity issues, and may permit management of the dispute before it escalates into a dispute that involves the entire community.

4. The effective holistic elements of the mediators in the Middle Eastern case can provide some benefits to the focused, specific, and narrow mediation approach that is followed by Western mediators, because of their limited involvement, knowledge of the social context, and history and nuances of the dispute.

In conclusion, it appears that there are few meeting points when comparing Western conflict resolution approaches with Middle Eastern approaches. However, the differences in the assumptions and perceptions of resolving conflicts are greater than the identified meeting points. This raises doubts about the applicability of the Western conflict resolution models and perceptions, which lack any consideration of the function of the values that underlie approaches of the people in the Middle East, that some scholars attempt or propose to apply in Middle Eastern conflicts.

■ Notes

1. The case study is described in Community Problem Solving Program (1989).

2. However, that Israeli soldiers and the legal system didn't intervene in the course of the dispute can be explained by two circumstances: many of the Druze community members serve in the Israeli army; and it was a conflict between two non-Jewish groups.

3. This section is based on the study by Sally Engle Merry (1989).

10

Traditional Conflict Management in Africa and China

Guy Olivier Faure

If negotiation is an activity as old as our world, its study is comparatively quite recent, for the first analytical works on the subject were published in the 1960s. Most of the current research leaves aside traditional negotiation that can be observed elsewhere than in North America and Western Europe. Nevertheless, there lies a whole human heritage of empirical know-how that should be collected before it vanishes and its memory fades.

The purpose of this chapter is to review the characteristics and distinctive features that are common to these types of negotiation. It seeks to distinguish what makes them typical of a certain class of negotiation by, at the same time, showing what makes them different from negotiation observed in western industrial societies and what they have in common that makes them fall into a homogeneous category of negotiation.

A cross-cultural approach is a difficult exercise because it has to overcome two major obstacles: triviality and parochiality. Trying to capture a maximum of characteristics under unifying concepts can lead under the plea of universalism to an ending with nothing very significant. At the other end, trying to be too specific leads to such a segmented reality that instead of having common features, one draws out only characteristics that differentiate each one of the studied types. To avoid the two difficulties, three analytical categories have been used: structure, values, and behaviors.

Behaviors are the visible part of the negotiation, what can directly be observed. They do not carry their own explanation with them. There is a need to investigate the process at other levels upstream to be able to establish some causal link. A negotiator's values constitute one of these levels because values conduct, orient, and provide meaning to behaviors. The third level to be considered is the structural level, which organizes and channels the negotiation process.

In addition, behaviors, values, and structural constraints are all influenced by culture at both its product and dynamic elements taking part in its evolution. Culture tells us not only what to do, what is desirable, and what should be done, but also what the meanings behind the moves are and how to understand a negotiation situation (Faure and Rubin 1993). If we look at structural elements such as codes and rituals, they are, as well, clearly products of society.

The propositions that follow come from observations drawn from two distinct cultures in which traditional practices are still very present: Africa and China. Typical situations to which those practices relate are family or marital conflicts due to disrespect, jealousy, abuse, adultery, basic duties that are not fulfilled, a spouse's gambling, a wife's spending too much money or not doing the housework, a childless wife or a wife giving birth only to females, a wife treated as a slave, a division of inheritance, or violent behavior. Other typical cases are neighborhood disputes involving loss of face, damages, stealing, violent acts, or simply parties who do not fulfill the obligations linked to a transaction.

■ Structural Elements in Traditional Negotiation

Negotiation can be viewed as a system made of components of various origins. Their main function is to structure the actors' action. Three categories of structural elements by which to describe and understand traditional negotiations can be distinguished: the cognitive aspects, the parties to the process, and their approaches to the problem.

Cognition governs the conduct of the negotiators, for it organizes thinking, introduces meaning, and, in doing so, structures behaviors. The holistic nature of the traditional approach is one of its most remarkable characteristics. Contrary to Cartesian analytical thinking, the traditional approach is most often global and aims at simultaneously capturing all the elements of a situation under the shape of a whole that is a priori nonfractional. Such an approach is expressed in the underlying philosophy of the concept of *ubuntu* presented by Masina. *Ubuntu* is based on the union of opposites and development of a diunital logic. It carries many similarities with the Taoist vision of the world anchored in the traditional Chinese culture. Unity is obtained by the complementarity of two principles that, far from excluding each other as is the case in western cultures, maintain their contradictory aspects. Good does not oppose evil; truth does not oppose untruth; beauty does not oppose ugliness; but they combine together. This type of holistic approach is especially fit for dealing with complexity. Negotiation may then become the space where an agreement formula will be devised and details will only be dealt with at the implementation stage (Zartman and Berman 1982).

The dominance of concrete thinking is another basic characteristic of traditional negotiators. If we consider discourses and arguments that are exchanged throughout the process, reasoning is grounded on images and metaphors. Contrary to what is often believed, metaphors are not a primitive and simplistic way of presenting arguments but a quite adapted way to capture complexity, such as the "needle and thread" image used by a Dinka chief to express relationships between parts of Sudan (Deng in this volume).

A metaphor illustrates a paradigm and gives it an additional strength for communicating and demonstrating. In the form of a narration, of a tale, of a saying, it is a concrete means of transmitting a particular logic that will make the outward sign of the demonstration. In doing so, the problem gets structured in a way that leads to a particular answer that can be highly effective.

The use of symbols during the negotiation also reflects a very specific mode of structuration specific to traditional societies. Symbols contribute to providing meanings and put emphasis on certain elements in a negotiation situation. Thus they rank priorities: when the sale of a family tree is qualified as a "homicide" (Uwazie in this volume), it demonstrates the profound meaning lying behind the object itself. Expression of choices through symbolic means such as a green or a dry twig among people from pastoral societies of northern Kenya carries particular strength. Throwing a paper crocodile to restore peace can also be understood as a clear symbolic signal (Kouassi in this volume). In addition, symbols provide basic material for the process itself, in which offers and counteroffers take place. For instance, authority symbols when mobilized at the right moment may reinforce the power position of one of the actors considerably. Ritually prescribed places such as the village square, the men's house, an imposing tree, a circle drawn in the center of the encampment, or an ancestral site may confer a specific importance to what is going to be performed.

Myths to which one refers in a negotiation anchor in a particularly meaningful way. By definition, the myth has a structuring function and can lead to position the global approach in a specific context that would be difficult to put into question by rational means. The myth draws its strength from the fact that it has no author but only tellers. The negotiator who refers to it typically operates among the tellers. It thus implies certain orientations toward a solution and prohibits others, according to the myth of internal logic. Myths can be so powerful that some of them are still being invented as tools for building the future (Osaghae in this volume).

Finally, memory, especially historical memory as transmitted from one generation to the next (unwritten records becoming part of the tradition), influences the actors' attitudes and the situation rationale in a significant way. In the case of a dispute, it is not unusual in some societies (Iranian, Beluch, or Chinese for example) to see people expressing grievances about things that happened more than a hundred years ago. A similar attitude is discerned when two clans started negotiating in the Somali desert, raising thorny issues from one hundred years ago (Menkhaus in this volume). The present, then, is no more than a simple moment in an enduring time flow, drawing its sense from something other than mere interaction between negotiators on a given matter.

The negotiation structure also consists of the number and the nature of the parties involved. One specificity of traditional societies is to include supernatural forces that will in turn modify negotiators' behaviors, for these only take place among humans. Conflicts among men may be even thought as originated by disputes among gods. For instance, the Bushmen believe that disputes are produced by the "bad gods who want to destroy the work of the good gods" (Ury 1990, 231). Gods may also take part in securing the correct implementation of the agreement. Thus, in a business contract signed in China during the Ming dynasty, six hundred years ago, a final codicil mentioned that "the party that breaks this contract will be persecuted by gods and men alike" (in Pye 1982). If more blood is spilled in a conflict in the Horn of Africa, god will punish (Tuso in this volume). People will come to terms with one another because of their fear of god (Kouassi in this volume). With the Bushmen, so long as the dispute is not resolved, nobody will be allowed to move away from the group. There is no way of avoiding going through a reconciliation, because any attempt to escape from the related procedures would "make the gods angry" (Ury 1990, 233).

As in the Greek mythology where gods constantly intervene in humans' business, in many traditional societies, the divine and the human are intermixed; gods and humans are in constant interaction. The negotiation microcosm is, in that case, a reflection of the social macrocosm. There is a continuum between material and spiritual forces that makes the world of spirits part of the human world. Ghosts and ancestors are major components of those forces and come to punish those who do not comply (Fred-Mensah in this volume). In a conflict between Nigerian women and the government, women threatened to demonstrate nude; they actually did so in South Africa, in July 1990. The political authorities gave up in Nigeria because they feared that it would attract ghosts (Osaghae in this volume), whereas they were simply shamed in South Africa.

More generally, conflict resolution by traditional means involves actors who do not take part in the process as individuals but because they belong to a certain tribe, clan, village, kinship, age group, brotherhood, or the like (Nader and Todd 1978). The negotiator is an element in a whole from which he cannot be disassociated. The individualistic perspective seldom applies and it is the full leverage and constraints of the group that the negotiator brings to the interaction in which he is taking part (Masina in this volume). As a consequence, what is at stake is not the negotiator's interests or reputation but those of the group he belongs to. In case of deadlocks, he can use the possibilities given by being part of a larger group to look, for example, for possible mediation if both parties belong to a common group. Such a function can be performed in Africa by the elders or in China by the *guanxi,* a network of people linked by a system of mutual obligations (Chen and Faure 1995, 46).

A structural element that plays a major role in conflict resolution processes in traditional societies is its public nature. Hearings, discussions, and deliberations are always carried out before an audience. Nothing of what is debated is kept confidential and the community witnesses all the proceedings as a dumb but essential counterpart. It is when confronted with the whole group that the culprit must express repentance (Masina in this volume). It is in front of the community and the elders that the culprit has to commit himself or herself by swearing an oath. In such a case, perjury would be not merely an offense to the victim but an insult to the whole group, a contempt of community.

Ad hoc mediators bearing special personal and social characteristics may intervene on occasions as the " ego of the community" (Kouassi in this volume). In the African tradition, men start as warriors and ultimately end up as peacemakers (Deng in this volume). The elders have a status, based on age and experience equated with wisdom, that provides them with enough authority to be the final decisionmakers in a conflict solved through arbitration. One can also notice that this role is always performed by men. Women are simply kept as part of the audience, as mere observers or to carry out men's decisions.

The overall organization of the negotiation is another structural component. It affects and governs the entire relation-building process. A typical approach for traditional societies is to operate by way of concentric circles in order to gradually define the scope of the negotiation. It is a method relying on successive, cautious attempts to go from the periphery to the core. The real issues of the negotiation progressively appear like a puzzle for which each player has only part of the pieces and tries to achieve a problematic adjustment (Faure 1995a). This approach has some high functional consequences such as making the process foreseeable to give time its influencing role and to save face for the parties in the dispute.

Finally, a normative way of thinking is developed by the actors. Rather than making attempts at understanding or at establishing some truth, it aims at implementing a kind of wisdom (Deng in this volume), a vision that goes beyond private interests or even transgresses principles when the cost of not abiding remains bearable. Thus, if one of the actors takes more than what the strict implementation of a principle would allow, the other may restrain himself or herself from protesting.

■ Traditional Negotiation Values

Values are situated at the deepest level of personality. They show what is desirable and what is reprehensible. According to prevailing interests and constraints, they orient the conduct of each negotiator. They prioritize basic choices and select types of behavior considered appropriate. A cross-cultural look at the negotiation values operating in traditional societies distinguishes four subsets organized around the following axes: relationship, restitution, identity, and risk aversion.

Preservation of the quality of the relationship, even at the expense of attaining the goal while dealing with the divergence, means that outcomes must provide a satisfying level of mutual satisfaction. As emphasized by Deng (Faure and Rubin 1993, 94), the Dinka chief in a negotiation does not act as a leader but as a "wise person able to perform a point of consensus." In the same way, in Chinese culture, a poor settlement between the parties to the conflict or a mediation, even costly, is more advisable than an arbitration that would be viewed as a sign that harmony has definitively been broken. Special respect given to age or hierarchical position is also a typical expression of social values aimed at maintaining the fundamental balance of a society. Harmony is such a crucial value that a hostile attitude between disputing parties can be as much penalized as the crime at the origin of the conflict. Thus, relations among members of the same community are never framed or dealt with according to a zero-sum logic.

The settlement of the dispute has to be achieved through consensus with the Tolai (Melanesia) because what is absolutely essential is to restore good relations among all the members of the group (Epstein 1971). Invented traditions demonstrate how necessary it can be to reinforce basic mechanisms in order to preserve harmony. Peace has to be reestablished not only among people but with the whole environment, including the animals and trees as mentioned in the chapters by Tuso and Osaghae. If not, supernatural forces will come and strike by means of natural catastrophes.

Preserving face is another major relational element. Saving the other's face, being careful about the other's image and reputation, means preserving the quality of the relationship and its perenniality. It is the appearance that raises contentious issues, for, beyond the objective data measuring gains and losses at the end of the negotiation, it is the look other people like third parties have at the situation that gives it sense and provides clues for social judgment. Thus, relationship comes first, before the quest for truth. Likewise, in a contract, the stability of the relationship and its friendly characters are more important than written legal commitments. Furthermore, abiding by these commitments depends very much upon the strength of the relationship that has been built. This is the reason that it is not unusual to have the Chinese, for example, renegotiating a contract just after having signed it.

Restitution is necessary to restore harmony, whereas in the Western world, punishment remains the prevailing concept. Compensation, even symbolic, carries with it an essential virtue in traditional cultures. Where people live in a dense network of narrow interactions, it provides an effective base for reconciliation. The purpose is to re-create the community balance that has been challenged and everyone has to play his part in this task. This is why an apology has to be made publicly, for the solution concerns the whole community, as it is for the commitment of the culprit. The group always has some responsibility for what people do, or do not do, as it plays a central role in the education of its members and the position they later on occupy.

Identity comes from community: We are, therefore I am (Masina in this volume; King-Irani in this volume). The negotiation is a situation in which one can have a sharp consciousness of one's own identity and the absolute necessity of preserving it. Often the real cause is not the explicit issue that the parties are discussing but the underlying stakes that raise identity problems (Deng in this volume; Lowi and Rothman in Faure and Rubin 1993). Giving up some objectives may lead to a challenge of one's own identity, a questioning of oneself. To negotiate, thus, involves another task, restating identity fundamentals and discovering a rule of compatibility between these and the subject of the dispute.

Risk aversion is often a well-shared value in negotiations held in traditional societies. Contrary to western values that give a bonus to risk taking and develop a special interest in a gambler's culture, here the game can be understood as a challenge of traditional order, as an act to enter into a zone of risk in which it is not advisable to expose oneself or one's own people. Thus, before undertaking any initiative, the negotiator will carefully assess its advantages and cost. If areas of uncertainty remain, the negotiator will refrain.

A typical way to reduce risks is to involve in the conflict resolution structure some powerful parties such as gods and ancestors who cannot be deceived without heavy consequences for the guilty party. Oath swearing, in that case, strengthens the commitment made by the offender, as the spirits, if angered, could strike by inflicting some natural calamity as noted in the chapter by Kouassi. Another way of dealing with risk is to prevent it by establishing a protective social and physical distance between the parties. Even within the household, privacy among the Fulbe pastoralists is created not by walls but by social distance and the management of space (Reisman 1977).

■ Behaviors in Traditional Negotiation

Tactical moves are the visible part of the negotiation process. They are concrete actions that express and embody the negotiator's decisions. Here again, there is a specific repertoire to which actors refer when negotiations occur in a traditional society. Among the recurring behaviors can be distinguished resorting to rituals, using rhetoric, giving indirect signals, making specific use of time, and, finally, integrating into the negotiation process non-work-related activities such as leisure, social activities, banquets.

Rituals and their integration in the negotiation process are ways of narrowly controlling the process, channeling it in order to avoid ending up in regrettable situations (King-Irani in this volume). Rituals frame behavior, raise the level of certainty of an action, and lead to what is socially more acceptable. They culturalize interactions by providing them with meaning beyond mere interest confrontation (Gulliver 1979). For example, a kola nut distribution at the very start of a conflict resolution introduces a symbolic order. In a similar way, religious rites and prayers made for reconciliation reinforces the ceremony status, as noted in the chapter by Tuso. Calling forth spiritual powers in a cleansing ceremony serves the same purpose as that shown by the Rendille of North Kenya, using milk to clean the blood that has been spilled and to wash away evil. In conflict mediation, ritual powers can be exercised through masks and other paraphernalia instilling a religious kind of awe (Little, quoted by Osaghae in this volume). Resorting to trance can also be a ritualized way to receive gods' advice about what to do to solve the dispute.

Ritual affirmation is a symbolic action to ensure that everyone shares what has been decided. The range of actions that can be implemented is extremely diverse: handshaking, embracing, kissing, oath taking, prayer, sacrifice, commensal drinking and eating. The closure of the ceremony may also include the sacrifice of an animal such as a goat or a sheep to re-create the unity of the group. Spilling animal's blood is a means of appeasing the anger of the group, gods, and ancestors. The collective consumption of the meat is another of the numerous rituals aimed at rebuilding the bonds between members of the same community in a kind of communion. In other cases, the drinking of a special concoction fulfills the same function (Kouassi in this volume).

Rhetoric is a means of implementing a situational regulation through discourse. Words do no tend to express an act such as a concession or demand, but they tend to be the act as such. Words do not reflect reality; they become the reality or, at least, part of it. Thus, rhetoric introduces, as in the African palaver, an additional resource at the negotiators' disposal (see Zartman 1996 on "diplomatic integration").

In conflict resolution processes whether in Africa or in China, oratorical processes are highly valued. Social wisdom is a spoken exercise that finds its legitimization in the admiration elicited among the listeners. The use of proverbs (Uwazie in this volume) strengthens the argument by embedding it in traditional wisdom. Calling people by terms of kinship, such as "Nephew," sets up an integrative mechanism that leads to a shift in problem framing.

Indirect signals are another distinctive attribute of traditional societies. Whatever may be its purpose (face saving, exploration, tricks, etc.), an indirect game is characterized by the use of weak signals, difficult to capture, often ambiguous. Such a practice is typical of high-context societies (Hall 1976) and it implies an important work of observation and decoding (Faure 1995b). Even the mediator in traditional Chinese society strives to do so, and takes care not to formulate too explicit suggestions.

The use of a metalanguage or of special ways to state facts, as in the case of a conflict between husband and wife among the Igbo of Nigeria, suggests rather than emphasizes, as noted in the chapter by Uwazie. The husband has an affair with a widow in the village and does not adequately provide food for the family. The wife, when acknowledging these two statements, is careful not to connect them, in order not to orient the conflict in a direction where chances for an agreement would be too small.

Traditional societies make very specific use of time, as has been underlined by many anthropologists (Gulliver 1979). Such an observation applies to a social interaction like a negotiation. Circular time that predominates in traditional societies opposes vectorial time that prevails in modern industrial societies. Circular time is a slow cumulative process where duration and associated functions leave their almost unnoticed imprint.

Long-term concerns dominate short-term benefits in the way elders aim to reestablish harmony in the family or in the community. Among the most remarkable traits characterizing an efficient mediator is his ability to find an auspicious moment to obtain the agreement of the parties to the dispute. As with the Chinese *feng shui* (geomancy), season, time, and location are essential parameters in the building of a stable agreement.

Finally, if, in industrial societies, negotiation can be summarized as a relatively homogeneous process, directly oriented toward a goal, in traditional societies, negotiation appears as a set of various subactivities among which non-work-related ones play an important part (Faure in Kremenyuk and Sjostedt forthcoming). Leisure, visits, cultural events, amusements, attendance at plays, and participation in banquets can be part of them. This mixing of activities within the negotiation setting can be highly functional with regard to the relationship that it helps to establish, reestablish, or strengthen. It makes efficient use of the nonlinear nature of the negotiation process and confirms the multiplicity of the levels at which it takes place.

Conclusion

A cross-cultural review of traditional practices in conflict resolution leads to a widening of the repertoire of observable conducts in current research focusing on situations related to industrial societies. It bears testimony to other cognitive and reflexive approaches of negotiation and refers to quite distinctive understandings of the process.

Holistic and nondualist approaches of negotiation situations leading to original methods of dealing with complexity have been emphasized. In the same perspective, the similar role played by metaphorical approaches has been underlined. The importance of symbols in the production of meaning and in the structuration of actions and choices has been shown. It is the same with the function fulfilled by myths and historical representations in legitimization procedures.

Actors taking part in the resolution of conflicts offer great diversity, for humans are joined by gods, ghosts, ancestors, and supernatural forces with all the authority they can put forward in facing the culprits. In the community of men, the strength of the collective bond is also a distinctive attribute of traditional negotiation settings, because the individuals cannot be totally separated from the group to whom they belong.

The global organization of the negotiation process also presents specificity, in particular by resorting to approaches by concentric circles aimed at gradually defining the scope of what is really at stake. The most respected values borrow more from the repertoire of normative wisdom than from means of establishing truth. The quality of the relationship and harmony among group members appear as priority objectives. Identity consciousness, face saving, and risk aversion are values that remain central to the orientation of practices in conflict resolution in traditional societies.

Finally, considering the third analytical layer in the negotiation process, the behavioral level, resorting to rituals as a means of keeping the conflict under control, or regulating it and reconciling the parties to the dispute, demonstrated real effectiveness. The oratorical art and use of rhetoric supported by popular wisdom contribute to the warming up and orienting of the resolution process.

A more frequent use of ambiguous or weak signals also achieves a functional outcome by limiting the verbal level of conflict. Traditional societies also make a broad use of time, vectorial or circular, to decide upon the propitious moment for decisionmaking. The ripe moment may meet the psychological expectation of the actors or may aim first at satisfying supernatural requirements. Ultimately, these societies make of the conflict resolution process a set of multiple procedures operating at different levels, thus orchestrating a complex functionality.

☐ *Traditional Societies' Practices and Western Approaches*

A set of common and coherent traits express ways by which African and Chinese cultures deal with their conflicts, outlining a significant and distinct profile. Behind the characteristics that make it unique and substantially different from the Western tradition, there is a central concept, a basic idea whose above-mentioned traits are just concrete manifestations. This governing idea lies in problem framing. In traditional societies, the dispute is not understood as in the West as a conflict between two parties but as a problem between an offender and the community. What is finally harmed is not a person but the whole group. As exemplified by the Bushmen of the Kalahari, the offender must ask forgiveness in front of the whole community (Ury 1990).

Then, the final purpose addresses what is at stake beyond the expressed grievance and harmony; it is not simply to punish, an action which would be viewed as harming the group a second time. Reestablishing harmony implies reintegrating the deviant members. Thus, social life coming back to a normal state, gods and humans will find again peace. The Arusha need to publicly emphasize common values and social norms of conduct. The ultimate matter is not justice but restoring good relations, cooperation among neighbors or members of the same age group (Gulliver 1979, 264). Considering American cases, the same author observes that American society shows no care for reestablishing common values and renewal of relationship.

In the West, identity depends achievementally on previous accomplishments. In Africa and Asia, identity is conferred ascriptively by the family, the village, or the tribe to which the person belongs. Thus, what varies dramatically is the concept of self. In Third World societies, usually based on collectivist cultures, the responsibility is never just individual. This is why the whole group feels concerned in Africa and this is also why, traditionally in China, the whole family was regarded as responsible for the wrongdoing of one of its members.

Peace and order in the group constitute an essential issue in collectivist cultures that are much more careful about harmony than individualist cultures are (Triandis 1994, 220). Collectivist societies prefer negotiation to going to court to settle a dispute (Leung 1988), probably because a negotiated outcome will not look and will not operate as a punishment. Usually, collectivist cultures will rather make use of indirect negotiation strategies, mainly because of face-saving concerns for them and for the other side (Ting-Toomey 1988). This again clearly shows the extreme care taken by these societies to limit as much as possible any disruption in the social equilibrium.

Such a vision of social relations, justice, and responsibility could lead to a new definition of negotiation applied to internal conflicts from a social regulation perspective. Negotiation could, thus, be defined as an interactive process set up by a group in order to resolve a divergence that has risen within. If the basic concept of negotiation carries differences with the classical western definition, does practice bear the same differences? The answer in that case has to be yes and no.

There are definitely similarities, common approaches such as what can be considered the most important stake in a negotiation and, especially when starting, the definition of the problem. As in decisionmaking, the whole process and outcome will strongly depend on the way the basic problem is formulated. For instance, in a case in Tanzania a man asks for a sum of money from his son-in-law who has recently returned home after having spent a year away as a migrant worker. Should this amount be understood as a courtesy gift that a young man should bring to his wife's father or should it be conceived as a complementary bride wealth payment? The final community attitude toward the problem leads to an issue definition that considerably orients the possible solutions of the problem (Gulliver 1979, 132–133). If problem definition is a common and essential feature in both cultures, African and western, the final purpose served by the community, the mediator, or the arbitrator is clearly different. Again, in the Tanzanian case, the final aim is not to blame, to punish, but to restore the social links. It is so important to the audience that even their own supporters exert pressure on the disputants to end the conflict as quickly as possible so that relationships would not be threatened.

Conflict management practice is performed differently in traditional societies, for they put the emphasis on other components than western societies do. Involving supernatural forces, resorting to collective rituals, abundantly using rhetoric, getting the whole community to participate, and dancing for consensus building give a very specific picture of what is done to strive for harmony. The degree to which the whole group, symbolically or physically, involves itself in the peacemaking process reveals its basic collective nature. For instance, in case of a dispute, hunter-gatherers such as the Bushmen call three or four people to ascertain the offense, and then they all go to admonish the culprit. This final action anchors the process in the community (Ury 1990, 231).

A collective process of a "powwow" type may also be enacted. Bushmen would call a *xotla,* held in the center of the encampment and marked by a circle of poles. Everyone there will question the disputants until they have solved their conflict (Ury 1990, 233). Ritual dances can play an important role in the resolution process, functioning as a catharsis. The community holds a dance in a circle and sings at the same time to get the gods taking the bitter feelings away. Thus, anger is gradually washed away and a consensus is crystallized (Ury 1990, 235).

Public proceedings may also play a preventive role to keep things in order, for it will be psychologically hard for the possible offender to withstand the beating of a village drum by the complainant to announce his grievance. Similarly in China, getting into a public argument strongly exposes one to a loss of face that, because it may involve the family reputation, will entail much higher costs than those concretely at stake. As a consequence, the principle of open proceedings plays a deterrent function.

An abundant use of public rhetoric also helps to lower the level of antagonism by helping the disputants to get rid of their stress and release the overall tension. However, the role of speech is not limited to this outcome. Often, it is the only means of action on the problem, for the final purpose is not to compel the deviant member but to convince him or her to behave differently.

These various ways to handle disputes have demonstrated their effectiveness throughout the ages. However, they can be applied only to conflicts within a community because it is social normative values that provide ground for effectiveness. When there is no sense of collective responsibility, there is no point of thinking in terms of reintegration and no social regulation can operate. When a conflict crops up at a macro level, such as intertribally or between states, there are no more superordinate values that can be emphasized to trigger the resolution mechanism. The social fabric produced by the culture is insufficiently dense and resistant to be able to serve as a referent for the purpose of reinserting the deviant member.

Traditional societies teach us something important when we consider the broad and unique repertoire of ways to approach and to solve their internal conflicts. More than the practical and somehow exotic aspects of dispute management, what is essential is the way they define and frame conflict. Their basic assumption contends that cooperation is the essence of human life, which, in turn, cannot be conceived outside the group. In Western societies, dynamics come far more from competition, making questionable any attempt to transfer some traditional practices, as far as their effectiveness is concerned. However, the inventory that has been presented here displays various means of achieving the construction of a satisfying balance in dispute settlements. In particular it introduces approaches focused on values borrowed from traditional wisdom. In doing so, it reveals part of the extent and richness of this human heritage that is nowadays essential to recognize and to disseminate.

PART 3

Applying Traditional Methods to Modern Conflict Management

11

Xhosa Practices of *Ubuntu* for South Africa

Nomonde Masina

> Indigenous Southern Africans were not a *tabula rasa* for white invaders or capitalists to civilize or to victimize. Over many centuries, they had been developing social forms and cultural traditions that colonialism, capitalism and apartheid have assaulted, abused and modified but never eradicated. One cannot understand how Africans have endured the fragmentation of their family life by migrant labor unless one has knowledge of their customary social values and networks. Nor can one fathom the vigor of black resistance to the apartheid state without knowledge of precolonial African ideas about the social and economic obligations of rulers and rights of subjects, and the basis of political legitimacy. (Thompson 1990, 2)

The quotation above summarizes the essence of this chapter. African traditions and philosophical approaches have continued to survive despite attempts at marginalization by colonialism, Christianity, and apartheid. *Ubuntu* is an understanding of African philosophy peculiar to South Africa. It represents the embodiment of the political, cultural, economic, and social dynamics of African society. This philosophy embraces both the spiritual and the material elements of human existence. Moreover, *ubuntu* has presented formidable and at times contradictory challenges to European discourses of dominance and understandings of the African reality. This chapter seeks to establish a foundational understanding of the principle of *ubuntu* and its application to conflict resolution.

■ *Ubuntu*

In the traditional African view, human existence is seen as unified, interconnected, and integrated. This view recognizes the dialectics in any given system (union of opposites—i.e., the good *and* the bad). To be out of harmony is regarded as harmful to the well-being and survival of the whole. In the *siNtu* custom, *ubuntu* as a concept permeates the whole fabric of society, thus yielding "both/and" conclusions, contrasted with the Christian idea of good or evil with its "either/or" conclusions.

Ubuntu is an indigenous social perspective/philosophy of all African communities of South Africa.[1] The perspective of *ubuntu* is not easily translatable into English. However, literally translated, *ubuntu* means "collective personhood" or "the art or virtue of being human." The fundamental characteristics of *ubuntu* are caring, compassion, unity, tolerance, respect, closeness, generosity, genuineness, empathy, consultation, compromise, and hospitality. "Ubuntu is an expression of our collective personhood, and invokes images of group support, acceptance, co-operation, care, sharing and solidarity" (Mbigi 1995, 57; see also Mbigi and Maree 1995, 2).

Ubuntu is in essence customary law whose breach brought on sanctions ranging from isolation to fines. The gravest transgression like witchcraft was followed by death. But the sanction element of *ubuntu* was rarely invoked because family and societal bonds were solidly communicated and therefore preemptive against major breaches. A persuasive corrective mechanism of deliberations within family, peer, and gender associations was therefore the most functional conflict resolution practice.

In traditional African societies, the belief in *ubuntu* is that one can be a person only through others. It is only in the spirit of *ubuntu,* with its emphasis of working together, that problems can be solved. Managing or resolving conflicts in African communities becomes an open process, in the sense that it includes the nuclear and extended families, and even the elders of the village, chiefs, and headmen as well. In support of this, Reuel Khoza (Christie, Lessem, and Mbigi 1993, 122–123) points out: "Ubuntu as an orientation to life is opposed to individualism and insensitive competitiveness. Neither is it comfortable with collectivism where collectivism stresses the importance of the social unit to the point of depersonalizing the individual. At the same time it places great importance on working for the common good."

In agreement with Khoza, Koopman (Christie, Lessem, and Mbigi 1993, 48) illustrates a distinction between a western approach and *ubuntu.* He notes that

> whites, by and large, are individualistic exclusivists. When managing conflict, therefore, we prefer to apply win/lose tactics, clear cut and defined structures and procedures. Mostly we alienate ourselves within conflict situations leading us to enter into 'negotiations' in order to control an outcome of 'rightness' and 'wrongness'. Africans by and large, are communal inclusivists. Managing conflict becomes an 'open' sum process involving immediate family, supervisors, elders, etc. within the framework of morals. This necessitates entering into a 'dialogue' from which a sense of 'fairness' and 'unfairness' towards other members in society can emerge.

African culture places a great emphasis on caring for people, as well as on being a good person in the community. It is very strong on collective solidarity and this can be captured by the Nguni proverb "umuntu ngumuntu ngabantu" (I am because we are). This means that society consciously takes responsibility for its "persons product."

Role of Chiefs, Counselors, and Headmen in Mediation

A dispute in a village between families, members of a family, or members of a tribe would be referred to the elders of the families, headman, chief, or king, depending on the nature of the conflict. The aggrieved person will state his or her case fully to the *inkundla/lekgotla*.[2] The defendant is called upon to meet the accusations and witnesses are heard. Interrogations follow until the truth is established. Discussions take place and an agreement is reached binding both parties. That the accused is also involved and his or her case is heard, makes it possible for both parties to accept the decision of the *inkundla/lekgotla*. The question is not who is going to win or lose, but how to attain a win-win outcome.

The *inkundla/lekgotla* as an institution of conflict management is communal in character; that is, the entire society is involved at various levels in the resolution of conflict. This is in stark contrast to western institutions of conflict mediation. In traditional courts there is no one appointed specifically to act as a public prosecutor or as counsel for either the defendant (*ummangalelwa*) or the plaintiff (*ummangali*). The *inkundla/lekgotla* constitutes the court, functioning both as jury and judge. "In traditional court procedure it is not only one man who urges the complainant to expatiate and who also cross-questions him on the case but many men; they may be the King's or the chief's or the headman's counselors. They may be visitors at the Royal quarters or they may be passers-by" (Qangule 1979, 40).

"The paramount chief . . . was . . . a principal force in unifying districts in a tribe (and) the petty headman still settles minor disputes between members of *imizi* under him by arbitration" (Hunter 1961, 393). The king or chief is always assisted by a small number of confidential advisers or council of elders who have authority to settle every kind of community problem. The counselors were elderly men of repute in their area, old men with court experience, men with oratorial powers, men of caliber, or men who were conspicuous for their wisdom and skill in debating cases. The headman was responsible to the chief for the peace, order, and good government of his area, in which he is the chief's representative. But he must himself refer all cases of serious difficulty to the superior authority of the chief, and appeal to the chief from his verdict is also possible.

□ Ubuntu *and Conflict Resolution*

In some cases where *ubuntu* functioned in conflict resolution situations during precolonial times, differences of opinion were settled amicably by means of dialogue within the community under the leadership of an authority figure. The fine imposed was generally in the form of cattle; capital punishment was rare. In other cases, punishment was absolute and automatic because the offense was beyond the pale of acceptable behavior. In a third group, conflict was unmanageable and was carried out to its own resolution.

Example 1 (on murder). Murder or serious bodily assault cases are called "blood cases" and are always referred to the king or chief, for they are looked upon as injurious to him. Before judgment is pronounced, the counselors will state the pros and cons of the case to the king or chief. It is seldom that the king or chief disagrees with the opinion of his counselors; if he does, either his personal views are accepted and become the finding of the court (*inkundla*) or a compromise will be reached and a modified judgment given. However, there have been cases where a king, chief, or headman did not consult with other members of the community. In such cases they became targets of attack from community members and were deserted by their subjects (Hunter 1961, 393–394). Effective government can result only from harmonious cooperation between him and his people. In Xhosa, *inkosi yinkosi ngabantu*—"a chief is chief by grace of his tribe."

The king or chief will then state the number of cattle to be paid: he has lost one of his followers, so restitution must be made (Soga 1931, 32–33). The chief will be the one to decide how many cattle to be given to the bereaved family; the rest belong to him. Traditional courts sought to arrive at a settlement rather than pronounce judgment. The emphasis is on rehabilitation and reconciliation and on restoring harmony in the community, rather than on punishment (win-lose).

Example 2 (on theft). Somebody has stolen a cow, a goat, or a sheep. The owner of the stolen animal will spread the message in the community and report the case to the headman. When the suspect is caught, the trial will begin. The owner of the stolen animal will be asked to present his case, after which the accused will be asked to tell his or her side of the story. Both parties, together with witnesses, will be cross-examined in order to establish the truth. If the accused is found guilty by the *inkundla/lekgotla,* he or she will have to replace the animal.

What then does one learn from the above example? The culprit is humiliated in front of the members of the community. He is shown by the *inkundla* how he has offended the community at large, deviating from the values of the community. This will then contribute to his mending his ways and correcting his antisocial behavior. By replacing the animal, for example, Xhosa people say "*ulihlawule ityala*" (He has paid the debt). "The offender against community law pays the fine imposed upon him, and returns again to public life. He is received with open arms. No stigma is attached to him for he has paid the penalty, and by so doing has made restitution" (Sega 1981, 44–45).

On the other hand, if the same case was referred to the European-type courts of law, the offender would not be emotionally involved in the loss. The case would be referred to the police, who would investigate the matter: if the accused is found guilty, he might get a jail sentence but no corrective social effect would have occurred with regard to the offender because of the technical procedures of the western system. The system does not have the capacity to tap one's inner fear of rejection by one's community.

Example 3 (on damage). Cattle entered a person's yard and damaged crops; the owner of the crop is entitled to compensation. The parties concerned may settle the matter between themselves, or if they cannot agree, the matter can be referred to the headman or chief.

Example 4 (on minor's theft). Small boys who have committed an offense normally get a few lashes. For instance, a boy who has stolen cattle is sentenced to thrashing. The idea is to show other young people that they get the punishment instead of their parents paying the fine. An older person will be required to replace the cattle. A man can also be fined an additional cow for the headman, chief, and their counselors for having wasted their time in trying to solve the problem.

Example 5 (on quarrels). Men or women may fight or use foul language. In such cases they may be fined because of their behavior—men fined by men, and women by women. They may be fined barrels of home-brewed liquor (*umqombothi*), a goat, a sheep, or a cow, depending on the degree of the crime. The *umqombothi* fine paid by men will only be drunk by men, and women by women. Another punishment is a prohibition to attend a social gathering (*imigidi*) for a few months. The headman might also alert headmen in other villages of the decision taken so that the party cannot attend any of their ceremonies.

Example 6 (on marriage). The spirit of *ubuntu* also expresses itself in marriage ceremonies. One does not just marry one's partner. In African societies, marriage is a collective union of two extended families, even though it is the bride and groom who agree to marry each other. It is a contract between two families as much as between the two individuals concerned. A bride or groom has to be accompanied by other members of the family, and right from the start, outside facilitators are used to help negotiate *ikhazi* and resolve conflicts.[3] Because of the communal character of customary law, the nearest male relatives of the parties play an important role in all stages of negotiations. The role of the facilitator or go-between, *unozakuzaku,* is permanent in the marriage and in the relationship between the extended families. During the marriage ceremony, advice is given to the bride and groom by representatives of both parties. The bride is advised (*ukuyala*) to behave, be gentle, be faithful, and so on. She is actually told that she is going *uyakwanja zotha umlilo*—"where eagles dare."[4] So she has to *nyamezela*—"to stay to the bitter end."

In the event of marital problems, elders or the go-between (in this case called *umlamli*) are always called to solve the problem. If the problem cannot be solved, the wife can always go back to her family to seek protection. In this case, the husband is expected to send members of his family to negotiate her return (*ukuphuthuma*). Both families will meet in a forum of *inkundla* to resolve the conflict. If the correct atmosphere has been created during negotiations of *ilobola,* the matter might be talked over and settled as between friends. The woman's family usually persuades their daughter to remain with her husband.

Sometimes parties in conflict take sides and concentrate more on defending their member than on solving the problem. They will start blaming each other's child for the problem. When the problem solving becomes deadlocked, both parties invite neighbors who are not related to them to listen to facts and come up with a solution. These neighbors are supposed to be neutral mediators who are concerned with reaching a solution acceptable to both parties. If a solution cannot be reached even by neighbors, the marriage dissolves.

Several types of conflict are more resistant to resolution, such as when a wife is sent away by her husband for adultery or witchcraft, or when she deserts him of her own accord and refuses to return. In other cases, there is less room for discussion and conciliation. Here fairness means justice because the offending behavior has transcended acceptable norms. *Ubuntu* means the authoritative restoration of equilibrium and acceptable conduct to a momentarily troubled society.

Example 7 (on rape). In the case of rape (*isihewulo*), the girl will be referred to old women for inspection. If indeed there is evidence of rape, the old women of that village will go to the boy's home. The parents of the boy will immediately know that something wrong has happened. Those women will forcefully take a female cow from the boy's home and take it to the girl's family. The cow cannot be kept at the girl's place for breeding; it will have to be slaughtered immediately and consumed by women.

Example 8 (on incest). Among the transgressions that threaten the integrity of the tribe is incest (*umbulo*). Xhosas look upon it as an ill-omened action and disgraceful. The punishment is again paying a certain number of cattle.

Example 9 (on witchcraft). Trials for witchcraft (*umuthi*) are conducted by the priest-diviners. The findings of the priest-diviners are communicated to the king or chief. Not all the cases of witchcraft are communicated to the king or chief. Authority can also be given by subordinate chiefs. The type of punishment that the accused would be given was never imprisonment, because prisons did not exist. Capital punishment was imposed in cases of witchcraft because a witch was feared to be a menace to society.

> The primary aim of Xosa law, and presumably bantu law in general, is to preserve tribal equilibrium. The law, therefore, guides the individual towards keeping the tribe from disintegration. Any punishment administered for disturbing the balance of tribal life is of a constructive or corrective character: to restore what has been lost in stability by the action of an individual or individuals. It is very noticeable how this idea is ingrained in the fibre of the people. The ethical question scarcely counts, restoration is the principal thing. . . . [A] sorcerer's crime may be against an individual or community, but from its very nature it becomes an attack on the tribe. The stability of the tribe is threatened, and the ordinary process of law, and its punishments, is unable to meet a case of this nature. Hence abnormal methods are adopted . . . vengeance follows immediately on the commission of the crime, in the form of death. No fine is adequate for a crime of this nature. (Soga 1931, 44–45)

The king or chief can even confiscate the entire property of tribespeople found guilty of witchcraft or other grave crimes such as murder.

A third category of conflicts refers not to individual acts that break society's norms but to disputes among groups within or outside the society. When these disputes occur between parts of the larger society, with no clear right or wrong, they will be mediated so as to restore harmony to society. When a part of society revolts against authority, however, the reaction is unambiguous and win-win ideas are put aside. Similarly, when the conflict pits one society against a different ethnic group, its pursuit is its only means of resolution.

Example 10 (on intergroup conflict). In a homogeneous society where there are different clans, there is normally a paramount chief who acts as an arbitrator when there are problems between the clans. The decision of a paramount chief is generally accepted because of the level of respect he holds. In Xhosa culture, supposing *Amantinde* clan fights *Amaxesibe* clan, the different chiefs in those villages will call a meeting, *imbizo,* to discuss the problem.[5] If the clans fail to solve the problem, the king will call the *imbizo* with his *amaphakathi* (councillors) of all the men in the village and solve the problem to bring about peace.

Example 11 (on rebellion). Rebellion in society means a fight to the death between enemies. The consequence would be expulsion or decimation. In most cases rebels are chased out of the territory, or if they run away from the tribe on their own accord and are caught, they are taken away to the great place, the king's place, and charged a large number of cattle or their property confiscated.

Example 12 (on war). When there is about to be war between ethnic groups, the chiefs of different tribes warn all members of their tribe that war is impending. Warriors are summoned for a general meeting, where the king or chief informs them of the enemy and the cause of war. Stabbing and throwing assegais would then be cleaned and sharpened before the war takes place. War would then be declared between the enemies. The tribe that wages war never alerts its enemy lest the enemy uses witchcraft (*umuthi*) to defend itself. If there is war, there is immediate attack. The tribe that wins the war loots all the enemy's cattle, which are brought to the king or chief and belong to him.

■ *Ubuntu,* Conflict Resolution, and the New South Africa

The result of the new economic and technical ideas and impositions upon the African has been the loosening of kinship ties and obligations and the narrowing of traditional duties of the individual. European values have been additive to, rather than substitutive of, indigenous values. It is a common phenomenon these days for a single individual to incorporate within himself or herself European and indigenous forms of behavior or goals, each being held to be applicable according to circumstances. Western values like using courts for divorce have been adopted. Couples who wish to divorce no longer need permission from their families. Young people, more often than not, still get married the traditional way (women still demand that *lobola* be paid for them) but they stay as a couple away from their in-laws, unlike the traditional practice where a married couple would stay with the man's family. It was easy for the man's family (*onozakuzaku*) to intervene when there was a problem between the married couple because the couple was staying with the man's family. Nowadays families of the couple find it more difficult to be involved because they do not want to be taken as intruders. It is then up to the couple to involve both families, relatives, or friends when there is a crisis. The couple is free to use whatever method it is comfortable with at that time depending again on the nature of the marital problem(s). They can choose to go to the court for a divorce, or seek help from other people to save the marriage. One might even find a situation where one party wants to save the marriage and does what one possibly can to save it, but if the other party wants to break up, the marriage is bound to dissolve. The same result could also happen differently in traditional society if a woman eloped with another man or kept going back to her family every time she was mistreated by her husband's family, or the husband mistreats her until she finally decides to leave him.

But *ubuntu* is also undergoing progressive development and expansion under twentieth-century conditions of the free-market system and a new democratic dispensation in South Africa. The need to work together, respect and resolve conflict with the ultimate aim of reaching a win-win outcome as opposed to a zero-sum solution has informed—just to mention a few—the quest for reconciliation and the debate on the death penalty, and the drafting of the 1995 Labour Relations Act. In an attempt to address the processes of change in South Africa, which is essentially resolving conflicts brought about by apartheid, South Africans have relied upon the concept of *ubuntu.*

But this also represents an expansion of the *ubuntu* ideas beyond their original scope. In traditional application, as seen in the examples, *ubuntu* reconciliation and harmonization was reserved for internal relations within Xhosa society, and war, to be won, was used outside. Under the new dispensation, *ubuntu* practices are extended outside the ethnic and even racial group. But the extension is new only in form, not in spirit, for the win-win practices of reconciliation and harmonization are used to form a new society, overriding tribal and racial bounds and building a new humanity (*ubuntu*).

One example is the Truth and Reconciliation Commission (TRC), established in 1995 to create a judicial structure to address injustices committed by both those fighting for liberation in and outside South Africa and those fighting for the apartheid system. The Commission deals with cases of human rights violations, amnesty/indemnity, reparation, and rehabilitation. Its principal objective emphasizes the need to create a nonadversarial relationship between offenders and their victims. The primary aim of the TRC is to heal the wounds of those who have lost loved ones during the apartheid period, in accordance with the principles of the country's new Constitution and its stress on the need for national reconstruction. "The . . . Constitution [chapter II, sections 9–10 of the final Constitution of 1996] lays the secure foundation for the people of South Africa to transcend the divisions and strife of the past, which generated gross violation of human rights, the transgression of humanitarian principles in violent conflicts and a legacy of hatred, fear, guilt and revenge. These can be addressed on the basis that there is a need for understanding but not for vengeance, a need for reparation but not retaliation, a need for *ubuntu* but not for victimization" (TRC 1995, 5). The TRC is trying to obtain full disclosure of past human rights violations. It started by hearing testimony from victims and their families; some of them were crying uncontrollably at the TRC hearings as they expressed the pain they have suffered as a result of human rights abuse.

Most of the accounts were shocking, but most victims wanted more to know the truth than to ask the TRC to punish those who caused harm to their families (*New Nation,* 20 December 1996, 3). When one woman, during a TRC hearing, mentioned that she had forgiven the killers, Archbishop Desmond Tutu said to her: "You make me so proud, mama, to be a black person like you" (*Mail and Guardian,* 7 February 1997, 24). This sign of forgiveness gives a clear promise of reconciliation. Some of the horrible stories told by families of victims include people who were killed because they were suspected of being police informers; people who were tortured, stoned, and killed and later their corpses burned; people who were murdered because they knew too much; people who were shot and blown to pieces by hand grenades; people who were subject to tire necklace killings during the liberation struggle, mainly by young activists against suspected informers; innocent children and women killed because there were in a wrong house; people who were killed in the bloody pre-election train attacks. The list is seemingly endless.

Some victims and families have opposed amnesty for perpetrators, but still go along with the TRC's program in order to learn of the circumstances under which their loved ones died. Other families protest that they cannot allow people to push reconciliation down their throats and complain about "the imposition of a Christian morality of forgiveness" (*Sunday Times,* 23 February 1997, 26).

After the victims and their families had given their testimony to the TRC, the focus shifted from victims of human rights abuses to perpetrators who applied for amnesty. In some cases perpetrators had to be served with subpoena by the TRC to give their side of accounts to help victims know the truth. Some revelations were shocking. Perpetrators told how they killed, gassed, tortured, drugged, poisoned, burned, beat to death, mutilated, and threw bodies of victims into a river or buried them. Those were some of the horrors revealed by those applying for amnesty.

The theory behind the TRC is that by telling the truth and revealing the cruel acts committed, perpetrators have told themselves, "Never again." It is important that the TRC ensure that the truth unearthed leads to atonement, reconciliation, and forgiveness. At the end of the day, the Commission is rebuilding the nation through truth, peace, and reconciliation. What the TRC has done so far has not been easy. Some perpetrators still refuse to apologize for what they have done or to appear before the TRC. In Archbishop Tutu's words (*Sunday Times,* 8 December 1996, 22):

> In reviewing the amnesty process, the reluctance of political leaders of all persuasions to submit applications is the issue which gives us the most concern. We can probably get to the truth without them; their subordinates are coming forward in sufficient numbers for us to put together most of the puzzle without them. But, in hiding behind their foot soldiers, political leaders are squandering an important opportunity for reconciliation.

It is also reported that some victims and their families are still waiting to be compensated. Hlengiwe, chairperson of the TRC's Reparation and Rehabilitation (*New Nation,* 31 January 1997, 4), said, "For people to heal, they have to get reparation, otherwise reconciliation is defeated . . . the situation is now desperate. While victims are waiting, perpetrators have been granted amnesty." Some victims will have to wait for years. The TRC will have to finish its investigations and then make recommendations to the president for victims to be compensated.

□ *The Debate on the Death Penalty*

The Constitutional Court considered the elements of *ubuntu* when deciding to strike down the death penalty. Judge Johann Kriegler quoted the Constitution to support his views on the death penalty, pointing out that society has moved from victimization to humaneness (*ubuntu*). Judge Thole Madala (*Sunday Times,* 11 June 1995, 23) also pointed out aspects of *ubuntu,* arguing that while a murderer might not have shown his or her victim mercy, society should not take its values from the murderer. Society should instead "impose" its *ubuntu* on the victimizer. The Constitutional Court opposed the death penalty, declaring it inconsistent with the Constitution and, in its first two years, it denied the death penalty in some cases as unconstitutional. In the case of families who applied to have the TRC's amnesty provision declared unconstitutional, the Constitutional Court rejected the applications.

President Nelson Mandela has asserted that capital punishment is a barbaric method and would not be used in South Africa (*Mail and Guardian,* 14 February 1997, p. 3). George Fivas, the South African police chief, has also argued that there is no connection between capital punishment and the rate of crime.

The issue shows how the new South Africa is prepared to change its practices in accordance with traditional African ways of managing conflict, giving offenders the chance to present their side of the story, accounting for their behavior, acknowledging that they have offended victims, repenting for their conduct, and finally asking for forgiveness. This process, according to the chairman of the Truth and Reconciliation Commission, Archbishop Tutu, will heal the wounds of the victims. The Department of Correctional Services finally dismantled the gallows in November 1996, since capital punishment had been abolished.

□ *The 1995 Labour Relations Act (LRA)*

The most important element in the 1995 Labour Relations Act is its effort to obtain a balance between employers and employees, to alleviate the conflict between business and labor, and to facilitate a more cooperative relationship between workers and employers. Before the drafting of the 1995 LRA, conflict was managed through win-lose tactics of structures such as industrial councils, conciliation boards, and industrial courts (Zartman 1994). These are structures through which industrial conflict was institutionalized. These structures were in turn taken by employees and employers to be cumbersome, expensive, and sometimes inconsistent. The inconsistency of some judgments of the industrial court brought unhappiness to both management and labor, and something had to be done to promote sound industrial relations.

The 1995 LRA introduced workplace forums for employers to consult with the employees, to try to reach consensus, and to decide jointly on matters affecting the company. In their explanatory memorandum, the authors of the legislation pointed out that

> South Africa's reentry into international markets . . . demanded that we produce value-added products and improve productivity. . . . If we are to have any hope of successfully restructuring our industry and economy, then management and labor must find new ways of dealing with each other.

They further pointed out that

> the [Act's] solution is to create workplace forums where workers and management shift their focus from adversarial collective bargaining on all matters to joint problem solving and participation on certain subjects. The purpose is to create a dialogue between the parties so that they can work more effectively together in order to improve living standards and productivity. (LRA, expl. memo)

The idea behind the act is that both parties should cooperate with each other and work as a team. They should respect each other, try to change their attitudes toward one another, and make relevant compromises. They should move from adversarial relations to consensual relations, these being the ways in which African communities operated. The point is not that joint problem solving is new to labor-management practices or that it is unique to South Africa, but that in South Africa, its introduction is part of a traditionally inspired focus on building a new South African community.

■ Conclusion

Ubuntu at the philosophical level seeks to find a balance between self and other, the destructive and the creative, good and bad. It moves away from the thinking of social relations in dualistic oppositions, that is, an either/or situation, good versus bad, black versus white, self versus other, in seeking to resolve conflict. The purpose of *ubuntu* is to work toward a situation that acknowledges a mutually beneficial condition. Its emphasis is on cooperation with one another for the common good as opposed to competition that could lead to grave instability within any community. It emphasizes the whole and not the part(s). It describes the feeling of the worth of the community and a shared fellowship of men and women. South Africa at present is trying to move away from confrontation and is developing a new system based on the African principle of *ubuntu.* Both the president and the deputy president are promoting reconciliation to all South Africans in order to transform and build a new society—the rainbow nation (to use Archbishop Tutu's phrase).

Notes

1. In South Africa's eleven official languages, *ubuntu* would be used in Xhosa and Zulu, *botho* in Tswana, Southern Sotho (Seshoeshoe), and Northern Sotho (Sepedi), *uvhutu* in Venda, *uvunhu* in Tsonga, *ubundu* in Ndebele, *ubunftu* in Swazi, *brotherhood* in English, and *broederskap* in Afrikaans.

2. The *inkundla/lekgotla* could be the respected males in any family, or outside family members, the headman, the chief, counselors, and other respected members of the community.

3. *Ikhazi* involves the *ilobola/bogadi* that is given by the groom to the wife's family and on the other side, the brides' family will give her the *ilobola;* this is not a commercial transaction. There is no way that a person can be bought. It is a way of extending a hand to the other family and building friendship. Even with the bride's family, they have a saying that goes "We have not lost a child, but have gained a son-in-law." *Inkomo yobulunga* is a cow given to a woman by her people as a kind of dowry. It is regarded as sacred (pertaining to rightness) and may not be taken away by the husband or even confiscated by a chief or headman. It is there to protect her and her family.

4. This means that the bride is going to a place where in-laws will be very difficult to please; a tough place where people will go all out to destroy her and enjoy such scenes. It is a place where one is going to get challenges; in short, "where eagles dare."

5. *Imbizo* is a gathering of all males of a community at the chief's or king's place (tribal or district meeting) to solve a major problem that affects the community as a whole. Other important matters (*iindaba zomzi' weNkosi*) that are not necessarily problems are also discussed there.

12

Traditional Conflict Management in Contemporary Somalia

Ken Menkhaus

The solution to a conflict
is talking about the conflict
—Somali proverb

Nowhere in Africa has the debate over the utility of traditional conflict management mechanisms been more pronounced and consequential than in the Somali crisis (Farah with Lewis 1993; Sahnoun 1994; Bradbury 1993; SDRA/MCC 1994; Prendergast 1994; Gilkes 1994; Menkhaus 1996; Lyons and Samatar 1995; Thakur 1994; Spear and Keller 1996). There, the outbreak of civil war in 1988 and the total and protracted collapse of the state in early 1991 led to one of the worst humanitarian crises of the century, which in turn led to a massive international peacekeeping operation (UN Operation in Somalia, UNOSOM) and dozens of local and national peace initiatives between 1992 and 1995. Those many peace conferences triggered a sharp debate between advocates of a "grassroots" approach and supporters of a "top down" peace process in Somalia.

This chapter will attempt to cull from the Somali experience some of the most significant conceptual and theoretical advances that were generated in the debate over traditional conflict management in that country. These debates over definitions, concepts, and frameworks helped to clarify and refine our general understanding of "traditional" actors and processes, and have immediate comparative relevance in conflict zones beyond Somalia. The chapter will then highlight some of the practical, applied lessons learned regarding traditional conflict management in complex emergencies. Some of these lessons may have relevance to other conflict zones in Africa; others may be unique to the Somali culture and context.

Several theses emerge from this analysis. First, and most important, the Somali case demonstrates that traditional conflict resolution can survive the disruptions and social transformations of complex emergencies and play a useful role in conflict management. Second, while traditional conflict mechanisms remain one of the most enduring, trusted, and effective institutions in Somali society, their effectiveness is situational, not universal. They are bound by, among other things, the level of conflict at hand (more apt to manage and resolve localized or regional conflicts than national-level ones), the nature of the conflict, and the interests of local constituencies in peace. These situational variables help to explain why traditional peacemaking has enjoyed much more success in the North than in the South. A third thesis affirms that what we have come to understand as traditional conflict management actually represents a synthesis of time-honored practices and new techniques, as communities adapt their customs to cope with fundamentally new types of conflict. For the sake of simplification I refer to this hybrid process as "traditional" (rather than burdening the reader with a term like "neo" or "quasi" traditional); but the evidence from the Somali case clearly suggests that these practices are adaptable and dynamic, not static and timeless. Finally, the Somali case study reminds us that actors most often identified with "traditional" peacemaking—in Somalia, clan elders—are fluid, not fixed, social categories, whose political agendas and interests may or may not coincide with peace. Though elders have a recognized and honored role in peacemaking, they can under certain circumstances be obstacles to peace and proponents of conflict. Great care must therefore be taken not to idealize traditional peacemakers.

■ Key Features of "Traditional" Somali Conflict Management

Somali political culture features a very prominent and elaborate role for conflict management, in large measure because precolonial Somalia was a stateless, decentralized, nomadic society in which conflict between clans over pasture and wells was endemic. Procedures for managing these conflicts were thus vital as a means of preventing chronic violence in this anarchic pastoral setting. Not surprisingly, conflict management and negotiation in Somalia remain high art forms.

A wide range of social structures and cultural practices play a role in what has come to be understood as "traditional" conflict management in Somalia. The highly acclaimed art of poetry in Somalia, for instance, can be a forceful weapon for promoting peace or inciting war; likewise, the practice of interclan marriage builds maternal links between rival clans and bestows upon women a special role as trusted and protected intermediaries. For our purposes, four key social structures are highlighted: the practice of blood compensation, or *diya*-payments; the role of clan elders in managing interclan conflicts; the binding power of the social contract negotiated between two lineage groups known as *xeer;* and the consultative mechanism of the *shir,* or assembly. Historically these traditional conflict management mechanisms were only partially successful; precolonial Somalia was rife with armed conflicts and long-running blood feuds.

☐ Diya-*Paying Groups*

Somali social organization comprises a complex web of affiliations and identities, including class, regional, religious, and occupational cleavages. But none has been so revitalized in the current crisis in Somalia as lineage, or clan identity. Somalis identify themselves within a vast family tree that is defined at the highest level by six large clan families, each of which breaks down into clans, subclans, and primary lineages. This fluid, cascading lineage identity can be mobilized at different levels, depending on the nature of the conflict at hand. The most stable lineage unit is the *diya*-paying group, which can number between several hundred to several thousand close relatives, bound to collectively pay or receive blood compensation, or *diya,* if one of their members commits or is a victim of a crime (Lewis 1988, 11).

Even under a functioning colonial and postcolonial judicial system, the *diya*-system continued to serve as the primary structure through which personal grievances from livestock raiding to murders were peacefully resolved through compensation rather than retaliation. Typically, for instance, the murder of a man would be compensated by the payment of one hundred camels by the *diya*-paying group of the accused murderer to the *diya* group of the deceased. Such an exchange would be the result of lengthy negotiations between elders of the two groups, and in cases when agreement could not be reached, a blood feud leading to retaliatory attacks was usually the result. But the fear of revenge attacks, and the opportunity to prevent or terminate cycles of revenge killings through *diya*-payments, permitted a modicum of order and security in historically stateless Somalia and has continued to function even after the Siad Barre regime abolished and outlawed *diya*-payments. The high costs of compensation also served as a deterrent for potential miscreants; since their clansmen bore the collective costs of compensation, peer pressure to observe social contracts was strong within *diya* groups.

☐ *Clan Elders*

The central actors in traditional conflict management in Somalia are clan elders—prominent adult males representing the lineage groups involved in talks. They can include notable religious leaders—sheikhs or *wadads*—as well. Their rise to a position of influence and eminence is based not on hereditary status but on a lifetime of earned reputation as effective negotiators, trusted mediators, moving orators, or wise and pious men. The social category of "elder" is quite fluid, a source of considerable confusion for outsiders. Individual Somalis were and are capable of wearing more than one hat—businessmen could under certain circumstances be viewed as elders, as could politicians and others.

In some regions of Somalia, the highest level council of elders is called the *guurti* or *akhyaar;* more localized, subclan councils are active as well. Clan elders are skilled negotiators on behalf of their clans; their role is essential in the crafting of accords and the resolving of disputes between lineages. Most localized disputes, such as stolen property, were and continue to be taken to elders for mediation or arbitration, but larger regional clan conflicts have also long been the domain of clan elders. In both colonial and postcolonial governments, paid positions were created in an effort to co-opt or replace potentially troublesome clan elders (Farah 1993, 14–29).

□ *Xeer*

Customary law, or social contracts, both within and between *diya*-paying groups were and remain central in establishing norms, expectations, and obligations in the absence of formal state law enforcement. *Xeer* often draws on aspects of Islamic Shari'a law, but is viewed by Islamist groups as a deviation from Shari'a. Traditional reconciliation efforts generally produce such a social contract between the reconciling groups. Readers more familiar with international relations than Somali anthropology may find it useful to liken *xeer* to customary international law, or to "regimes" in international organization. In both instances, there is no political force with the punitive capacity to enforce these accords; but in both cases, there are negative consequences for actors who choose to violate the code of conduct. And both *xeer* and international regimes provide a certain level of predictability, confidence building, and cooperation in an otherwise anarchic environment.

□ *Shir*

Traditional clan assemblies, known as *shir,* are the consultative processes that make traditional Somali peacemaking so relatively democratic and open. These assemblies can either call all adult male members of a lineage (at any level of segmentation) to discuss and ratify a position, or can involve a meeting between elders of two or more lineages. *Shir* are lengthy processes in which all present have the right to express their views. Because they are held in the midst of the community and are open for all to observe, and because they ensure a thorough process of consensus building and consultation, traditional assemblies produce accords that possess a high level of legitimacy and binding power.

Collectively, these various practices and social institutions form the core of what Somalis and outside observers mean when they refer to "traditional" conflict management. Importantly, this list underscores a key distinction between traditional *processes,* such as clan assemblies, and traditional *actors,* especially the elders. That distinction has come to matter in recent years, as elders have sometimes been drawn into nontraditional peace conferences, and traditional assemblies have been used by nontraditional actors (factional and militia leaders).

■ Traditional Conflict Management and Peace Initiatives in the Somali Crisis

One of the most notable aspects of the current Somali crisis is the protracted and complete collapse of the state. Many observers see in this crisis a "return" to the decentralized, pastoral anarchy of precolonial Somalia. While this view is oversimplified—Somalia's current situation is radically different in many ways from the nineteenth century, and cannot be accurately portrayed as a "return" to anything—it does underscore that traditional Somali social structures, which evolved within a context of statelessness, have now been again thrust into a radically decentralized, quasi-anarchic political environment. At issue is the extent to which these traditional mechanisms for managing conflict in precolonial anarchy have the capacity to manage late-twentieth-century anarchy.

Since the collapse of the state in January 1991, dispute mediation, arbitration, and punitive sanctions at the micro level (individual, family, and neighborhood or village level) have been performed almost exclusively by clan elders. To be sure, in zones of the country hardest hit by civil war and occupation by outside militias, especially in the southern interriverine area, local elders were left powerless. Indeed, the empowerment of heavily armed teenage gunmen (known as the *mooryaan* in the South, and the *dey-dey* in the North) came at the direct expense of elders, who have only gradually been able to reassert some level of authority over these elements. In some instances alternative sources of quasi-judicial authority have supplanted traditional mechanisms—Islamic courts have grown in strength in parts of Mogadishu and elsewhere, for example, and in rare cases formal governmental authorities (either regional, factional, or self-designated national) perform some judicial roles. But throughout the country, whatever localized dispute management exists is largely accomplished through traditional means.

But if it is true that elders play a dominant role in the handling of individual or neighborhood disputes, it is less the case that traditional processes have been central to the resolution of larger conflicts involving armed hostilities between clans or factions, or political conflicts at the regional and national level. Traditional conflict management at the macro level has played a prominent role at several key junctures in Somalia's long-running crisis, but has been most notable for its exclusion from most internationally sponsored peace conferences. It has been drawn on most effectively and extensively in the North, in the self-proclaimed secessionist state of "Somaliland."[1] It also enjoyed a relatively short period of prominence as the preferred UN strategy for peace building in southern Somalia in mid- to late 1993, with mixed results.

□ *Civil War Diplomacy, 1988–1990*

From 1988 to January 1991, Somalia was rocked by a widening civil war that began in brutal fighting in the northwest and gradually spread throughout the countryside, eventually engulfing Mogadishu by late 1990. External efforts to negotiate an end to the worsening fighting were tepid—the concurrent end of the Cold War led to dramatically reduced interest in Somalia on the part of international actors. The only significant initiative was made by a group of former civilian politicians from the 1960s and prominent businessmen. Known as the Manifesto Group, these Somalis called for an interim government and an end to hostilities, a proposal met by harsh measures by the Barre regime. Traditional clan elders were not brought into this process, despite the fact that armed liberation movements were defined almost entirely along clan lines. Clan elders had simply never played a role in conflict management at the national level, and were perceived (probably accurately) by the Manifesto Group as inexperienced and unhelpful at that level of political negotiation. Two decades of marginalization, manipulation, and co-optation of clan elders by the Barre regime had further weakened the potential role of traditional conflict management mechanisms in the late 1980s.[2]

□ *Grassroots Reconciliation Efforts in Northern Somalia, 1991–1993*

In northern Somalia, traditional conflict management processes and players experienced a dramatic resurgence in the years following the fall of the Barre regime. The faction that eventually drove the national military out of the North, the Somali National Movement (SNM), recognized both clan identity and the role of clan elders in its constitution, in stark contrast to the Barre regime, which had formally outlawed "tribalism" (Bradbury 1993, 67, 74). In the National Charter, the Upper House of the government is defined as the "Council of Elders," and is charged with the responsibility "to encourage and safeguard peace" as well as creating and enforcing codes of conduct (*xeer*) among clans. The *guurti*'s de facto role in maintenance of the peace is thus enshrined in the formal structure of the Somaliland state.

The SNM's deference toward clan elders was due in part to the important role played by the *guurti* in helping to organize the Isaaq clan's defense against Barre's forces in the 1988–1990 war (Farah 1993, 18–19). The greater strength of traditional social institutions in the North may also be a function of two other elements: the North's relative isolation from the socioeconomic changes and urbanization imposed on southern Somalia and the North's greater ethnical homogeneity and demographic stability. The small number of clans in the region have a history of interaction and did not have to cope with the destructive and highly armed anarchy and looting that plagued southern Somalia.

As a result, traditional processes and actors have been at the fore of nearly all major reconciliation initiatives in the North. The decision to declare secession for Somaliland was itself made at the Grand *Shir* of northern clans. Following the outbreak of intraclan fighting in the North in late 1991, a series of traditional peace meetings was held, culminating in the Boroma Conference from January to May 1993. These talks were convened by the *guurti* of the northern clans and succeeded in resolving current armed conflicts, compensating groups that lost livestock or kinsfolk, selecting a new president for Somaliland, establishing security arrangements in the region, resolving grazing and property disputes, and formulating a "National Peace Charter" that establishes a social contract or *xeer* for all of the people of Somaliland (Bradbury 1993, 67–68, 73–74). By any standard, this was an impressive accomplishment for a traditional peacemaking mechanism facing entirely new types of political challenges.

A second important series of traditional peace talks occurred in the region of Sanaag in northern Somalia; like the Boroma Conference, its success has also been widely cited as evidence of the vitality of traditional conflict management in Somalia. This round of seven peace meetings, held between August 1992 and June 1993, brought together four major clans in a disputed eastern territory of Somaliland in order to confirm peace between them and to establish a regional administration. Smaller, bilateral peace meetings between reconciling clans eventually culminated in a meeting of over four hundred participants at the town of Erigavo, which produced an accord to institutionalize the cease-fire through promotion of free movement, free trade, access to common grazing and water sources, and resolution of property disputes (Bradbury 1993, 91–93, 97; SDRA/MCC 1994). Like the Boroma Conference, the Sanaag meetings received small but vital levels of financial support from several international NGOs.

The hybrid nature of the Sanaag peace process is noteworthy; while centered on traditional processes and social actors, it provided important support roles for "nontraditional" participants, like intellectuals and local nongovernmental organizations, as well. At the core of the proceeding were two hundred elders, who formed the main council of delegates; they represented their clans' interests in negotiations. A small group of honored clan elders formed a "Council of Sultans and Garaads," or *guurti,* to serve as mediators. A chairing committee of eight members administered the meeting, while preparatory committees, composed largely of younger intellectuals, assisted in the drafting of accords and the resolution of technical political matters beyond the purview of the elders. This practice of creating a division of labor between elders, who handled general negotiations, and intellectuals, who were given roles in committees to hammer out technical problems relating to local administration, police, and other matters of the state, proved to be a useful synthesis of old and new processes that was repeated in other Somali peace meetings.

Though neither the Boroma nor the Sanaag peace conference proved to be an unqualified success—each met with problems of implementation and universal acceptance—they represented two of the most durable and comprehensive peace processes undertaken in the Somali crisis. That both of them were essentially "traditional" in both process and in leadership provided compelling evidence for advocates of traditional, bottom-up approaches to peace in Somalia. Yet only a few of the dozens of peace initiatives sponsored by the UN and others during the international intervention in Somalia from 1993 to 1995 drew on traditional conflict management.

□ *The Failure of Traditional Mechanisms in Southern Somalia, 1991–1992*

The success of traditional peace building in the North stands in stark contrast to the virtual absence of durable reconciliation efforts (traditional or otherwise) in war- and famine-racked southern Somalia in 1991 and 1992. Given the horrific levels of violence and suffering in the South, conflict management there was needed more desperately than anywhere else in the country. International diplomacy was conspicuously absent in southern Somalia in 1991 and 1992 for geostrategic and bureaucratic reasons (Clarke 1993; Menkhaus and Ortmayer 1999). But why were traditional Somali peace-building mechanisms unable to better manage the conflict?

Some analyses have emphasized the destructive impact of militarization in southern Somalia as an explanation. In an environment in which nearly every teenager possessed an automatic weapon, and in which use of that weapon was essential to secure basic foodstuffs for one's family, relations between elders and youth were bound to be transformed. Indeed, elders in the South did often complain that the proliferation of guns in the hands of young men and boys destroyed the respect and authority of the elders. While it is true that the level of weaponry in the South was overwhelming, and that this complicated the work of elders, that alone cannot fully account for the marginalization of traditional authority in 1991–1992 southern Somalia. Elders in the North faced similar levels of arms in the hands of bandits and idle youth, and yet were eventually able to command the clan to control those youth.

A more compelling answer lies in the issue of invasion. Unlike northern Somalia, southern Somalia was (and largely remains) under conquest and occupation by warring clan militias, none of which have legitimate historical claims on the cities and agricultural land over which they have fought.[3] As a result, local clan elders found themselves attempting to negotiate with young militiamen and bandits from distant clans rather than with "peer" elders. Local elders were, moreover, negotiating from positions of extreme weakness, as their communities typically had few weapons or organized defense forces. The teenage gunmen of the conquering clans had little respect for traditional peace building, nor did they desire such mediation. Their livelihood depended on an economy of plunder and extortion that would presumably be threatened by peace. Traditional authority and peacemaking in the South were not destroyed by the dynamics of conquest, but were at least temporarily marginalized in the first years of the crisis.

In most of the interriverain region, the clan elders did not—at least initially—accompany young militiamen whose forays ranged far beyond the traditional homelands of their clans. Only later, with the peace imposed by UNOSOM, did clan elders in Mogadishu begin to reassert a role in managing interclan conflict, though they were never able to override the prerogatives of the militia leaders in their clans. Most importantly, however, elders of clans that had gained valuable real estate in southern Somali cities and agricultural zones were constrained by the fact that their constituents stood to gain little and lose much in any peacemaking that entailed return of or compensation for property lost in the years of warfare. Since elders first and foremost serve as negotiators representing their clan, they were understandably unwilling to promote reconciliation under those terms. Indeed, in several cases, elders of clans that were clinging to hard-fought and valuable urban or agricultural territory won by conquest were among the most recalcitrant actors in peace initiatives, even more so than faction leaders, whose broader political strategies rendered them at times more amenable to peace treaties with formal rivals (Menkhaus 1999).

□ *Top-Down Reconciliation Efforts, 1993–1995*

The vast majority of internationally sponsored peace initiatives in Somalia had little or nothing to do with traditional conflict management. Instead, they typically were held in posh hotels in distant regional capitals (Addis Ababa, Nairobi, Djibouti, Cairo) among invited factional and militia leaders, and featured formal peace conferences and negotiating procedures in conformity with standard international diplomacy rather than Somali custom. There were many well-reasoned arguments for this approach. First, it was argued that meetings had to be held outside of Somalia for security and logistical reasons; less persuasively, it was also said that the factional leaders needed to be distanced from hard-liners in their communities in order to be convinced of the merits of reconciliation. Second, the choice of participants—factional and militia leaders—was justified on the realpolitik argument that these were the players holding the guns, and therefore they had to be central to any peace process. *Washington Post* correspondent Jennifer Parmelee (1993) captured the spirit of this view:

> Time and again, I asked the powers that be—the U.N., the United States—"Aren't you giving these guys [the militias leaders] too much prominence?" The reply invariably came back: "They're the players. We've got to play ball with them." And so, the world waltzed with the warlords.

Elders, community leaders, and other grassroots representatives of Somali civil society were perceived as too weak to enforce accords on militia leaders. While this argument had merit, it tended to overlook the fact that the factional and militia leaders, too, exercised very little control over their alleged constituencies. It also confused the militias' capacity to destroy and disrupt with an ability to govern, a crucial distinction that was never fully appreciated by the UN. Finally, standard diplomatic procedures were justified on the grounds that traditional Somali assemblies were unwieldy and far too time-consuming, often lasting months rather than days or weeks. This complaint reflected an unfortunate tendency on the part of the UN to confuse its timetables and political needs with the best interests of the Somali people. The two were far from synonymous.

Thus, in the most internationally visible and politically significant peace conferences from 1992 through 1995, elders and traditional peace processes were conspicuously absent. In the most important of these meetings, the Addis Ababa Conference on National Reconciliation convened by the UN in March 1993, Somali and international advocates of grassroots peace building were outraged that the UN invited only representatives of fifteen self-styled political factions, with no role whatsoever for elders and other community leaders. The UN was constrained by the insistence of General Mohamed Farah Aideed and other militia leaders that only they had the right to participate; but the UN eventually acquiesced to external pressure by belatedly permitting the participation of over two hundred Somali community leaders as observers to the proceedings.[4] Though not permitted to sign the final agreement, the community leaders' presence at the proceedings had a moderating effect on the factions. In particular, though faction leaders sought to establish direct factional control over the composition of the proposed Transitional National Council (TNC), they were compelled to sign an accord that left open the selection process by which regional representatives to the TNC would be chosen. Many grassroots advocates inferred from the accord that local communities would thus be able to select their representatives, much in the same manner as clan assemblies did in Somaliland. But in following days, the factions met in isolation from community leaders and drafted an addendum to the accord that asserted that regional representatives to the TNC would be selected by the factions, not by local constituencies. The episode was startling evidence of the chasm between the interests of factions and civic society in Somalia.

Outside Somaliland, it appeared, Somali faction and militia leaders simply were unwilling to share significant political power with traditional authorities. Indeed, representatives of the political factions were among the most caustic critics of traditional peace processes, contending that "elders" were illiterate nomads with no business in the affairs of state, and that foreigners who advocated traditional peace processes were promoting clannism and backwardness in Somalia.[5] Their skepticism about elders and traditional conflict resolution procedures found receptive ears in international diplomatic circles, where most UN and foreign ministry officials were more comfortable with "modern" peace conference proceedings and with factions that, at a minimum, possessed stationary with English-language letterhead and representatives dressed in suits. Ironically, it was often African diplomats who expressed the most disdain for "traditional" methods and who viewed elders as embarrassing anachronisms rather than potential peacemakers. The elders' strongest advocates tended to be Western nongovernmental organizations with strong peace and justice agendas and long experience working in Somalia.

Over the course of its three-year presence, the UN Operation in Somalia (UNOSOM) hosted a long string of factionally based, national reconciliation conferences. Each was heralded as a diplomatic breakthrough, only to fail in the implementation stage. It soon became apparent that these expensive peace conferences had grown into something of a cynical cottage industry for faction leaders, who demanded—and received—sizable reimbursements from the UN for "travel expenses" for themselves and their entourage. The factions signed onto but failed to implement peace accords in part because they had no interest in their implementation, and in part because they lacked the political capacity to enforce the accords they signed. The UN and other external parties continued to sponsor them out of desperation, hoping that eventually one effort might bear fruit and salvage what had become a disastrous peacekeeping mission in Somalia.

Traditional Peace Building in Southern Somalia, 1993–1994

For advocates of a grassroots approach to peace building, the dismal track record of UN-sponsored, top-down, faction-based peace conferences stood in stark contrast to the successful history of traditional peace building in the isolated North and served as additional evidence that traditional conflict mechanisms held greater promise in Somalia. During one brief period, from May 1993 to early 1994, UN diplomats grew more receptive to this alternative approach and attempted to provide assistance to traditional peace meetings in southern Somalia. The reason for this short-lived receptiveness was essentially political. At that point in time, the UN was locked in a deadly conflict with General Aideed and his faction, the Somali National Alliance. Aideed was perceived, probably accurately, as one of the main obstacles to national reconciliation; he was in particular violently opposed to any political process that drew authority away from factions and toward local communities and elders, in large part because his clan—which militarily occupied a large section of interriverain land it did not have historic rights to—stood to lose the most from any process that invited local control over local politics. Once the UN found itself at war with Aideed in south Mogadishu, it embraced a political strategy in which it portrayed itself as an advocate of grassroots democracy and a champion of a civil society that was held hostage by warlords. That led the UN to sponsor a number of local and regional peace conferences featuring traditional procedures and clan elders. But in early 1994, when the UN sought accommodation with a temporarily resurgent General Aideed, one of the prices he exacted was the complete cessation of bottom-up political processes in the country. Thereafter the UN dealt exclusively with factions in its reconciliation efforts and pointedly ignored leaders from Somali civil society, a policy that led to repeated failure up to the final departure of UN forces in March 1995.

In those instances when the UN provided support to traditional conflict management, the results were mixed. By far the most important such initiative was the Jubaland Peace Accord, held from June to August 1993 in the port city of Kismayo. The long-running armed conflict over this valued city and region constituted one of the most intractable and dangerous flash points in Somalia. Like the Sanaag peace conference, the Jubaland peace conference entailed a creative fusion of traditional processes and contemporary procedures, and a symbiotic relationship between clan elders, "intellectuals," and other civic leaders.[6] International agencies provided vital logistical support but otherwise kept a low profile. Broad principles of the reconciliation were handled by a daily plenary session of elders, while specific technical aspects of implementation were farmed out to committees formed by intellectuals, who generated proposals for the elders' consideration. The broader public was kept informed and actively involved through meetings with their elders in town each evening, which gave the proceedings a level of public ratification that was conspicuously absent in peace conferences held outside Somalia. In addition, in order to publicly rebuild and reaffirm old friendships across clan lines, elders held a series of "peace feasts" with one another in Kismayo, a powerful and effective "track two" peace-building tactic.[7]

Faction and militia leaders from the two groups in conflict were kept out of the actual proceedings, though they used intermediaries as best they could to influence the outcome. Significantly, the elders of the Ogadeni clan openly broke with the Ogadeni faction and its militia leader Colonel Omar Jess to pursue peace, at considerable personal danger. Their bold move to sue for peace without the backing of their clan militia was a gamble, since their rivals, the Mijerteen and Marehan clan elders, maintained close relations with their militia leader, General "Morgan." The Ogadeni elders took such a risk, and were willing to negotiate from a position of weakness, because their military stalemate with Morgan's forces had left their clan members destitute and displaced in squalid refugee camps outside the city.

The Jubaland Peace Accord was a partial success, but some crucial aspects of the agreement could not be implemented due to the rejection of the accord by some militias. In particular, though the major clans involved in the accord were willing to share the city of Kismayo again, they could not agree to an allocation of seats in the town council and in the local, UN-funded police force. Later, in February 1994, when elders sought to reinvigorate the accords through the convening of a new peace assembly, one militia leader purposefully disrupted the *shir* by provoking armed conflict with the opposing clan. That action led to renewed hostilities, the forced expulsion of the Ogadeni clan from the city, and the discrediting and marginalization of moderate elders on both sides of the conflict. This disappointing outcome highlighted the fact that clan elders, pursuing peace in the interests of their communities, could not directly challenge the interests of militias without risking retaliatory measures. The militias, whose interests in continued warfare, plunder, and anarchy were so often in conflict with the needs of their clan members, had the ability to disrupt proceedings in which they felt marginalized.

Nonetheless, a number of grassroots peace initiatives were successfully concluded in southern Somalia during UNOSOM's tenure, in Afmadow, Bardhere, Baidoa, and elsewhere. For UN officials, however, these local and regional peace conferences proved a disappointment. The expectation of international diplomats was that localized, traditional reconciliation processes would serve as the building blocks for national reconciliation; this was often characterized as a "bottom-up" approach to peace. But local and regional peace accords typically remained precisely that—local and regional—with little upward momentum.

For international diplomats, local and regional peace accords possessed little intrinsic value on their own; they were valuable only as first steps toward national reconciliation, which would yield the "real" prize—the reestablishment of a Somali central state, the ultimate criterion by which the UN peace operation would be judged a success or failure. But for local communities and the elders representing them, the obverse was true. National reconciliation had no intrinsic value—indeed, it was often looked upon with fear and distrust as a process that could culminate in a return of an oppressive and parasitic central state. Rather, it was local and regional accords that promised immediate and tangible benefits, by reopening commerce and roads between neighboring clans, insuring shared access to pastures, attracting investment, and reducing the risk of raids on livestock. Reconciliation patterns reflected communal interests that remained highly localized in Somalia.

■ Lessons Learned: Conceptual and Practical Contributions of the Somali Experience

How, then, does the Somali case help to inform our ability to conceptualize and generate theories about traditional conflict management in Africa? And what practical lessons can be drawn from the Somali experience? As a single country case study, it can do no more than suggest propositions that comparative research in other African settings can test and refine. Some of the most significant of these propositions include the following:

- "Traditional" conflict management is a misnomer; what we term "traditional" procedures are usually a synthesis of old and new styles of diplomacy. This should not be surprising, since traditional practices that did not exhibit an ability to adapt and change would be of limited use in coping with the very new types of conflicts confronting Africa in the late twentieth century. Care must be taken to avoid conceiving of traditional and modern diplomacy in strictly dichotomous terms.
- In defining "traditional conflict management," care must be taken to distinguish between traditional *processes* and traditional *actors*. This distinction was only gradually discerned by international observers in Somalia, who tended to confuse the two.
- A distinction should be made between "grassroots" and "traditional" peace processes; these two concepts are frequently but incorrectly used interchangeably. Advocates of grassroots peace building envision participa-

tion by a broad spectrum of civil society, including "nontraditional" actors—women's NGO groups, intellectuals, and professional groups—whose involvement in reconciliation efforts are by no means traditional.

• The interests and political agendas of traditional actors in conflict management can be understood only through situational analyses rather than through arguments based on the intrinsic nature of social groups. Elders and other traditional peacemakers in peace are usually a force for reconciliation, but not under certain conditions. Policies that *assume* that elders and other traditional peacemakers are always a force for peace will occasionally be unpleasantly surprised, and reflect a naivete about the complex political agendas of these groups and individuals.

• To the extent that the role of traditional leaders such as elders is to represent their community in peace talks, their ability to promote peace is constrained by the material interests of the communities to which they belong. Analysis of the motives and interests of traditional peacemakers must be rooted in an astute assessment of their constituencies. Elders, poets, and other traditional peacemakers can coax and inspire ambivalent or fearful constituencies to embrace peace, but they cannot be expected to move their communities to accept peace if it is clearly harmful to their material interests.

• The authority of traditional conflict mechanisms to broker and enforce peace accords in the chaos and social transformation associated with complex emergencies is also situational, not predetermined. The Somali case suggests that several variables are key in constraining the authority of traditional social authority, including military occupation by "outside" groups and high levels of militarization. The Somali case also suggests that traditional conflict management mechanisms in complex emergencies are incapacitated in the early, most disruptive stages of the crisis, but reassert at least some of their previous authority over time.

• Likewise, the relationship between traditional peace builders and other political figures and groups is crucial to the potential influence of these actors, but is also variable, not fixed. Most analyses of the Somali conflict have tended to embrace one of two points of departure—either that relations between elders and the militia leaders of their clans are inherently conflictual, or that clan identity is so strong that elders and militia leaders of the same lineage virtually always act in unison. But closer examination reveals a much more complex and fluctuating relationship between traditional leaders and their counterparts in factions and militias.

• The Somali case strongly suggests that the capacity of traditional peacemaking processes is strongest at the local and regional levels, and weakest at the national level, reflecting the process of state collapse it was hoped to correct. This is not to say that aspects of traditional conflict management have no role in national-level peacemaking, only that the Somali experience did not give evidence of such a role. Accurate assessments of the potential of traditional approaches to conflict management must take into account these different levels of reconciliation.

• The Somali case also strongly suggests that traditional conflict management is much more effective in instances when reconciliation is the end in itself, rather than a necessary step in a state-building process. Where elders were asked to help broker peace between two or more clans with the aim of reintegrating the communities and reopening trade, those general goals were viewed in positive-sum terms, and thus enjoyed wide communal support. But when elders were asked to broker peace accords that also included agreements on the allocation of seats in district or regional councils, the process was transformed into a zero-sum contest. The fixed number of seats on local councils forced each clan to quantify its relative importance at the district and regional level, and each clan had fairly inflated notions of the "piece of the pie" to which it was entitled by reason of demographic size, historical rights, or military prowess.

• Traditional conflict management mechanisms tend to be process-oriented, not product-oriented; that is, they tend to focus on *managing* rather than *resolving* conflict. In this sense, they are somewhat more realistic than standard international diplomacy, with its emphasis on peace treaties that definitively end a conflict. The process orientation of traditional conflict management tends to produce negotiations somewhat akin to the General Agreement of Tariffs and Trade—that is, ongoing rounds of talks that revisit and renegotiate issues. This approach to conflict management, particularly the tendency to begin renegotiating freshly minted accords, fits poorly with international diplomatic timetables and approaches. International peacemakers seeking rapid, tangible, and fixed results in negotiations are almost certain to be disappointed by traditional conflict management.

• Finally, the Somali case underscores the fact that to be successful, traditional conflict management in Africa needs external support, but only if provided with great caution and in small amounts. Nearly all of the traditional assemblies that produced successful reconciliation in Somalia generated bills for food, transportation, and other incidentals that local communities, already beset by the devastation of war, could ill-afford to pay. External support to defray these costs—which were astronomical by local standards, but quite modest by international ones—dramatically reduced the pressure on participants and allowed them to focus on substantive issues. Support for transportation was especially valuable in convening elders from great distances. But too much external support actually exacerbated conflict, by inviting jealousies, misuse of funds, and fears of external favoritism or manipulation.

Notes

1. "Somaliland" consists of the former British colony of the same name, which unified with the Italian colony of Somalia to the south at independence in 1960. The decision by the residents of the northwest unilaterally to declare independence in May 1991 came following years of civil war, oppression, and genocide in northwest Somalia at the hands of the Barre regime. The largest clan in the northwest, the Isaaq, had been singled out for harsh treatment, and led the move for secession. Not all clans in northwest Somalia have accepted the declaration of an independent Somaliland, however, and most Somalis living in southern Somalia vigorously object. As a result, no foreign countries have extended it diplomatic recognition as of 1998.

2. For instance, though the practice of paying a stipend to elders and sultans was initiated by Italian colonial authorities, the Barre regime went much further, creating a new, government-appointed position called *nabadoon* (literally, peacemaker) to replace traditional community leaders.

3. Specifically, Hawiye clans hailing from the central region of the country have occupied and settled much of the interriverine area, inhabited primarily by the Digil-Rahanweyn, Dir, Benadiri, Barawan, Bantu, and other—generally weak, agricultural or urban—clans. Hawiye clan members have also essentially transformed the formerly multiclan cities of Mogadishu, Merka, and Brava into Hawiye-dominated urban areas. In the process, thousands of homes and farms belonging to Somali families of other clans have been appropriated by the newcomers. Further south, the Marehan clan has occupied Rahanweyn real estate in the town of Bardhere and surrounding farmland, while a complex, shifting coalition of clans (especially the Ogadeni, Harti, Marehan, and Hawiye) jostle to occupy land and buildings in Kismayo and the adjacent Jubba River valley.

4. This last-minute addition to the proceedings was facilitated by the fact that a UN Humanitarian Conference on Somalia had just been completed in Addis Ababa, so that many of the community leaders invited to that meeting were already in place to attend the National Reconciliation Conference when asked.

5. Author's field notes, 1993–1994. The author served as Special Political Adviser in the UN Operation in Somalia for nine months and was present at a number of these peace conferences.

6. The social category of "intellectual" was as fluid as that of "elder." Any Somali possessing a university degree could be considered an intellectual. This group of "professionals" sought to portray themselves to international peacekeepers and funding agencies (especially funding agencies!) as nonpartisan and above the fray of clan politics, but in reality their allegiances and interests were highly variable; some were truly dedicated to the good of the whole Somali community and risked their lives for peace, while others worked directly for warlords and were among the most dangerous provocateurs of interclan violence.

7. The concept of "track two" diplomacy was first introduced by Davidson and Montville (1981–1982, 145–157). For a recent refinement of this approach, see Diamond and McDonald (1996).

13

Applying Traditional Methods to Modern Conflict: Possibilities and Limits

Eghosa E. Osaghae

The fate of Africa and Africans was arguably never more gloomy and desperate than it has been since the late 1970s. Many states have all but collapsed, battered in the main by fratricidal wars, intractable political conflicts, and economic insolvency. The people have become more pauperized and hopeless, helpless victims of violent wars, repressive and corrupt governments, and economic adjustments that have had devastating and conflict-worsening consequences. At the core of this pathetic state, which is threatening to further degenerate in many cases, are the violent conflicts that have torn many countries apart. It is the futility of efforts to resolve the conflicts in these countries that has partly provoked the search for more creative and contextual approaches to conflict resolution in Africa.

There are of course other important reasons that traditional systems of conflict management need to be more thoroughly investigated and incorporated into modern conflict resolution efforts. One is that doing so will help to mitigate the disenabling effects produced by the perception of United Nations and Western powers' conflict resolution and management initiatives as extensions of foreign intervention of the (re)colonization kind. This perception by anticolonial and anti-imperialist elites and warlords is reinforced by the larger context of economic and political adjustments imposed by Western countries and other multilateral organizations, which have rendered many insolvent African states new colonies in all but name. The delegitimizing implications of this perception, which were underplayed for a long time, and the ways in which the incorporation of traditional conflict management strategies into mainstream strategies can help to reduce the problems have recently been identified in the search for better conflict management in Africa (see Spear and Keller 1996).

Second, from the perspective of indigenous knowledge, the incorporation of traditional systems not only helps to contextualize conflict management but also facilitates the participation of local peoples who are usually left out of search-for-peace processes and ensures the sustenance of endangered indigenous formations. Without such contextualization and local participation, interventions in unfamiliar terrain may actually exacerbate rather than reduce conflicts (Smock and Crocker 1995). Recent studies of traditional organizations—hometown associations, cultural organizations, ethnic unions, women's societies, and so on—as integral parts of modern civil society in various parts of Africa, show the enormous benefits and potentials of traditional conflict management strategies, especially in the case of ethnic conflicts, which have so far remained substantially untapped (Agbaje 1990; Barkan 1994; Osaghae 1996a; Gboyega 1997; Agbese 1996).

This chapter attempts a critical examination of this new line of thought, which, because of the seeming inadequacies of strategies that have so far been applied and the increasingly desperate levels of conflicts that have been reached, has become very attractive. We begin by trying to situate the "traditional" in African discourse in terms of its definition on the one hand, and its relevance and dominance of the sociopolitical landscape on the other. This framework sets the frontiers and parameters within which traditional systems of conflict management will be searched for and analyzed. Next, an attempt is made to (re)construct a paradigm of traditional conflict management from the works of anthropologists, historians, and other social scientists who have studied conflict resolution in several traditional African societies. Then we shall come to the question of possibilities and limits. Given the world of difference between the so-called traditional society and the present (modern) formations, how can traditional strategies be made relevant to contemporary conflict situations?

■ Conceptualizing the Traditional in Africa

Very few scholars of African society would deny that most people on the continent remain attached to traditional ways of life. This is true not only of the predominant rural populations but also of urban dwellers and the elites who retain their rural and primordial ties and loyalties through the various ethnic and cultural associations that proliferate in the urban civil society landscape. At the political level, traditional attachments are largely responsible for the centrality of so-called traditional practices in the legitimizing strategies adopted by several leaders in Africa. They have manipulated traditional institutions and practices and reinvented traditions to mobilize and sustain support. Indeed, the force of tradition is very dramatic and acute in the contestation for, and retention of, (state) power. Heads of states have been known to rely heavily on witch doctors, marabouts, and powerful juju men who in some cases live in state houses at government expense (Bretton

[1967] elaborates on how Ghana's Nkrumah relied on fetish to retain power); witchcraft, divination, secret societies, and rituals feature very prominently in elections and rivalries among politicians and political parties; warring factions and guerrilla armies strengthen internal solidarity and fight their wars through rituals, secret oathings, and other traditional practices (Grundy 1971); and so on.

Tradition is all too clear in present-day African politics and this, in itself, is sufficient reason to consider traditional sources of conflict management. After all, traditional strategies of conflict management are employed at the subnational level in most countries, especially in those where so-called traditional rulers are still respected (in some of them, there are no alternatives to traditional systems). Little (1967, 185) discovered from his study of the Mende of Sierra Leone that the authority of the Poro society (as well as the Sande and Humui, other secret societies that serve as cultural arbiters) is still widely used to resolve conflicts: "Nowadays . . . serious 'palavers' concerning the chiefdom as a whole are talked over in the bush [by a Poro tribunal], irrespective of whether or not they come up for public attention, or the official notice of the government." Laurrent Kabila apparently refused to meet Mobutu Sese Seko face-to-face in 1997 for fear of juju.

Even at the national level, attempts have been made in some countries to entrench "traditional" ways. Although these were mostly designed to perpetuate rulers in power, they nevertheless promoted elements of indigenous conflict management practices. A case in point was the adoption of Poro secret society (and its equivalent for women, Sande society) as a national society by President Tubman in Liberia as part of his indigenization and patrimonialist project. Subsequently, the ritual authority of the grand master of the society, whom Liberians referred to as the "Big Devil," which had important conflict-resolving roles, was extended to parts of the country where the society did not previously exist (Walter 1969; Little 1973; Osaghae 1996b). In Nigeria, traditional rulers have been upheld by all postcolonial governments, particularly military governments, to strengthen patrimonialist structures at the grass roots.

The point is, if tradition can be made to work for political stability by keeping rulers in power, there is no reason why it cannot be made to work for conflict resolution. But the question of tradition is not so simple and straightforward. To begin with, what is meant by "traditional" in Africa, where colonialism and other external influences have transformed social formations in such fundamental ways that there is very little that may be considered authentically indigenous and traditional? In his ideal-type classification of the postcolonial social structure in Africa—into transformed indigenous social structure, migrated social structure, and emergent social structure—Ekeh (1983) denies the survival of any *purely* traditional social structure. Even the current so-called institution of traditional rulership belongs to the category of transformed indigenous social structure, as the colonial authorities, especially the British and Germans, extended, imposed, and generalized traditional rulership (or chieftaincy) on places where it was previously unknown.

This is the main point of the "invention of tradition" school championed in African studies by Terence Ranger: "The invented traditions of African societies—whether invented by the Europeans or by Africans themselves in response—*distorted the past but became in themselves realities*" (Ranger 1983, 212, emphasis added). Can a distorted past be regarded as traditional? The answer, even from the point of view of the invention school, is "yes," since, as Hobsbawm (1983, 2) puts it, the "object and characteristic of 'traditions' including invented ones, is invariance." Although invariance is used here to distinguish the traditional from the customary, which Hobsbawm says is more innovative and receptive to change, it should be taken to suggest that traditions are relatively more enduring and resistant to change rather than simply permanent and unchanging.

The "traditional" may then be defined as simply the legacy of the past, including the changes and transformations that this past may have gone through. The reconstruction (or invention) of this past is, however, a selective process, as the relevant legacy comprises only those aspects that the inventors wish to emphasize or employ to chosen ends. This meaning of what is traditional is clear enough from the efforts of governments in Africa, both in the colonial and in the postcolonial periods, to construct "traditions." The same approach is found in the works of anthropologists and historians for whom tradition refers essentially to the presence of the past in the workings of society. Following Weber's (1977) ideal-type category, "traditional" refers to behaviors, institutions, and practices that derive from the past. Perhaps this is what Hobsbawm wants to convey in characterizing traditions as invariant, but it is obvious that the very process of invention makes traditions as subject to change as customs. As anthropologists and historians show, the process of social change is in large part a process of changing traditions and customs, a process of refinement that involves preservation of some traditions and transformation or discarding of others.

The search for traditional strategies of conflict management then looks for the past in present-day social formations that can be applied to modern conflicts, and stresses the *indigenous* content. The essence of this is to separate practices and institutions that may have crept into the legacy of the past from external influences such as Islam, Christianity, capitalism, and other western influences from those that are essentially autochthonous. For example, customary law, which in this case represents the traditional, is usually separated from common (English) law and Shari'a law, notwithstanding the refinements that it went through under colonial rule and in the process of codification. Such indigenous formations, which, from what has been said, can rarely be found in a *pure* form, will, as much as possible, be emphasized in characterizing the "traditional." To go back to Ekeh's useful classification, it is the transformed *indigenous* social structure (including nontransformed indigenous social structure, where it can be found), rather than the migrated and emergent social structure, that should be searched for traditional conflict management strategies.

Traditional Strategies of Conflict Management in Africa

Insights into conflict management in traditional African societies and the strategies they involved are provided mainly by the works of the anthropologists and historians who have studied several groups in different parts of the continent (notable examples include Beattie 1960; Bohannan 1957; Bohannan and Bohannan 1953; Evans-Pritchard 1940; Fadipe 1970; Fortes and Evans-Pritchard 1940; Gluckman 1955, 1963; Latham 1973; Little 1967; Mair 1962; Nadel 1942; Nader and Todd 1978; Offiong 1989; Nader 1994; Schapera 1943).

The various studies show that notwithstanding the differences in sociopolitical organization and levels of development, the nature of conflicts and the strategies devised to deal with them in traditional African societies present striking similarities. These similarities are attributable to the common social formations in the societies that derive from what is popularly called a preliterate worldview or thought system. With regard to religion, for example, Busia (1967, 4) points out that "it is possible to discern common religious ideas and assumptions about the universe held throughout Africa, and which provide a world view that may be described as African." The main differences, in terms of the needs and nature of conflict management, generally follow Fortes and Evans-Pritchard's (1940) classification of traditional polities into centralized (or state) systems and noncentralized (or stateless) systems:

> In [centralized systems], it is a balance between different parts of the administrative organization. The forces that maintain the supremacy of the paramount ruler are opposed by the forces that act as a check on his powers. . . . A different kind of balance is found in [noncentralized states]. It is an equilibrium between a number of segments, spatially juxtaposed and structurally equivalent, which are defined in local and lineage, not in administrative terms. . . . Divergence of interests between the component segments is intrinsic to the political structure. . . . The stabilizing factor is not a superordinate juridical or military organization, but is simply the sum total of inter-segment relations. (Fortes and Evans-Pritchard, 1940, 11, 14)

By their very natures, then, political conflicts tended to be more prevalent in the more egalitarian and open noncentralized systems than in centralized systems. In spite of the differences arising from political organization, the basic elements of conflict management, as already indicated, were quite similar. These similarities will be the focus of our characterization and discussion of traditional systems of management.

Management is related to the nature of conflicts. The applicability of traditional strategies to modern conflicts is determined, among other factors, by the extent to which the nature of modern conflicts can be shown to be similar or comparable to conflicts in traditional societies. If, indeed, as authors like Bozeman (1976) have tried to show, modern conflicts are a direct consequence or continuation of past formations and tendencies, then traditional strategies may be more relevant to managing modern conflicts than we have been willing to acknowledge.

Anthropological accounts generally paint a conflict-endemic picture of African traditional society, especially those of the noncentralized genre. Such terms and phrases as "feuding," "internecine wars," "tribal wars," "regicide," "fear- and death-inducing conflicts," and "inherent civil wars" have been devised to underline this fact. The point is made that the traditional society is not only in a perpetual state of the "war of all against all," but that warring is an integral part or instrument of conflict resolution and management. Many disputes, it is said, are resolved when one faction or party vanquishes the other, through open fighting, sorcery, or some other mythical means, as in the case of dueling, through which the Lugbara of Uganda resolved family disputes (Middleton 1966). Hence Gluckman (1963, 87–90) regards the incessant civil wars that arose from interunit conflicts and succession disputes among the Zulus of South Africa as unifying civil wars. Not only were cleavages an aspect of the integration of the political system; he also asserts that the nation could be stable only if its component sections were hostile.

It would, however, be mistaken to conclude on this basis that conflict was the original condition of traditional society in Africa as some authors have done (see Bozeman 1976). To begin with, there was something of a simplistic stereotype (of the African "savage") that guided most of the anthropological studies. When this is put alongside the Western precepts that underlay the studies and led the authors to distorted accounts when structures akin to those of familiar western judicial and administrative processes could not be found, then it is easy to appreciate the exaggerations and oversimplifications that characterize some of the anthropological works. As Bretton (1958, 47–48) noted long ago, "the overly zealous application to underdeveloped areas of research methods derived from experience in advanced, highly developed countries, leads to the promulgation of wholly unrealistic theories" (also see Lofchie 1968).

In addition, anthropological studies have generally tended to ignore or undermine external factors, specifically relations with European and Arab traders and colonizers, in analyzing the so-called warring state of African traditional societies. Because of this, slavery and slave trade, the introduction and massive supplies of weapons of mass destruction, *divide et impera* policies, colonial wars and conquests, the violent processes of imposition of the colonial state and economy, and the subsequent elaboration of institutions and practices of violence—military, police, prisons, forced labor, and so on—all of which instigated or exacerbated and perpetuated extant and latent conflicts and are therefore crucial to any attempt to understand the nature of conflicts in traditional societies, have often been underplayed. As I have argued elsewhere (Osaghae 1995), external interferences and interventions have historically constituted "the fire behind the smoke" in ethnic and other political conflicts in Africa, and accordingly deserve to be emphasized in the analysis of aggravated conflicts. In particular, the arms trade and supplies that have since the late sixteenth century transformed the nature of conflicts in various parts of Africa to unprecedented levels of violence, and the complicity of competing foreign powers in conflict situations, need to be factored into explanations of conflict in traditional societies.

Despite these flaws in analysis, anthropological and historical accounts suggest that the nature of conflicts in traditional societies was in consonance with their levels of precapitalist development, and that, by their very nature, the so-called internal wars were part of the "natural" process of conflict resolution. Gluckman (1955), for example, points out that the hostility that underlay feuding created a sort of balance (of terror?) that prevented perpetual open fighting. Besides, succession disputes or lineage feuds that were said to be the main sources of conflicts did not occur all the time. Moreover, conflicts among individuals, lineages, clans, segments, and units of empire-states over socioeconomic and political benefits and privileges are not abnormal. Stedman's (1991b, 367–368) point about modern conflicts in Africa is equally applicable to conflicts of old: "Conflict in Africa arises from problems basic to all populations: the tugs and pulls of different identities, the differential distribution of resources and access to power, and competing definitions of what is right, fair or just." The manner of the conflicts—so-called wars and feuds—was a function of the nature of the political systems, especially the nature of political competition and succession to power, as well as the role of external actors.

If conflict seemed to be endemic to the social fabric, this has to be understood as a consequence of the organic character of traditional African society (this is apart from the disastrous effects of external influences pointed to earlier). The importance attached to kinship and lineage often meant that conflicts of a particularist nature, including individual conflicts, had the potentials of involving the whole society, segment, clan, or village. This organic character also explains the social fabric approach to resolving conflicts evident in the emphasis on consensus on law and morals, conciliation, and reinforcement of solidarity in juridical and mediation practices. Even assuming that traditional African society was so conflict-ridden, it must be taken as a mark of the efficacy of conflict management techniques (even if, as it is said, these sometimes involved more conflict) that the societies survived and were stable. This then could also be taken as a justification for examining traditional strategies, especially if modern conflicts that, by the same token, could be regarded as pervasive, are similar to those of the past.

The sources of conflicts in traditional societies were varied and complex. At the micro level, individual, family, and lineage disputes usually ensued from personal differences and quarrels, marital problems, rituals, day-to-day competition for scarce resources such as the right to land for farming, grazing, and settlement. At the macro level, conflicts involved the constituent units of the polity: states in the case of centralized systems and segments, clans, and villages in noncentralized systems. The pattern and range of conflicts oscillated between the different levels especially in noncentralized systems producing what has been termed a system of segmentary opposition or movement between fusion and fission in which conflicting parties at the subunit level are united against another unit at a higher level, but fall back to local conflicts once the level of relations change. The archetype of this pattern of conflicts is the Nuer system of feuding (see Evans-Pritchard 1940). The commonest sources of conflicts at the macro level included succession disputes and power struggles among the units and claimants to power (claimants were usually sons of late kings, members of rival royal homes among which power rotated, or simply usurpers).

In terms of the struggles for power, which is said to have been the most prevalent source of political conflicts, Gluckman talks of a "rebellious structure" of traditional polities:

> The possibility of rebellion is something that king, subordinate rulers, and subjects have to take into account all the time. Thus, we have to see rebellion as an ever present, persistent process influencing day-to-day political relations. . . . There is always the likelihood of some section breaking out and seeking independence, either because it is too weak to attack the king or because the king's party may flee after defeat. (1963, 36)

Despite the exaggeration in calling rebellion a persistent process, Gluckman makes the point that the struggle for power, whether at the individual level or the level of polities, was at the core of political conflicts in traditional societies. The same is of course true of modern political conflicts, even though the magnitude and intensity of these conflicts are more expansive. A description of tendencies in modern African states—applicable to the United States, Britain, France, Russia, or any polity—closely resembles that of Gluckman's above:

> The internal policies of African states are pragmatic . . . not only because the leadership is subject to sudden changes, but also because each African leader . . . has the implicit yet uncertain mandate to modify his programs so that he may stay in power, defy, defeat, or inactivate opponents, and forestall or manage feuds and conflicts as they arise. (Bozeman 1976, 28)

The first characteristic of traditional systems is that, like other strands of the preliterate traditional heritage, conflict management is experiential and undocumented. Bozeman (1976, 228) tells us that traditional forms of conflict management in Africa emanate from "established social practice" and "are therefore comprehensive references, virtually synonymous with the entirety of social life." The systems manifest in, and are propagated and preserved through, folklore, songs, rituals and other cultural and religious practices, sculpture and other art forms, and, in advanced forms, specific juridical institutions (see Otite 1978; Ayoade and Agbaje 1988). The Tiv of Nigeria, for example, have a system of "drumming the scandal," in which disputants, mostly neighboring patrilineal kinsmen, trade allegations in songs to each other's hearing. This often led to fighting, and whoever emerged victorious, won the dispute. The survival and presence of such abstract and mythical traditional formations in modern civil society has recently been described in terms of the concept of "infra politics," that is, the more hidden social formations that are consequential for politics in modern society (Scott 1990; also Fatton 1995).

Another characteristic that is also explicable in terms of the preliterate heritage is the mix or diffusion of conflict management systems in religious, social, cultural, and political practices. Most conflict management practices are ensconced in rituals and other religious observances, customs, spirit mediums, witchcraft, secret society activities, and so on. Mediators usually derive their authority from religious roles and functions, old age, or other distinctive personal qualities or claims. Among the Nuer, for example, a person called "man of the earth," who was basically a religious figure, could sometimes stop two disputing parties from fighting by threatening to curse them by the earth. The roles of secret societies, with their mythical and ritual powers, exercised through masks and masquerades, in conflict mediation have also been well documented (see Offiong 1989). The Poro society, which played a major role in resolving disputes among the Mende of Sierra Leone and several groups in Liberia, "instilled general awe of a religious kind, and derived its power entirely through the intercourse which its senior officials claimed to have with the world of spirits. They impersonated the latter with the aid of masks and other paraphernalia" (Little 1967, 183).

Another characteristic of traditional strategies was that they were localized and particularistic. This does not contradict the point made earlier that traditional conflict management systems were similar. While broad principles and inclinations were basically the same, the institutional manifestations and practices took on different forms as dictated by ecological factors, population density, political organization, economic relations, and so on. It is these institutional manifestations that were localized, based on the village and clan, the basic units of social organization in both centralized and noncentralized systems. In many cases, groups of proximate clans, villages, and smaller units linked by kinship and linguistic ties, or, as was more often the case, as subunits of a larger polity, shared similar management practices (this is the sense in which references are made to the Nupe, Tiv, Zulu, Nuer, and other peoples). Still there was no management strategy that was as widespread as, for example, the Swahili and Hausa languages, which spread through vast areas of the continent. Even supposedly powerful empires and kingdoms simply lacked the technology and manpower to extend dominant practices throughout their constituent units and vassal states. This characteristic has far-reaching implications for any attempt to apply traditional strategies to modern conflicts because, as we point out below, the particularistic nature of traditional strategies makes the adoption of any of the strategies likely to arouse suspicions of ethnic domination and hegemony in the multiethnic postcolonial state.

Traditional conflict management was often hinged on an intricate balance of interests—among the constituent units of a polity, contestants to power, factions, various institutions including women's organizations, age grade, and secret societies. The way in which the balance of forces worked to prevent conflicts and ensure peace and social order has been described thus:

> Peace arises from the existence of many kinds of relationships, and the values attached to them all by custom. These ties divide men at one point; but this division in a wider group and over a longer period of time leads to the establishment of social order. . . . In this way custom unites where it divides, cooperation and conflict balancing each other (Gluckman 1955, 23).

Stated in such terms, the balance in traditional societies is analogous to the balances among different groups in civil society that sustain modern liberal democracies referred to by students of pluralism, crosscutting memberships and loyalties of the various groups and all.

Conscious of the possible criticism of oversimplification (after all, countries like Nigeria that have complex differentiations at all levels experience complex conflicts, though the focus here is on much smaller societies and groups), Gluckman is quick to point out that divided loyalties are not always in themselves sufficient to prevent disputes or social dislocation, not least because, as he says, loyalties and interests are hardly so beautifully balanced. Nevertheless, "The greater the division in one area of society, the greater is likely to be the cohesion in a wider range of relationships—provided that there is a general need for peace, and a recognition of a moral order in which this peace can flourish" (Gluckman 1955, 25).

The overall principle was to forestall the concentration of power in the hands of one or a few individuals or political units and ensure that none of the conflicting parties was unduly disadvantaged. Some legal anthropologists indeed point to the plurality of norms among the diverse units of a polity such as the Tswana of Botswana studied by Comaroff and Roberts (1977, 1981) that permits the construction of alternative and competing realities to be advanced by parties to a dispute, as being supportive of resolution. Paul Francis (1984, 81) has elaborated how this works:

> While access to political office is apparently governed by ascriptive rules, the way in which subsidiary norms overlay and qualify the primary ones allows flexibility in the construction of claims, giving rival candidates the rhetorical means to advance their own claims and gainsay those of others, and making access to political office in reality a competitive process.

At the more general level, the checks and balances that served to prevent the abuse of power held in trust by the king and exercised only in the name of the community, as well as the famous feuding system in acephalous societies that involved a complex "warring" of factions or units in such a way that none got much more powerful than the rest, are some of the ways in which the balancing principle was upheld.

Another important characteristic of traditional conflict management, which derived from the organic solidarity of the societies referred to earlier, was the emphasis placed on value consensus and social cohesion as essential elements of conflict prevention. Management of conflicts, especially the judgments entailed in dispute mediation, had an important social function—to reassert and cement the bonds of unity that were perceived to be threatened by conflict. Thus, judgments were not simply about determining who was right or wrong or apportioning blame; they were more about conciliation and trying to ensure that the predisposing or propelling factors for conflict were eliminated if possible. At the widest range, Gluckman (1955, 23) tells us that "cohesion [was] stated in ritual terms—supported by mystical retribution—where values [were] unquestioned and axiomatic. Hence ritual reconciliation and sacrifice often follow[ed] the settlement of a quarrel, and ritual methods [were] used to reach adjustment."

Value consensus complemented social cohesion. In fact, consensus on the meaning of good, bad, just, unjust, acceptable, reprehensible, and so on, which was itself a product of shared history, customs, and kinship ties among others, was sine qua non for conflict management, especially the settlement of disputes. The emphasis on consensus can be seen in the famous "elders' meetings" held under trees, public or village assemblies, and other gatherings that dealt with serious conflicts in the (village) community. These meetings, examples of which are the "palaver hut" meetings of the Vai and Kpelle peoples of Liberia and the *Kgotla* of the Tswana (Peters 1984), which revolved around the chief, who served as spokesman of consensus, did not end until consensus was reached on how to resolve conflicts. Thus, mediation involved negotiations to arrive at settlement acceptable to conflicting parties. Furthermore, judgments were usually based on the customs of the people, and those delivering them—third-party arbitrators—were expected to know not only the issues in contention but also how to apply customary law to resolve them. This was in addition to being highly respected men (and women in some cases) of high status and influence. The Oromo of Ethiopia had a specially designated chief arbiter under the Gada age-grade system who arbitrated disputes between leaders of the Gada system on the one hand and wealthy landowners on the other, as described in the chapter by Tuso. The Amhara also had a similar setup for resolving disputes over land ownership (Bozeman 1976, 266).

At higher levels, say at the courts of kings and chiefs, mediation involved the king, who was regarded as the custodian of customs assisted by his advisers, elders and assistants who were themselves highly knowledgeable in the customs and ensured that decisions were not taken that were contrary to the norms. Moreover,

> The ideals of office required that the leader should be impartial and judge or act without bias, that he be wise in applying the general rules of law justly to the particular circumstances of dispute. Above all, he had to have the courage to take a decision and face the possible dislike, or even anger, of those who lost by his decision. (Gluckman 1955, 36)

Consensus was not always guaranteed, however. Sometimes, mediations were rejected by one or more of the parties in conflict because they were not based on correct interpretations of customs. At such times, further and wider consultations involving higher (temporal and spiritual) authorities, enlarged elders' councils, secret societies, rituals, and the like, were called for, and judgments reached had to be accepted in the overall interests of the community. In more serious cases like rebellion, invasion of territory, and violent struggles to be king where consensus was far-fetched or, where it was not, where one of the disputants remained intransigent, few options existed besides open fighting and war.

The foregoing presents, in broad outline, the essential elements of conflicts and conflict management in traditional African societies. In the section that follows, we come to the central concern of this chapter: How applicable are traditional systems and strategies of conflict management to modern conflicts in Africa?

■ Limits and Possibilities of Applying Traditional Strategies

For proponents of contextual conflict management, who seem to have received a great boost from the failure of conventional peacekeeping operations in Somalia and Rwanda, there can be no question about the relevance of traditional practices and the need to incorporate them into mainstream conflict management strategies. An examination of the larger question of the relevance of traditional thought systems and institutions to modern times (Osaghae 1989) leads to the conclusion that notwithstanding the phenomenal transformations of African societies and the introduction of new state structures and (peripheral) capitalist formations, traditional thought and institutions provide a necessary backdrop for present political practices and can as such be selectively put to positive use. Making a similar point, the historian Afigbo (1986) argues that the relevance of the African past can be assured only when historians succeed in reconstructing a *usable* and *problem-solving-oriented* past rather than ferreting out facts and more facts about a glorious Africa of old. That he says is both the poverty and challenge of African historiography. In other words, as much of what is said to be traditional is invented, the "traditional" can be constructed in such a way as to give prominence to the most expedient and positive aspects, while discarding, if possible, the negative aspects of the past.

It can be argued that traditional means of dealing with conflicts are mainly applicable to, and useful in, resolving simple disputes: matrimonial disputes, intrafamily quarrels, land disputes, and the like, which are not as complex or threatening as the conflicts of national and even supranational proportions. This argument underestimates the volatility of so-called simple conflicts that can quickly degenerate to involve most groups in the community because of the organic character of traditional communities. One lesson to be learned from the social fabric approach to conflicts and their management that characterizes traditional management in Africa is that simple and larger scale or complex conflicts are actually two sides of the same coin and mutually reinforcing. Consequently, resolution of day-to-day conflicts helps to ensure the stability needed for the prevention or resolution of more serious and expansive ones—in short, resolution of more serious conflicts is impossible without management of less serious conflicts at the lower levels.

A good example of this was the resolution of the crisis in the eastern regional branch of the National Council of Nigerian Citizens, one of the major political parties of colonial and immediate postcolonial Nigeria, that threatened the constitutional order in the country in 1952 and 1953, through recourse to the Igbo *Igbandu* system, under which the party leaders swore on oath to be loyal to Nnamdi Azikiwe. Besides, experience gained from familiarity with resolving conflicts at lower levels is always found useful at higher levels of engagement, which probably explains the preference of the warlords in Liberia for reconciliatory bodies headed and composed mainly by chiefs and other traditional authorities. But usefulness is a function of ultimate goals—reconciliation versus dominance—which explains the severe attitudes of warlords to local conflict management mechanisms in southern Somalia, as reported by Menkhaus in the preceding chapter.

Attempts have indeed been made to apply traditional strategies of conflict management to modern conflicts of a more complex nature at national levels with varying degrees of success. Examples include the centrality of the Baganda kingdom to the resolution of political conflicts in Uganda, the statutory involvement of traditional rulers in conflict management bodies at the local, state, and federal levels in Nigeria, and the attempts by the post-apartheid government of South Africa to employ the good offices of the king of Zululand to resolve the violent conflicts in the KwaZulu/Natal Province. One of the most recent of these, which has become the standard reference point, is the role played by clan elders in reconciling warring factions in northern Somalia, as noted by Menkhaus. At several points in the Liberian civil war, traditional rulers were involved in the search for peace along the lines of the famous "palaver hut" reconciliatory meetings. Although this had limited success, there is no doubt that the intervention of traditional leaders, with all the mythical powers they are assumed to have, made negotiations among the warlords possible.

On the other hand, there seem to be serious and even insurmountable obstacles to the application of traditional strategies to modern conflicts. These limits derive for the most part from the characteristics of conflict management in traditional societies as discussed in the previous section. The first of these is that management strategies were localized and particularistic, and that in spite of the similarities and common assumptions they involved, few, if any, strategies were generalized beyond local boundaries. The absence of a generalized model of conflict management may indeed be regarded as one of the weaknesses of traditional systems, but this does not prevent us from elaborating on and extending successful models if some of the difficulties discussed below can be overcome. In the alternative, a wholly new and eclectic model, built from composite elements of various relevant models, can be constructed, as is suggested in the concluding section of this paper.

In the postcolonial period, traditional conflict management strategies remain localized, although the exigencies of colonial rule necessitated the generalization of practices among enlarged ethnic groups. This was how, for example, the Ogboni society, which was originally Oyo, became a Yoruba institution, extending to the Egba, Ekiti, Ibadan, and so on. In effect, the strategies remain located in ethnic groups and this, in the circumstances of intense ethnic rivalry in African states, makes the adoption of one strategy more likely to be seen as a continuation of ethnic hegemony (especially where the strategy adopted comes from the ethnic group of the incumbent head of state). Forster (1994) points to the experience of Malawi where President Banda's so-called cultural nationalism was seen by many as an attempt to perpetuate the domination of his Chewa group. In circumstances like this, the adoption of supposedly traditional strategies of conflict management is more likely to worsen and exacerbate, rather than ameliorate, political conflicts.

The relevance and applicability of traditional strategies have been greatly disenabled by the politicization, corruption, and abuse of traditional structures, especially traditional rulership, which have steadily *delegitimized* conflict management built around them in the eyes of many, and reduced confidence in their efficacy. Kofele-Kale's (1981) finding from his Cameroonian study that most people in urban and rural areas prefer modern-judicial approaches—courts, police, and gendarmerie—to customary-traditional approaches in resolving disputes, is reflective of this growing tendency. The co-optation of traditional rulers as agents of the state, and their manipulation to serve partisan ends, which dates back to colonial times, not to mention the corruption of modern traditional rulers, have considerably reduced the reverence and respect commanded by this institution and, therefore, the ability of traditional rulers to resolve conflicts.

To take an interesting example, attempts by the African National Congress (ANC)-led government of national unity in South Africa to employ the good offices of the king of Zululand in resolving the violent wars in the KwaZulu Province of the country had very limited success because of fears by the Zulu-based opposition Inkatha Freedom Party (IFP) that the king supported the ANC and was being used by the party. A similar situation exists in Nigeria, where successive governments, but especially military governments that lack grass-roots support, have struggled to keep traditional rulers (labeled as "fathers of the nation") on their payrolls as mobilizers of support. This has obliterated the perceived neutrality of these rulers, which was a crucial requirement in their traditional conflict resolving roles, in the eyes of opposition groups. Even in cases of land dispute where, being the traditional custodians of land, traditional authorities are the key arbitrators, their neutrality has been compromised by their miscarriage of justice in favor of those offering the highest payoffs or bribes.

The limit placed by localization is reinforced by the fact that modern states in Africa, with the diverse groups that compose them, do not have the common moral and customary order on which conflict management is hinged in the traditional society (a similar point is made by Gluckman [1955] in his consideration of the possibility of applying Nuer feuding strategy to resolving international conflicts). The experience of Somalia, whose uniethnic situation was for a long time regarded as a recipe for unity, peace, and stability, has demonstrated the whole point about localization and absence of a moral order: national consensus was difficult precisely because of the interclan differences reinforced, as they were, by religious cleavages. It was even more difficult to find common grounds for reconciling the warlords from diverse groups who were the major actors in the conflicts in Liberia, Sudan, Somalia, Sierra Leone, and so on—the Charles Taylors and Alhaji Kromahs, John Garangs, Farah Aideeds, and Foday Sankohs. This in turn points to another area where traditional conflict management systems had shortcomings, since contests for power were often only resolved through splitting the polity and vanquishing the rivals.

Finally, the expansive nature of modern conflicts also limits the extent to which traditional strategies can be applied. Although most present-day conflicts, like those in traditional society, center on struggles for power and succession disputes among powerful individuals and groups, the wide range of actors and forces, including external ones, as well as the national and sometimes regional scope of the conflicts, render expedient traditional strategies inadequate. This partly explains why the traditional strategies applied in northern Somalia have had only limited success. The same can be said for Liberia, Sierra Leone, Burundi, Rwanda, Uganda, and Angola, where the involvement of peacekeeping forces and other foreign interests has removed the primary responsibility for resolution from the domestic arena.

■ Conclusion

The challenge remains to construct an eclectic model of conflict management that draws from common values and perceptions of conflict and its management all over Africa, and that incorporates various relevant and time-tested strategies as a possible way of overcoming most of the limitations identified above. This is a necessity if Africans themselves have not only to play a more active role in the resolution of their own conflicts but also to contribute to the growing demand for more creative models of management all over the world. Important ingredients for formulating more comprehensive and expedient traditional strategies that are relevant to the circumstances of modern conflicts—in the manner of inventing traditions—abound in the various anthropological and historical works. These could then be pieced together (there is of course nothing that prevents us from updating empirical knowledge beyond the classical accounts of colonial anthropology—in fact we should do so) to construct what would essentially be an African model of conflict management. The common assumptions that underlie and guide conflict management systems in traditional societies provide a necessary first step in this regard.

A significant development in this regard is the formulation of the philosophy of *ubuntu* by black scholars and activists in South Africa, as discussed in the chapter by Nomonde Masina. *Ubuntu,* according to its exponents, summarizes the philosophy that underlies governance, including conflict management, in traditional African society. Its central organizing principles are trust and sharing, especially popular participation in decisionmaking, which go to the very heart of the organic solidarity of traditional society (see Sindane n.d.; Khoza 1994; and Vilakazi 1991). In these terms, *ubuntu* is similar to formulations of African socialism in the 1960s. The (re)construction of *ubuntu* is still in its early stages and, like Nyerere's *ujamaa* and other earlier attempts to invent traditional social formations, its formulation is still far from coherent or even clear. But it has generally been well received as a potentially authentic African contribution to the theory and practice of democratic governance, and some criticism of being too basic and simplistic to meet the challenges of complex organization and conflicts can be met through further elaboration. Whatever the responses to it may be, *ubuntu* is an example of how traditional systems could be reconstructed to serve the needs of present-day requirements of conflict management.

14

Conclusions: Changes in the New Order and the Place for the Old

I. William Zartman

War and peace, and the skills they require, are positive values in African societies, as in all others. They have to be: they are the means of survival. War is the ultimate means. African societies defend themselves against neighboring societies' warring, and war against neighbors' defenses. They repress dissidence in their midst and put down the rebels who rise up against them. Manhood means becoming a warrior and is associated with youth. Idealized claims to the contrary, in this imperfect world no society lives by peace alone, in Africa or elsewhere: there are things worth fighting for, not the least of which is the right to determine one's own destiny as a society. Some African countries had to fight for their independence, the others receiving their sovereignty before fighting became necessary, and segments of some of these states now fight to control them or secede from them, to make sure that their destiny is in their own hands.

Yet war is dangerous, inefficient, and, in the end, contradictory as a way to assure survival. It is much more effective if threats can be disarmed or deterred, escalation prevented, and conflict managed. War does not make sense against oneself; societies do not survive on suicide. War may well destroy the values it is mobilized to preserve while seeking to enhance them, whereas conflict management and prevention have less chance of doing so. Maturity means becoming a man or a woman to make peace and is associated with leadership. Peace remains the eternal ideal, the condition of heaven if not of earth, the goal for which even wars are fought. It is better to achieve peace by making and keeping it than by seeking it through war.

War and peace in common parlance are unequal terms: war is a means of pursuing a policy (von Clausewitz 1832/1968), whereas peace is a condition or situation. Hence the semantic uncertainties in defining peace and the resigned consensus on a default definition of peace as the absence of war. Instead, both should be seen as processes or strategies of achieving goals, the one by violent and the other by nonviolent means. Minimum goals are variously termed system maintenance, survival, stability, or security, in the language of various disciplines, but the implications of these terms are often misleadingly static or too conservative to be real. The challenge of such processes and strategies is to deal with change, whether it comes from new and different conditions in the world or from specific threats from within or without. Change, present or threatened, can be dealt with defensively or accommodatively, but the effectiveness of either effort depends to a large extent on the magnitude of the change compared with one's own capacities. Thus, conflict management practices need to be considered not just in and of themselves but in relation to the degree of change to which they respond, the magnitude of the conflict between the established order—its relations and its values—and the challenge to it.

Therefore, any society will seek means to maintain its existence and coherence by reinforcing community, whether this effort is called return to equilibrium or restoration of harmony or management of conflict. The terms and concepts that have been used to identify the components of this function often overlap—institutions, structures, hierarchies, values, among others—and have occasioned an enormous literature, often marked by feisty internal debates. The essence of these concepts, however, can be categorized into two major parameters, one referring to the relations, "place," structures, and institutions of order (including the behaviors within those relations, structures, and institutions), and the other referring to the values of order (including the values given to the relations, structures, and institutions). Conflict management can be analyzed and evaluated in regard to the two categories of relations and values.

■ Africa and Conflict Management Practices

Many of the practices associated with traditional African conflict management are classical mediation, or negotiation with a third-party catalyst, within a particularly strong integrative spirit. The process falls under the standard analysis of negotiation, direct or mediated; the distinguishing African characteristic is the positive-sum integrative thrust of the practices. There is a focus on reconciling the interests of all the contestants as noted by Uwazie, in a manner reminiscent of de Callières' (1716/1963, 100) famous injunction that "the secret of negotiation is to harmonize the interests of the parties concerned." Thus, even when the conflict involves a member against his or her society, there is an emphasis on recuperation and reinsertion of the errant member back into its place in society. The recovery of a dissident member can just as well be seen as the restoration of the harmony and integrity of the community, as the assertion of value consensus and social cohesion, as recorded by Tuso and Fred-Mensah, so that the management of the conflict favors the concerns of both parties.

Integration also operates on the negative side; if blame can be apportioned among the parties, then the recuperation of the member is a more evenhanded process, as recorded in Francis Deng's chapter. Society too bears its responsibility for the defection of its members, often ignoring preventive actions that could earlier have been taken to obviate the impending conflict; similarly, if the conflict is between members of society, provocation, inattention, and selfishness can all mitigate the one-sidedness of blame in the affair. Shared responsibility for the conflict becomes the basis for shared responsibility for the resolution.

There is a revealing similarity between these conceptions and treatment of intracommunity conflict and those of personal psychosis, or between social and mental illness in Africa (Ahyi 1997). "The culprit is perceived as the victim and in this capacity, is taken charge of by the group. What purpose would it have served to spell out the crude fact of the crime? A crude denomination, a positive designation of reality can lead to a deadlock, whereas a symbolic clothing could conversely allow preservation of social cohesion" (Hountondji 1997, 29). The African "model does accept responsibility for madness [conflict]. The mad person is taken over, reintegrated into the traditional milieu, brought back into the social fold; he lives together with others. His statements are understood, experienced, accepted. Where necessary, purification rituals are performed. The other [Western] model leaves the mad person on his own. He is accused, subjected to treatment" (Ahyi 1997, 229).

Thus, the mediator seeks a formula for an agreement—a common definition of the problem and the solution or a shared sense of justice to govern the solution (Zartman and Berman 1982)—that can define the terms of trade and serve as the basis for a positive-sum agreement between the parties, as noted by Fred-Mensah and Tuso. Cultivating and then working on the offender's desire for reintegration and society's desire for restored harmony, order, and justice, the mediator brings the two parties together in an outcome that meets both parties' interests. It is not the operation of the mediation process that is unusual in dealing with conflicts but its application to cases of breach of society's rules of conduct.

Nonetheless, the instances reported indicate a mixture between the reconciling equal-party type of negotiation and the administration of justice. Parties did not "plea-bargain" in the search for equal treatment, where the parties play outcomes against probabilities and a reduced sentence is bargained against the cost, inconvenience, and uncertainty of a trial, a concession/convergence process over the sentence itself (Williams 1996). In the African mediations, the sentence is nested within an integrative set of payoffs concerning the reinsertion of the offender back into the community and its values. Justice is very much part of the exercise, but as a compensation for loss, not as a retribution for offense.

In African traditional practices, sentence and reintegration are joined together by a third element, atonement. Conflicting parties recognize the error and consequences of their conflict and seek a return to the normalcy of the community. Conflicts are managed by the community, which makes a settlement of disputes the condition for reintegration of the parties, whether their conflict is directly with the community or indirectly so by the fact that they have breached the community's peaceful order with their dispute. Thus, they need to recognize their disruption and seek forgiveness for it. In these terms, the sentence is literally a settling of accounts, not a punishment. The most notable expression of this spirit is the blood money or *dia*-paying practice, but the same spirit underlies conflict management in other areas, as noted by Masina, Kouassi, and Uwazie. Whether crimes or accidents, conflicts are settled by compensation of a symbolically equivalent amount, which then is recognized to have restored order to the community. That recognition is two-sided: acceptance by the aggrieved party depends on acceptance—that is, atonement—by the aggressor.

The process of reconciliation can take the form of arbitration or negotiation, as well as mediation. In traditional African mediation, the agent is a neutral and powerless third party, armed with personal characteristics such as wisdom and integrity but without the means for providing inducements and sanctions—a moral mediator rather than a mediator with muscle, or in more standard terms, a mediator as formulator but not as manipulator (Touval and Zartman 1985; Zartman and Touval 1996). The mediator functions much as an ombudsman, intervening between authority and citizen, tempering justice with mercy and sentences with reintegration, as noted by Kouassi, Deng, and Tuso. Thus the mediator seems to have functioned mostly in direct conflicts between the community and a member, but also including a "reversed" situation of a conflict between an authority and the community.

At least as characteristic of African traditional conflict management methods is the use of arbitration or adjudication (Bilder 1997; Kressel and Pruitt 1989). Here the reconciliation function is practiced by an authority figure who mediates between conflicting parties but is empowered to make binding judgments. The purpose is not to render a judgment in law but to reconcile the conflicting parties and reintegrate the offender in the community and its norms. It is important to note, however, that the authority figures rarely acts alone but generally in council; in fact, some accounts emphasize that the king would be acting illegitimately if he exercised his authority without benefit of a council of elders or advisers with ties to the community and even to the conflicting parties. The space between the authority and the community is cushioned by community representatives who counsel authority.

Where there is no authority, the same reconciliation is accomplished by negotiation. This situation obtains in a number of different settings—within community relations where civil society handles its own conflicts without appeal to authority (Masina), in segmentary and other acephalic societies where central authority is absent and component units handle their relations between each other (Deng), or in intercommunity or interstate conflicts where the parties' sovereignty excludes any superior authority (Kouassi). Like arbitration, negotiation in African traditional conflict management is carried out by groups or councils representing the parties; the parties do not negotiate on their own behalf, but their representatives are in a higher position of authority. These groups collectively bear responsibility for the act of their member and collectively help to provide the compensation. Once again, the contestants are cushioned in the management of their conflict.

Even in negotiation, the parties appear to be operating to some extent within a recognized order and relationship and under a normative set of expectations. When operating within a community, whether independent or in place of a central authority, they observe and reinforce the norms and relations of the community. "The root notion of communitarian thought is that value stems from the community, that the individual finds meaning in life by virtue of his or her membership of a political community" (Brown 1992, 11). Or, in Masina's and Faure's terms, *Sumus, ergo sum* (We are, therefore I am). Even when operating between communities, the parties implicitly recognize a certain normative modus operandi that tells them what to do and what to expect, without which they would be unable to establish compensation. Such negotiations serve to reestablish relations, even if these are not the sort that could be referred to as community; they allow segmentary oı geographic neighbors to live side by side in peace again, after the disruption occasioned by the conflict. This normative understanding not only codifies relationships; it also serves as a formula for their negotiation, leaving further negotiations to fill in the details about the amount of the compensation, extenuating circumstances, and other idiosyncracies.

A loose community system in which the members band together to deal with a deviant party, reintegrating it back into the community, has a name in international relations: it is called collective security, a system that in reality has existed only rarely in global or even regional politics (Claude 1954; Wolfers 1956). However, within the United Nations system at rare moments such as the Korean and second Gulf Wars, within the Organization of African Unity (OAU) and some of its subregional components such as the West African Economic Community (CEAO) or the East

African Inter-Governmental Authority for Development (IGAD) on numerous occasions, and occasionally within other regional systems, collective security has been practiced. The point is not to note its rarity or the impetus that African experiences could give to it, but rather to recognize that even in as loose a group of actors as a state system, collective efforts to reintegrate deviant members can be effective, both through the use of war and deterrence, and through the exercise of conflict management.

African traditional conflict management techniques embody many of the mechanisms identified in concepts about mediation, arbitration, and negotiation. This is by no means to say that these are "Western" techniques that Africans have copied. In dual ways, the African experience invalidates such ethnocentric claims. On one hand, since these techniques and mechanisms evolved through African practice before the colonial interruption, it is clear that they are African inventions. It would be just as accurate to say that Western practices and concepts are copies of African creations as the reverse. Of course neither statement is accurate. The special techniques and practices of mediation, arbitration, and negotiation have independent sources that meet only when modern communications and interactions have brought the two lines of evolution in contact with each other, to discover that theirs is a universal human activity, property of no one, and therefore of all.

On the other hand, these methods are practiced in Africa within a very integrative or positive-sum spirit, in which conflict is viewed as a disruption of the community whose integrity needs to be restored. While this may require a punishment that is on the surface indistinguishable from Western sentencing, the overall goal appears quite different. Conflict is resolved by reincluding the offending member within the community, rather than excluding the guilty party. If harmony is involved in this exercise, it is not because it is a normal condition of African society; the community may be conflict-driven and even unable to handle its internal disputes (Ahyi 1997). But—and all the more so—harmony is a normative goal of society, in some sense a universal goal, and traditional Africa methods seek to restore it by integrative, inclusionary, and conciliatory methods.

■ Conflict, Community, and Modern Challenges

It is clear that African traditional conflict management techniques depend to a large extent on the existence of a community of relationships and values to which they can refer and that provide the context for their operations. Relationships are a precondition for the effective operation of the modes of conflict management as practiced traditionally in African arbitration, mediation, and negotiation. Arbitration presupposes a hierarchical structure, marked not only by a central authority figure but also by a respected council surrounding him that in some way represents the broader community. Mediation, although conducted by a moral figure without formal power who would appear to be outside any structure, nonetheless depends on relations of respect and deference between him or her and both the ruled and the ruler; his role depends on a ruler-ruled dichotomy within which he can operate. Even in the case of direct negotiation between conflicting parties, they are held together by relationships that provide the containing context for their conflict management, either tightly as within a sociopolitical community or loosely but still present between neighbors or other interacting entities. This is not to say that anyone has some relationships if one only looks for them; to the contrary, it is to note that conflict management, traditional African style, however tenuous, depends on using or building some relational context, however tenuous.

Similarly, traditional methods depend doubly on integrative values. Such values define the positive-sum context that infuses practices with a peculiar direction, establishing the spirit of the endeavor. More precisely, they also determine what is fair and legitimate and what is expected, and so set the parameters and the perimeters for solutions.

It has often been noted, as a result, that African traditional methods essentially focused on intracommunity conflict and worked because of the support given them by the community. If that is the extent of the practices, it leaves little to learn. In the absence of or as an alternative to a highly institutionalized system of laws and courts, African communities relied on customs and norms and found survival in a reinforcement of community cohesion. At most, their practices could give rise to an interesting debate over conciliatory versus confrontational methods of maintaining community norms, or of Eastern and Western styles of negotiation (Abu-Nimer).

But more important are issues outside this debate—the operation of traditional practices in areas where a strong community relation and spirit do not exist, such as interstate and internal against-system conflicts, and the lessons that these operations could have for current practice. If the dominant image of traditional ways of dealing with conflict within communities is reconciliation, the dominant picture for interstate conflict is war (Smith 1968; Boahen 1973). The harmony and time-honed practices of reaffirming social cohesion that characterized intracommunity conflict management had no equivalent in intercommunity relations. Nonetheless, conflict management did occur on occasion in Africa, at two junctures—in ending war and, more infrequently, in preventing war. Peace agreements of both kinds, like war, presuppose the existence of organized communities to make them (Turney-High 1949, 231–237). Occasional accounts available, as pointed out in Kouassi's chapter, indicate that wars ended with the same kinds of diplomatic practices as found around the world, mixed with some other practices special to African cases such as oathing and joking, noted by Wilson-Fall and Kouassi.

Arrangements for preventing conflict appear to be less frequent, or at least less frequently recorded, as noted in Kouassi's and Deng's accounts, and are more difficult to establish because neither the commonality of values that is expected as a basis for conflict management nor the practices and relationships that are necessary for its pursuit are present. Deng's account underscores the fact that preventive diplomacy was not a normal option; it was necessary to convince both sides of the value of making and maintaining peaceful relations, as well as the terms under which they were established. The tactics used were insightful and inspiring:

- Reach out to the other side.
- Treat the furthest away as well as you treat your own.
- Serve your own people by keeping the other party satisfied.
- Take the other party's interests into account as much as your own.

These are important, positive-sum precepts that can be useful in providing lasting peaceful relationships. They are important not merely as tactical pieces of advice but as a deeper attempt to set up a pattern of values to replace the absent community that is necessary to effective traditional conflict management. Whereas in intracommunity practices the normative basis and accepted mediating agent for conflict management had already been set and the practices both use and reinforce them in intercommunity relations, the conflict management practices must establish their own normative basis while or before dealing with the conflict itself. Not all good precepts and practices would serve both purposes. Only normative principles of equality or reciprocity would put the other party on notice concerning the integrative response expected to the first party's tactics.

Thus, when traditional conflict management has been applied to intercommunity conflicts, it works by building relationships where none exist, as noted by Fred-Mensah and Wilson-Fall. Marriages, hostages, and joking were simple devices for building relationships when conflicts were on a personal level, and even the widespread use of gifts was effective in creating dependencies of indebtedness that were so important in traditional relations. When conflicting parties are not tied together by shared values and interdependence, both aspects need to be created for conflict management agreements to be more than just a punctual exercise. Building interdependencies makes it impossible for parties to walk away from each other or to renew conflict without damaging themselves.

Activities in turn require norms to govern their ongoing functions, so that a normative base is gradually grown. The effectiveness of traditional conflict management depends on the existence of a relational and value context. The point is significant and will have important ramifications, but it should not be overread: relationships permit but do not guarantee success, either momentary or durable, in conflict management. They are necessary but hardly sufficient, as relationships from nuclear family to superpower can show.

It is the third category of conflicts that eludes the experience of African traditional conflict management, the conflicts against the community. Challenges to authority are challenges to the community itself, with both the ruler and the pretender trying to mobilize the network of relationships and values behind oneself and to undo the same network arrayed behind the opponent. Such conflicts are authority-destroying as they turn against the incumbent figures and structures and seek to delegitimize them. Traditional accounts show that rebellions and contests of authority are met with repression and that the spirit of conciliation stops at the seat of the ruler, as noted by Masina, Wilson-Fall, and Deng. With one exception, nothing in African traditional practices gives any help in dealing with conflicts against the community. Yet this is the type of conflict that is most prevalent at the present time.

The only conflict prevention practice that could deal with rebellion is avoidance, a traditional African tactic that takes advantage of the communitarian context in the negative. If a strong community spirit were not present, ostracism and other separating mechanisms could not be used effectively. Separation is used both as punishment and as a means of reducing conflicting contact, as noted by Wilson-Fall and Tuso; rather than continuing to live together in friction, parties split when harmonious relations cannot be restored.

Traditional Insights and Modern Conflicts

If the point about the communitarian basis for traditional African practices has been belabored in this conclusion, it is because it is so crucial to conflict management. Its importance is visible in both the positive and the negative: present, it provides the necessary if not sufficient element in managing conflict; absent, either it must be supplied or it characterizes the type of conflicts where traditional practices were powerless. It has been seen that traditional techniques were generally the same as modern methods of arbitration, mediation, and negotiation, but that the major distinction of African conflict management has been its use of an integrative ethos based on the values and relations of the traditional community. Yet modernization in itself breaks down the tissue of traditional society, and too often the efforts of the 1960s at nation building—that is, at building a new social tissue on a broader, more inclusive scale—have led in the 1990s to negative reactions rather than positive results. As a consequence, political leaders express their solidarities and grievances in terms of ethnic identities and vie for control of their ethnic communities, mobilizing them as political—and sometimes paramilitary—armies to vie for control of the state. The result is a succession of authority-destroying conflicts, the type that traditional conflict management measures are incapable of handling.

The lesson lies in traditional Africans' answer to their own problem: Where there is no community, relations and values must be built either before or during the conflict management process. Unfortunately, traditional practices leave little guidance about how this is to be done. Even more seriously, they are not well situated to give guidance on which challenges and changes are beneficial and which are unproductively disruptive. When the harmony and values of the community are disrupted by conflict from (or between) dissident members, as in intracommunity conflict, or even when communities are disrupted by conflict between them, as in intercommunity conflict, reaffirmation of community values and relations is a helpful basis for managing conflict.

But when conflict is associated with change, merely reasserting the values of the community is no guide to action. A normative judgment is needed to evaluate the conflict, and the community values themselves may be the subject of that judgment. Conflict management in these cases is the management of change, moving the community "forward" without violence. The spirit of traditional conflict management is conservative, maintaining the status quo, an appropriate stance in an era little marked by social and political change. The modern era is radically different, for better or worse, but "better or worse" is no help in determining which conflicts need managing in the direction of the status quo and which in the direction of change. Zaire's Mobutu, Somalia's Siad Barre and then Aideed, Rwanda's Bagosora (if not Habyarimana), Burundi's Nyangoro (if not Bagaza), Kenya's arap Moi, Togo's Eyadema, among others, all manipulated notions of communitarian solidarity against long-overdue change, and their opponents' weakness lay in their inability to mobilize the values and structures of the community behind the option they provided. There is a time for justice and a time for reconciliation, and the latter is not always the crowning value. Is there anything traditional practices can tell us about dealing with change?

• Traditional practice underscores the need of the sociopolitical community to assert itself, its identity, and its control of its norms. Whether change or status quo is involved, it is important that it be achieved without violence. Control of the context of conflict puts management on the "high ground" and provides a better position to defend rather than engaging in personal confrontation. If change can be grounded in the practices of the community, it has a higher chance of being accomplished without violence and in an evolutionary manner. In Zaire, for example, had the succession to Mobutu been accomplished through the Sovereign National Conference in the early 1990s or through elections in the mid-1990s, both following national procedures and norms, the excesses of the revolutionary transfer would have been minimized.

• Communities of course do not assert themselves; they are affirmed, defended, and circumvented by their leaders. Conflict management as managed change involves mobilizing and bringing along the community leadership. The notion of cushioning leadership groups is a useful ingredient in broadening responsibility and tying in networks from political as well as civil society. The Sovereign National Conferences of Mali, Benin, Niger, and others were such cushioning coups, often very large but effective in various ways in moving the state for various distances along the path of change.

• Traditional conflict management in Africa strongly emphasizes the importance of dealing with political figures before a conflict becomes military. In traditional terms, this means leaving conflict in the hands of elders who look to develop peaceful relations and out of the hands of younger figures who want to resolve the conflict in war. The wisdom of the approach does not diminish in shifting the conflict from a traditional to a modern setting, but that wisdom is often ignored. Political leaders by their nature are more apt to make deals, come to terms, and be open to positive-sum outcomes than military leaders, and when the conflict escalates to its military stage there is a greater tendency to hold out for military victory. In reality, of course, conflict evolution is much more complex than this simple dichotomy, but the distinction remains significant.

• The ombudsman seems to be an African invention, even if better known in the West by a Scandinavian name. Familiarity with the function of *dunku,* by various names, across the continent facilitates its operation, and may help to explain the entry accorded to former officials acting as moral mediators such as Jimmy Carter, Julius Nyerere, Canaan Banana, and Mohamed Sahnoun, among others. Familiarity does not guarantee success, of course, and these mediator missions have not produced uniform results. Traditional experience shows that they need a free hand to operate, to benefit from the access that their function receives. Sahnoun's mission in 1992 was making progress in dealing with the Somali conflict but authorization from UN headquarters in New York was withdrawn and the mission aborted (Sahnoun 1994; Lyons and Samatar 1995).

Traditional conflict "medicine" was good for its era. Its successes were certainly not universal, but it did make a major contribution to the maintenance of stability and commonality in African societies. Independently of developments in other parts of the world, it invented mechanisms of negotiation, mediation, and arbitration that have become part of the universal human repertoire for dealing with conflict. However, modern-type conflicts that arise from deep sociopolitical change elude its integrative attentions, as they elude the ministrations of other contemporary diplomacy. To these, traditional experiences, derived inductively from long centuries of on-the-job learning, can at best add some insights. Given the magnitude of the challenge, they are worthy of attention.

Bibliography

Abam, A. S. (1985). "A Political History of Okrika: From the 18th Century to 1960." M.A. thesis, University of Lagos.

Abel, Richard, ed. (1982). *The Politics of Informal Justice.* 2 vols. New York and London: Academic Press.

——— (1973). "A Comparative Theory of Dispute Institutions in Society." 8 *Law & Society Review* 2.

Abir, Mordechai (1980). *Ethiopia and the Red Sea.* London: Frank Cass.

——— (1969). *Ethiopia: The Era of the Princes; The Challenge of Islam and Re-Unification of the Christian Empire, 1769–1855.* New York: Praeger Publishers.

Adewoye, O. (1977). *The Judicial System of Southern Nigeria: 1854–1954.* Atlantic Highlands, NJ: Humanities Press.

Adjanohoun, E. J., ed. (1980). *Médecine traditionnelle et pharmacopé.* Agence de coopération culturelle et technique.

Adjido, C. T. (1984). "Psychologie médicale et pratiques traditionnelles." *Revue de psychologie médicale* 6 (16): 7.

Afigbo, A. E. (1986). *The Making of Modern Africa.* New York: Longman.

Agbaje, A. (1990a). "Travails of the Secular State." *Journal of Commonwealth Studies* 28 (3).

——— (1990b). "In Search of Building Blocks: The State, Civil Society, Voluntary Action and Grassroot Development in Africa." *Africa Quarterly* 30 (3–4).

Agbese, Pita Ogaba (1996). "Ethnic Conflicts and Hometown Associations: An Analysis of the Experience of the Agila Development Association," *Africa Today* 43 (2).

Agu vs. Ikewibe (1993). 3 *Nigerian Weekly Law Reports* Prt. 180.

Ahyi, Gualbert (1997). "Traditional Models of Mental Health and Illness in Benin," in Paulin Hountondji, ed., *Endogenous Knowledge: Research Trails.* Dakar: CODESRIA.

Akinteye, Akin, James Movel Wuye, and Muhammed Nurayn Ashafa (1996). *Zagon Kataf Crisis (Kaduna State, Nigeria): A Case Study.* Report developed under the auspices of Academic Associates/SEMA Ltd., Nigeria. Sponsored by the British Council.

Albert, Isaac O., Tinu Awe, Georges Herault, and Wuyi Omitoogun (1995). *Informal Channels for Conflict Resolution in Ibadan, Nigeria.* Ibadan: Institut Francais de Recherche en Afrique.

Alier, Abel (1990). *Southern Sudan: Too Many Agreements Dishonoured.* Exeter, England: Ithaca Press.

Amadi, E. (1982). *Ethics in Nigerian Culture.* Ibadan, Nigeria.

Amir, Y. (1976). "The Role of Intergroup Contact in Change of Prejudice and Ethnic Relations," in P. A. Katz, and D. A. Taylor, eds., *Elimination of Racism: Profiles in Controversy.* New York: Pergamon.

Anderson, James (n.d.). *Islamic Law in Africa.* London: Frank Cass.

Andreski, S. (1954). *Military Organization and Society.* London: Routledge and Paul.

Arendt, Hannah (1958). *The Human Condition.* Chicago: University of Chicago Press.

Assimeng, Max (1981). "The Structure of Politics," in *Social Structure of Ghana: A Study in Persistence and Change.* Accra: Ghana Publishing Corporation.

Atsime, Georgis. (1987). *Ye Galla Tarik* [The History of the Oromo People] (two volumes). Originally written in Amharic and undated, the work was translated and edited by Báiru Tafla. Weisbaden: Franz Steiner Verlag.

Aueback, Jerold (1983). *Justice Without Law?* New York: Oxford University Press.

Avruch, Kevin (1999). *Culture and Conflict Resolution.* Washington: United States Institute of Peace.

Avruch, Kevin, et al., eds. (1991). *Conflict Resolution: Cross-Cultural Perspectives.* New York: Greenwood Press.

Ayittey, G. (1991). *Indigenous African Institutions.* Irvington-on-Hudson, NY: Transnational Publishers, Inc.

Ayoade, J. A. A., and A. A. B. Agbaje, eds. (1989). *African Traditional Political Thought and Institutions.* Lagos: CBAAC.

Ayodele, Tella (1976). "Les pratiques méducakes traditionnelles en Afrique." *Ethiopiques* no. Special 168-75 (November).

Azar, Edward E. (1990). *The Management of Protracted Social Conflict: Theory and Cases.* Brookfield, WI: Gower.

Ba, Ahmadou Hamptaté (1986). *Jaawaambe, Traditions Historiques des Peul Jaawaambe.* Centre Régional de Documentation pour la Tradition Orale (CELH-TO): Niamey, Niger.

Bacow, L., and M. Wheeler (1983). *Environmental Dispute Resolution.* New York: Plenum.

Bahrey (1954). "History of the Galla," in C. F. Beckingham and G. W. B. Huntingford, eds. and trans., *Some Records of Ethiopia, 1553–1646.* London: Hakluyat Society.

Bariso, Tadesse (1988). "Traditional Warfare Among the Guji of Southern Ethiopia." M.A. thesis, Michigan State University.

Barkan, Joel D. (1994). "Resurrecting Modernization Theory and the Emergence of Civil Society in Kenya and Nigeria," in D. E. Apter and C. G. Rosberg, eds., *Political Development and the New Realism in Sub-Saharan Africa.* Charlottesville and London: University Press of Virginia.

Barkan, Joel D., et al. (1991). *"Hometown" Voluntary Associations, Local Development, and the Emergence of Civil Society in Western Nigeria.* Nairobi, Kenya: Institute for Development Studies, University of Nairobi.

Bartel, L. (1983). *Oromo Religion, Myths and Rites of the Western Oromo of Ethiopia.* Berlin: Dietrich Reimer Veerlag.

Bates, Darrell (1979). *The Abyssinian Difficulty.* Oxford: Oxford University Press.

Bates, Robert H. (1983). "The Preservation of Order in Stateless Societies: A

Reinterpretation of Evans-Pritchard," in *Essays on Political Economy of Rural Africa.* New York: Cambridge University Press.
Baxter, Paul T. W. (1983). "The Problem of the Oromo or the Problem for the Oromo," in I. M. Lewis, ed., *Nationalism and Self-Determination in the Horn of Africa.* London: Ithaca Press.
——— (1978). "Boran Age-Sets and Generation-Sets: Gada, a Puzzle?" in Paul T. W. Baxter and Uri Almogor, eds., *Age, Generation and Times: Some Features of East African Age Organizations.* New York: St. Martin's Press.
——— (1975). "Some Consequences of Sedentarisation for Social Relationships," in T. Monod, ed., *Pastoralism in Tropical Africa.* IAI (London): Oxford University Press.
Beattie, J. (1960). *Bunyoro: An African Kingdom.* New York: Holt, Rinehart and Winston.
Bellot, Jean Marc (1980). *Kel Tamasheq du Gourma Nigerien et Peul du Torodi: Société Agro-Pastorales en Mutation (Republique du Niger).* Thèse de IIIème cycle, mars. Université de Bordeaux III, Géographie.
Bengham, G. (1985). *Resolving Environmental Disputes: A Decade of Experience.* Washington: The Conservation Foundation.
Bep, Olivier-Bever (1986). *Medicinal Plants in Intertropical Africa.* New York: Cambridge University Press.
Berkovitch, Jacob (1997). "Mediation in International Conflict," in I. William Zartman and J. Lewis Rasmussen, ed., *Peacemaking in International Conflict.* Washington: United States Institute of Peace.
———, ed. (1995). *Resolving International Conflicts: The Theory and Practice of Mediation.* Tel Aviv: Leonard Davis Institute.
Beshir, Mohamed Omer (1968). *The Southern Sudan: Background to Conflict.* London: C. Hurst and Company.
Bible Society of South Africa (1985). *Good News Bible* (Edition with Deutoronocanonicals Apocrypha).
Bilder, Richard (1997). "Adjudication," in I. William Zartman and J. Lewis Rasmussen, ed., *Peacemaking in International Conflict.* Washington: United States Institute of Peace.
Black, D., and M. Baumgartner (1978). "Self-help in Modern Society." *Law & Human Behavior* 2.
Blake, R., H. A. Shepard, and J. Mouton (1964). *Managing Intergroup Conflict in Industry.* Houston: Gulf.
Blalock, Hubert M. (1989). *Power and Conflict.* Newbury Park, CA: Sage Publications.
Boahen, Adu A. (1973). "Traditional African Diplomacy and Diplomatic Techniques." Paper submitted to the International Congress of Africanists, third Session, 9–19 December. Addis Ababa, Ethiopia.
——— (1966). *Topics in West African History.* London: Longman.
Bohannan, L., and P. J. Bohannan (1953). *The Tive of Central Nigeria.* Ethnographic Survey of Africa. London: International African Institute.
Bohannan, P. J. (1957). *Justice and Judgement among the Tiv.* London: Oxford University Press.
Bonte, P., and G. Galaty, eds. (1991). *Herders, Warriors and Traders: Pastoralism in Africa.* Boulder, CO: Westview Press.
Boutwell, Jeffrey, Michael Klare, and Laura Reed, eds. (1995). *Lethal Commerce: The Global Trade in Small Arms and Light Weapons.* Cambridge: The Committee on International Security Studies.

Bozeman, A. B. (1976). *Conflict in Africa: Concepts and Realities.* Princeton: Princeton University Press.
Bradbury, Mark (1993). *The Somali Conflict: Prospects for Peace.* Oxfam Research Paper No. 9 (October).
Bretton, Henry (1967). *The Rise and Fall of Kwame Nkrumah: A Study of Personal Rule in Africa.* New York: Praeger.
——— (1958). "Current Political Thought and Practice in Ghana." *American Political Science Review* 52 (1).
Brietzke, Paul (1982). *Law Development and the Ethiopian Revolution.* London: Bucknell.
Brown, Chris (1992). *International Relations Theory: New Normative Approaches.* New York: Columbia University Press.
Bulhan, Hussein A. (1985). *Frantz Fanon and the Psychology of Oppression.* New York: Plenum Press.
Buliyar, John Rigano (1995). "Towards Ethnography of Peace and Conflict Resolution among Pastoral Communities of Kenya." Unpublished paper for USIA-Africa Exchange Program (May).
Burton, John W. (1986). *Resolving Deep-Rooted Conflict: A Handbook.* New York and London: University Press of America.
——— (1980). "Atuot Age Categories and Marriage." *Africa* 50 (2).
——— (1969). *Conflict and Communication: The Use of Controlled Communication in International Relations.* London: Macmillan.
Burton, John W., and Frank Dukes, eds. (1990). *The Conflict Series: Resolution and Prevention; Human Needs Theory; Practices in Management, Settlement and Resolution; Readings in Management and Resolution.* New York: St. Martin's Press.
Bush, Robert, and A. Baruch (1996). "The Unexplored Possibilities of Community Mediation: A Comment on Merry and Milner." *Law and Social Inquiry* 21 (3).
Busia, K. A. (1951). *The Position of the Chief in the Modern Political System of Ashanti: A Study of the Influence of Contemporary Changes on Ashanti Political Institutions.* New York: Oxford University Press.
Bussani, Mauro (1996). "Tort Law and Development Insights from the Case of Ethiopia and Eritrea." *Journal of African Law* 40.
Cain, M. (1985). "Beyond Informal Justice." *Contemporary Crises* 9.
Canter, R. S. (1978). "Dispute Settlement and Dispute Processing in Zambia: Individual Choice Versus Societal Constraints," in Laura Nader and H. F. Todd, Jr., eds., *The Disputing Process in Ten Societies.* New York: Columbia University Press.
Capelletti, M., ed. (1978). *Access to Justice.* Vol. 4. Milan: Guifre.
Caplan, Lionel (1995). "The Milieu of Disputing: Managing Quarrels in East Nepal," in Pat Caplan, ed., *Understanding Disputes: The Politics of Argument.* Providence: Berg Publishers.
Caplan, Pat (1995). "'Law' and 'Custom': Marital Disputes on Northern Mafia Island, Tanzania," in P. Caplan, ed., *Understanding Disputes: The Politics of Argument.* Providence: Berg Publishers.
Chaliand, Gerard (1982). *The Struggles for Africa: Conflict of Great Powers.* New York: St. Martin's Press.
Chanock, Martin (1985). *Law, Custom, and Social Order: The Colonial Experience in Malawi and Sabia.* Cambridge: Cambridge University Press.
Chatterjee, Partha (1999). "Community in the East," in I. William Zartman, ed., *Concepts of Political Science.* New York: Macmillan.

Chen, D., and Guy Olivier Faure (1995). "When Chinese Companies Negotiate with Their Government." *Organization Studies* 16 (1).

Christie, P., R. Lessem, and L. Mbigi (1993). *African Management: Philosophies, Concepts and Applications.* Randburg, S.A.: Knowledge Resources (Pty) Ltd.

Clarke, Jeffrey (1993). "Debacle in Somalia: Failure of the Collective Response," in Lori Damrosch, ed., *Enforcing Restraint: Collective Intervention in Internal Conflicts.* New York: Council on Foreign Relations.

Claude, Inis (1964). *Swords into Plowshares; The Problems and Progress of International Organization.* New York: Random House.

Cohen, Abner (1974). *Two-Dimensional Man: An Essay on the Anthropology of Power and Symbolism in Complex Society.* Berkeley: University of California Press.

Cohen, David W. (1991). "'A Case for the Basoga': Lloyd Fallers and the Construction of an African Legal System," in Kristin Mann and Richard Roberts, eds., *Law in Colonial Africa. Social History of Africa.* Portsmouth, NH: Heinemann.

Cohen, Raymond (1997). *Negotiating Across Cultures: Communication Obstacles in International Diplomacy.* Washington: United States Institute of Peace.

Cohen, Ronald (1961). "Marriage Instability among the Kanuri of Northern Nigeria." *American Anthropologist* (New Series) 63.

Colosi, T. R., and A. E. Brekly (1986). *Collective Bargaining: How It Works and Why.* New York: American Arbitration Association.

Colson, Elizabeth (1995a). "Introduction: Anthropology and the Study of Disputes," in Pat Caplan, ed., *Understanding Disputes: The Politics of Argument.* Providence: Berg Publishers.

——— (1995b). "The Contentiousness of Disputes," in Pat Caplan, ed., *Understanding Disputes: The Politics of Argument.* Providence: Berg Publishers.

——— (1977). "The Invocation of Norms in Dispute Settlement: The Tswana Case," in I. Hammett, ed., *Social Anthropology and Law.* ASA Monograph 14. London: Academic Press.

——— (1976). "From Chief's Court to Local Court," in Myron Aronoff, ed., *Freedom and Constraint.* Amsterdam: Van Gorcum.

——— (1970). *The Plateau Tonga of Northern Rhodesia (Zambia): Social and Religious Studies.* Manchester: The Institute for Social Research, University of Zambia.

——— (1953). "Social Control and Vengeance in Plateau Tonga." *Africa* 23.

Comaroff, John L. (1978). "Rules and Rulers: Political Processes in a Tswana Chiefdom." *Man* 13.

Comaroff, John L., and Simon Roberts (1981). *Rules and Processes: The Cultural Logic of Dispute in an African Context.* Chicago: University of Chicago Press.

Community Problem Solving Program (1989). "Community Problem Solving Case Summaries," vol. 2.

Coogler, O. J. (1978). *Structured Mediation in Divorce Settlement: A Handbook for Marital Mediators.* Lexington, MA: Lexington.

Copson, Raymond (1994). *Africa's Wars and Prospects for Peace.* London: Sharpe.

Cooter, Robert D. (1989). "Inventing Property: Economic Theories of the Origins of Market Property Applied to Papua New Guinea" (draft). Berkeley: University of California.

Coser, L. (1956). *The Function of Social Conflict.* New York: Free Press.

Couloumbis, T. A., and J. Wolde (1978). *Introduction to International Relations: Power and Justice.* New York: Pella.

Crawford, J. R. (1969–1970). "The History and Nature of the Judicial System of Botswana, Lesotho and Swaziland: Introduction and the Superior Courts." *South African Law Journal* 87.

Crocker, Chester A., Fen Osler Hampson, and Pamela Aall, eds., (1996). *Managing Global Chaos.* Washington: United States Institute of Peace.

Cruikshank, Jeffrey, and Lawrence Susskind (1988). *Breaking the Impasse: Consensual Approaches to Resolving Public Disputes.* New York: Basic Books.

Cunnison, Ian G. (1956). "Perpetual Kinship: A Political Institution of the Luapula Peoples." *Rhodes-Livingstone Journal* 20.

Dahrendorf, Rolf (1968). *Essays in the Theory of Society.* Stanford: Stanford University Press.

Danzig, R. (1973). "Toward Creation of Complementary, Decentralized System of Criminal Justice." *Stanford Law Review* 26 (1).

Darkoh, Michael (1964a). "The Economic Life of Buem, 1884–1914." *Bulletin of the Ghana Geographical Association* 9 (1).

——— (1964b). "Recent Trends in the Economic Geography of Buem." *Bulletin of the Ghana Geographical Association* 9 (2).

Davidson, William D., and Joseph V. Montville (1981–1982). "Foreign Policy According to Freud." *Foreign Policy* 45 (Winter).

deCallières, François (1716/1963). *On the Manner of Negotiating with Princes.* Notre Dame: University of Notre Dame Press.

de Craemer, W. (1977). *The Jamaa and the Church: A Bantu Catholic Movement in Zaire.* Oxford: Clarendon.

Deng, Francis M. (1995). *War of Visions: Conflict of Identities in the Sudan.* Washington: The Brookings Institution.

——— (1993). "Northern and Southern Sudan: The Nile," in G. O. Faure and Jeffrey Rubin, eds., *Culture and Negotiation.* Newbury Park, CA: Sage.

——— (1992). "Cultural Dimensions of Conflict Management and Development: Some Lessons from the Sudan," in Ismail Serageldin and B. Taboroff, eds., *Culture and Development.* Proceedings of a World Bank international conference, 2–3 April.

Deng, Francis M., and I. William Zartman, eds. (1991). *Conflict Resolution in Africa.* Washington: The Brookings Institution.

——— (1986). *The Man Called Deng Majok: A Biography of Power, Polygyny and Change.* New Haven and London: Yale University Press.

——— (1982). *Recollections of Babo Nimir.* London: Ithaca Press.

——— (1980). *Dinka Cosmology.* London: Ithaca Press.

——— (1978). *Africans of Two Worlds: Dinka in Afro-Arab Sudan.* New Haven and London: Yale University Press.

——— (1974). *The Dink and their Songs.* Oxford: Oxford University Press.

——— (1971). *Tradition and Modernization: A Challenge for Law among the Dinka of the Sudan.* New Haven and London: Yale University Press.

Dentan, Robert K. (1968). *The Semai: A Nonviolent People of Malaysia.* New York: Rinehart and Winston.

Derman, William (1973). *Serfs, Peasants and Socialists.* Berkeley: University of California Press.

de Souza, Simone (1997). "Fruits, Seeds and Miscellaneous Ingredients Used in the Pharmaceutical Practice of Benin," in Pauline Hountondji, ed., *Endogenous Knowledge: Research Trails.* Dakar: CODESRIA.

Dia, Mamadou (1996). *Africa's Management in the 1990s and Beyond: Reconciling Indigenous and the Transplanted Institutions.* Washington: World Bank.

Diamond, Louise, and John McDonald (1996). *Multi-Track Diplomacy: A Systems Approach to Peace.* West Hartford, CT: Kumarian Press.
Diemé, Sebastien (1992). *Contribution à l'étude de la pharmacopée traditionelle diola.* Pharmacy thesis, University of Dakar.
Dike, K. O. (1956). *Trade and Politics in the Niger Delta.* London: Oxford University Press.
Diop, Abdoulaye Bara (1981). *La société wolof.* Paris: Karthala.
Dipire, Marguerite (1970). *Organisation Sociale des Peuls.* Paris: Plon.
Donnelly-Roark, P. (1998). "Indigenous Knowledge Systems in Sub-Saharan Africa: An Overview." *IK Notes* 1 (October).
Doob, L., ed. (1970). *Resolving Conflict in Africa: The Fermoda Workshop.* New Haven: Yale University Press.
Doornbos, M. R. (1975). "Land Tenure and Political Conflict in Ankole, Uganda." *Journal of Development Studies* 12 (1).
Druckman, Daniel (1997). "Negotiating in the International Context," in I. William Zartman and J. Lewis Rasmussen, ed., *Peacemaking in International Conflict.* Washington: United States Institute of Peace.
Dupire, Marguerite (1969). *Organisation sociale des Peuls.* Paris: Plon.
Ejitiwu, A. and T. Kpone (1989). "Atlantic Trade," in *Land and People of Nigeria Rivers States.* New York: Port Harcort.
Ekeh, Peter P. (1994). "Conflicts between the Cattle Fulanis and the Local Farmers: A Case Study of Enugu State." Unpublished report.
Elias, T. O. (1956). *Nature of African Customary Law 269.* Manchester: Manchester University Press.
Eliot, T. S. (1949). *Notes Towards the Definition of Culture.* New York: Harcourt Brace.
Epstein, A. L. (1971). "Dispute Settlement among the Tolai." *Oceania* 51.
Erekasima, E. V. (1966). "Cultural Institutions," in *Southern Nigeria in Transition.* London: Cambridge University Press.
Estes, Ralph (1996). *Tyranny of the Bottom Line: Why Corporations Make Good People Do Bad Things.* San Francisco: Berrett-Koehler Publishers.
Evans-Pritchard, E. E. (1968). *Nuer: A Description of the Modes of Livelihood and Political Institutions of a Nilotic People.* London: Oxford University Press.
——— (1940a). "The Nuer," in Meyer Fortes and E. E. Evans-Pritchard, eds., *African Political Systems.* London: Oxford University Press for the International African Institute.
——— (1940b). "The Political System," in *The Nuer: The Description of the Modes of Livelihood and Political Institutions of a Nilotic People.* Oxford: The Clarendon Press.
Fadipe, N. A. (1970). *The Sociology of the Yoruba.* Ibadan: The University Press.
Fallers, Lloyd A. (1969). *Law without Precedent: Legal Ideas in Action in the Courts of Colonial Busoga.* Chicago: University of Chicago Press.
——— (1957). "Some Determinants of Marriage Stability in Busoga." *Africa* 27.
——— (c. 1956). *Bantu Bureaucracy: A Study of Integration and Conflict in the Political Institutions of an East African People.* Cambridge: Heffer.
Farah, A. Y. (1994). "Roots and Reconciliation: The Capacity of Lineage Leaders in Peacemaking in Somaliland." Paper presented at a conference on "The Challenge of Peacemaking in Africa: Conflict Prevention and Conflict Resolution," Addis Ababa, Ethiopia, 12–15 September.
——— [with I. M. Lewis] (1993). *Somalia: The Roots of Reconciliation: A Survey*

of Grassroots Peace Conferences in North West Somalia/Somaliland. London and Djibouti: ActionAid.

Farnsworth, N. R., et al. (1985). "Medical Plants in Therapy." *Bull.* WHO 63(6): 695.

Fatton, Robert, Jr. (1995). "Africa in the Age of Democratization: The Civic Limitations of Civil Society." *African Studies Review* 38 (2).

Faure, Guy Olivier (1999). "Joint Ventures in China and Their Negotiation," in Victor Kremenyuk and Gunnar Sjostedt, eds., *International Economic Negotiation.* London: Elgar.

——— (1995a). "La Négociation Chinoise: Aspects Cognitifs et Stratégiques." *Intercultures* 29/30: 7–24.

——— (1995b). "Nonverbal Negotiation in China." *Negotiation Journal* 11 (1).

Faure, Guy Oliver, and Jeffrey Rubin, eds. (1993). *Culture and Negotiation.* Newbury Park, CA: Sage.

Feirman, Steven (1990). *Peasant Intellectuals.* Madison: University of Wisconsin Press.

Felstiner, W. (1974). "Influences of Social Organization on Dispute Processing?" *Law & Society Review* 9 (1).

Field, Margaret Joyce (1960). *Search for Security: An Ethno-Psychiatric Study of Rural Ghana.* Evanston: Northwestern University Press.

Fisher, R. J., Elizabeth Kopelman, and Andrea Kupfer Schneider (1994). *Beyond Machiavelli: Tools for Coping with Conflict.* Cambridge: Harvard University Press.

Fisher, Roger, and William Ury (with Bruce Patton, ed.) (1991). *Getting to Yes: Negotiating Agreement without Giving In.* 2d ed. New York: Penguin Books.

Fisher, Ronald J. (1981). "A Third Party Consultation Workshop on the Indian Pakistanian Conflict." *Journal of Social Psychology* 112.

Flanigan, Beverly (1992). *Forgiving the Unforgivable: Overcoming the Bitter Legacy of Intimate Wounds.* New York: Macmillan Publishing Company.

Folger, Joseph P., et al. (1993). *Working through Conflict.* New York: Harper Collins Publishers.

Forman, S. (1972). "Law and Conflict in Rural Highland Equator." Ph.D. dissertation, University of California, Berkeley.

Forster, P. G. (1994). "Culture, Nationalism, and the Invention of Tradition in Malawi." *Journal of Modern African Studies* 32 (3).

Fortes, Meyer (1969). *Kinship and the Social Order.* London: Aldine.

Fortes, Meyer, and E. E. Evans-Pritchard, eds. (1940). *African Political Systems.* London: Oxford University Press, for the International African Institute.

Franchette, Sylvie (1996). *Migrations, Intégration Spatiale et Formation d'une Société Peul Dans le Fouladou.* Paris: O.S.T.R.O.M.

Francis, P. (1984). "New Directions in the Study of African Law: Review Article." *Africa,* 54 (4).

Frantz, Charles (1975). "Pastoral Societies: Stratification and National Integration in Africa." *Africa* 47 (4): 432.

Fred-Mensah, Ben Kwame (1996) "Changes, Ambiguities and Conflicts: Negotiating Land Rights in Buem-Kator, Ghana." Ph.D. Dissertation, Johns Hopkins University.

French, Hilary F. (1993). "Costly Tradeoffs: Reconciling Trade and the Environment." *World Watch Paper* 113 (March).

Frost, Brian (1991). *The Politics of Peace.* London: Darton, Longman and Todd, Ltd.

Fuller, Lon (1978). "The Forms and Limits of Adjudication." *Harvard Law Review* 92 (2).
Galaty, G., and P. Bonte, eds. (1991). *Herders, Warriors and Traders: Pastoralism in Africa.* Boulder, CO: Westview Press.
Gallais, Jean (1969). "Les Peuls en Question." *Revue de Psychologies de Peuples* 3: 231–251.
Gboyega, Alex (1997). "Nigeria: Conflict Unresolved," in I William Zartman, ed., *Governance as Conflict Management.* Washington: Brookings.
Geertz, Clifford (1983). *Local Knowledge.* New York: Basic Books.
Gibbs, J. L. (1963). "The Kpelle Moot." *Africa* 33 (1).
Giddens, Anthony (1991). *Modernity and Self-Identity: Self and Society in the Modern Age.* Stanford: Stanford University Press.
Gilkes, Patrick (1994). *The Price of Peace: Somalia and the United Nations 1991–1994.* London: Save the Children-UK.
Giorgis, Atsime (1988). As cited in Gadaa Melba's *Oromia.* Khartoum.
Githens, T. S. (1949). *Drug Plants of Africa.* University Park: University of Pennsylvania Press.
Gluckman, Max (1970). "Social Control and Vengeance in Plateau Tonga," in *Plateau Tonga of Northern Rhodesia (Zambia): Social and Religious Studies.* New York: Manchester University Press.
——— (1965a). *Politics and Ritual in Tribal Society.* Chicago: Aldine Publishing Company.
——— (1965b). *The Ideas in Barotse Jurisprudence.* New Haven: Yale University Press.
——— (1963). *Order and Rebellion in Tribal Africa.* [Collected essays with autobiographical introduction]. New York: The Free Press of Glencoe.
——— (1959). *Custom and Conflict in Africa.* Glencoe, IL: Free Press.
——— (1956). *Custom and Conflict in Africa.* Oxford: Basil Blackwell.
——— (1955). *Law and Authority in a Nigerian Tribe.* London: Oxford University Press.
Goldberg, S., et al. (1985). *Dispute Resolution.* Boston: Little, Brown, and Co.
Goldsmith, Sir James (1994). *The Trap.* New York: Carroll and Gray Publishers, Inc.
Good, Charles M. (1987). *Ethnomedical Systems in Africa: Patterns of Traditional Medicine in Rural and Urban Kenya.* New York: Guilford Press.
Grande, Elisabetta, ed. (1995). *Transplants, Innovation, and Legal Tradition in the Horn of Africa.* Torino: Harmattan-Italia.
Griffiths, J. (1985). "Four Laws of Interaction in Circumstances of Legal Pluralism: First Steps towards an Explanatory Theory," in A. Allott and G. Woodman, eds., *Peoples, Law and State: The Bellagio Papers.* Dordrecht: Foris Publications.
Grillo, Trina (1991). "The Mediation Alternative: Process Dangers to Women." *Yale Law Journal* 100.
Grundy, Kenneth (1971). *Guerrilla Struggle in Africa: An Analysis and Preview.* New York: Grossman.
Gulliver, P. H. (1979). *Disputes and Negotiations: A Cross-Cultural Perspective.* New York: Academic Press.
——— (1978). "Process and Decision," in P. Gulliver, ed., *Cross-Examinations: Essays in Memory of Max Gluckman.* Leiden: E.J. Brill.
——— (1977). "On Mediators," in T. Hamnett, ed., *Law and Social Anthropology* (ASA 14). London: Academic Press.
——— (1975). "An Arusha Land Dispute," in M. Karp, ed., *African Perspectives.* Boston: African Studies Program, Boston University.

——— (1969). "Disputes Settlement without Courts: The Ndendeuli of Southern Tanzania," in Laura Nader, ed., *Law and Culture and Society.* Chicago: Aldine.

——— (1963a). *Social Control in an African Society.* Boston: Boston University Press.

——— (1963b). "Land Shortage, Social Change and Social Conflict in East Africa." *Journal of Conflict Resolution* 5.

Hall, E. (1976). *Beyond Culture.* New York: Doubleday.

Hampson, Fen Osler (1996). *Nurturing Peace.* Washington: United States Institute of Peace.

Hanf, Theodor (1993). *Coexistence in Wartime Lebanon: The Decline of a State and the Rise of a Nation.* London: The Centre for Lebanese Studies and I.B. Taurus and Co., Ltd.

Hanlon, Joseph (1996). "Strangling Mozambique: International Monetary Fund 'Stabilization' in the World's Poorest Country." *Multinational Monitor* 17 (7, 8).

Harff, Barbara (1993). "Minorities, Rebellion and Repression in North Africa and the Middle East," in Ted Gurr, ed., *Minorities at Risk: A Global View of Ethnopolitical Conflicts.* Washington: United States Institute of Peace.

Harrington, Christina B. (1985). *Shadow Justice: The Ideology and Institutionalization of Alternatives to Court.* Westport, CT: Greenwood Press.

——— (1982). "Delegalization Reform Movements: A Historical Analysis," in R. Able, ed., *The Politics of Informal Justice.* Vol. 1. New York: Academic Press.

Harris, G. (1978). *Casting Out Anger: Religion among the Taita of Kenya.* Cambridge: Cambridge University Press.

Harrison, David (1988). *The Sociology of Modernization and Development.* London: Unwin Hyman.

Hassan, Mohammed (1983). "The Oromo of Ethiopia, 1500–1800: With Special Emphasis on the Gibe Region." Ph.D. dissertation, University of London.

——— (1981). "The Oromo Nation under Amhara Colonial Administration: Past and Present." Unpublished paper (June).

Havel, Vaclav (1992). "The End of the Modern Era." *New York Times,* 1 March.

Haynes, J. M. (1981). *Divorce Mediation: A Practical Guide for Therapists and Counselors.* New York: Springer.

Heald, S. (1989). *Controlling Anger: The Sociology of Gisu Violence.* Manchester: Manchester University Press.

Henderson, K. D. D. (1965). *Sudan Republic.* London: Ernest Benn Limited.

Henk, D. (1996). *Peace Operations: Views from Southern and Eastern Africa.* Carlisle, PA: Center for Strategic Leadership.

——— (1988). *Kazi ya Shaba: Choice, Continuity and Social Change in an Industrial Community of Southern Zaire.* Ph.D. dissertation, University of Florida.

Hewstone, M., and R. Brown, eds. (1986). *Control and Conflict in Intergroup Encounters.* Oxford: Basil Blackwell.

Hinnant, John (1977). "The Gada System of the Guji of Southern Ethiopia." Ph.D. dissertation, University of Chicago.

Hobsbawm, Eric (1983). "Introduction: Inventing Traditions," in E. Hobsbawm and T. Ranger, eds., *The Invention of Tradition.* New York: Cambridge University Press.

Hobsbawm, Eric, and Terence Ranger (1992). *The Invention of Tradition.* New York: Cambridge University Press.

Hofrichter, Richard (1987). *Neighborhood Justice in a Capitalist Society: The Expansion of the Informal State.* New York: Greenwood Press.

Holan, Douglas (1994). "Staying 'Cool' in Toraja: Informal Strategies for the Management of Anger Hostility in a Nonviolent Society." *Ethos* 16.
Hooker, M. B. (1975) *Legal Pluralism.* Oxford: Clarendon Press.
Hoover, James J. (1978). *The Seduction of Ruwej: Reconstructing Ruund History.* Ph.D. dissertation, Yale University.
Hountondji, Paulin, ed. (1997). *Endogenous Knowledge: Research Trails.* Dakar: CODESRIA.
Howell, P. P. (1962). *A Manuel of Nuer Law.* London: Oxford University Press, for the International African Institute.
——— (1954). *A Manual of Nuer Law.* London: Oxford University Press.
——— (1951). "Notes on the Ngork Dinka." *Sudan Notes and Records* 32, pt. 2.
Hultin, Jan (1996). "Perceiving Oromo: 'Galla' in the Great Narrative of Ethiopia," in Paul T. Baxter et al., eds., *Being Oromo and Becoming Oromo.* Lawrenceville, NJ: Red Sea Press.
Hume, Cameron (1994). *Ending Mozambique's War: The Role of Mediation and Good Offices.* Washington: United States Institute of Peace.
Hunter, M. (1961). *Reaction to Conquest.* 2d ed. London: Oxford University Press.
ibn Khaldun, Abd al-Rahman (1377/1967). *An Introduction to History.* Princeton: Princeton University Press.
Isichei, E. (1976). *A History of the Igbo People.* New York: Academic Press.
Issa-Salwe, Catodisalaam M. (1992). *The Collapse of the Somali State: The Impact of the Colonial Legacy.* London: HAAN Publishing.
Jeffrey, M. (1956). *Ibo Warfare.* London: Heinemann.
Jenco, Lawrence Martin (1995). *Bound to Forgive: The Pilgrimage to Reconciliation of a Beirut Hostage.* Notre Dame, IN: Ave Maria Press.
Johnson, Douglas H., and Gerard Prunier (1993). "The Foundation and Expansion of the Sudan People's Liberation Army," in M. W. Daly and Ahmad Alawad Sikainger, eds., *Civil War in the Sudan.* London: British Academic Press.
Jones, G. I. (1963). *The Trading States of Oil Rivers: A Study of Political Development in Eastern Nigeria.* Oxford: Oxford University Press.
Kalu, O. U. (1978). "Precarious Vision: The African Perception of His World," in *Readings in African Humanities: Cultural Development.* Enugu, Nigeria: Fourth Dimension Publishers.
Kelman, Herbert (1997). "Social-Psychological Dimensions of International Conflict," in I. William Zartman and J. Lewis Rasmussen, ed., *Peacemaking in International Conflict.* Washington: United States Institute of Peace.
——— (1972). "The Problem-Solving Workshop in Conflict Resolution," in R. Merritt, ed., *Communication in International Politics.* Urbana: University of Illinois Press.
Kelman, Herbert, and S. Cohn (1976). "The Problem-Solving Workshop: A Social-Psychological Contribution to the Resolution of International Relations." *Journal of Peace Research* 13 (2).
Kenyatta, Jomo (1938). *Facing Mountain Kenya: The Traditional Life of the Kikuyu.* London: Heinemann.
Kerharo, J., and G. Adam (1974). *La pharmacopée sénégalaise traditionnelle.* Paris: Vigot.
Kerharo, J., and A. Bouquet (1950). *Plantes médicinales de la Cote d'Ivoire et Haute Volta.* Paris: Vigot.
Khairallah, Daoud (1994). "Secular Democracy: A Viable Alternative to the Confessional System," in Deidre Collins, ed., *Peace for Lebanon? From War to Reconstruction.* Boulder, CO: Lynne Rienner Publishers.

Khoza, R. (1994). *Ubuntu: African Humanism.* Johannesburg: HSRC discussion paper.

Kirk-Greene, A. H. M., and S. J. Hogben (1996). *The Emirates of Northern Nigeria.* London: Oxford University.

Knuston, Karl (1967). *Authority and Change: A Study of the Kallu Institution among the Mecha Galla of Ethiopia.* Gotenborg: Ethnografiska Museet.

Kofele-Kale, Ndiva (1981). *Tribesmen and Patriots.* Lanham, MD: University Presses of America.

Kokwaro, M. O. (1995). *Luo Traditional Conflict Management and Resolution.* Washington: Center for Indigenous Knowledge/United States Information Agency, Africa Exchange Program.

——— (1976). *Medical Plants of East Africa.* East African Literature Bureau.

Kolb, D. (1983). *The Mediators.* London: MIT Press.

Koopman, A. (1993). "Transcultural Management: In Search of Pragmatic Humanism," in P. Christie, R. Lessem, and L. Mbigi, *African Management: Philosophies, Concepts and Applications.* Randburg, S.A.: Knowledge Resources (Pty) Ltd.

Korten, David C. (1996). *When Corporations Rule the World.* West Harford, CT: Kumarian Press.

Kressel, Kenneth, and Dean G. Pruitt (1989). *Mediation Research.* San Francisco: Jossey-Bass.

Krige, E. J., and J. D. Krige (1943). *The Realm of a Rain-Queen.* London: Oxford University Press, for the International African Institute.

Krige, J. D. (1939). "Some Aspects of Lovedu Judicial Arrangements." *Bantu Studies* 13 (2).

Kriger, Norma J. (1992). *Zimbabwe's Guerrilla War: Peasant Voices.* Cambridge: Cambridge University Press.

Kuper, Hilda (1963). *The Swazi: A South African Kingdom.* New York: Holt Rinehart and Winston.

Kymlicka, Will (1992). *Liberalism, Community and Culture.* Oxford: Clarendon Paperbacks.

Laitin, David D., and Said S. Samatar (1987). *Somalia: A Nation in Search of a State.* Boulder, CO: Westview Press.

Lambo, T. A. (1961). "A Form of Social Psychiatry in Africa." *World Mental Health* 13 (4): 190–203.

Lan, David (1985). *Guns and Rain: Guerillas and Spirit Mediums in Zimbabwe.* Berkeley: University of California Press.

Landeck, Jonathan K. (1991). "Contribution to Culture-Based Curriculum Development in Agricultural and Extension Education: Perceptions of Soil Management and Conservation by Farmers in Fuuta Jalon, Guinea, West Africa." Ph.D. dissertation, University Microfilms.

Laplatine, F. R. (1976). *Maladies mentales et thérapies traditionnelles en Afrique.* Paris: Delange.

Lappe, Frances M., and J. Collins (1978). *Food First: Beyond the Myth of Scarcity.* Rev. ed. Boston: Houghton-Mifflin.

Lasswell, Harold, and Abraham Kaplan (1950). *Power and Society.* New Haven: Yale University Press.

Latham, A. (1973). *Old Calabar, 1600–1891.* Oxford: Clarendon Press.

Laue, James, and Gerald Cormick (1978). "The Ethics of Intervention in Community Disputes," in Gordon Bermant, Herbert Kelman, and Donald Warwick, eds., *The Ethics of Social Intervention.* Washington: Halsted.

Laue, James, and Diane Bendahmane, eds. (1987). *Conflict Resolution: Track Two Diplomacy.* Washington: U.S. Government Printing Office.

Lawry, Steven W., James C. Riddell, and John W. Bennett (1984). "Land Tenure Policy in African Livestock Development," in James Simpson and Phylo Evangelou, eds., *Livestock Development in Sub-Saharan Africa.* Boulder, CO: Westview Press.

Laylin, J. G., and R. L. Bianchi (1959). "The Role of Adjudication in International River Disputes: The Lake Lanoux Case." *American Journal of International Law* 53 (1).

Leach, Edmund (1954). *Political System in Highland Burma: A Study of Kachin Social Structure.* London: Athlone.

Lederach, John Paul (1995). *Preparing for Peace: Conflict Transformation Across Cultures.* Syracuse: Syracuse University Press.

Legesse, Asmarom (1987). "Oromo Democracy." Paper presented at conference on Oromo Revolution, Washington, DC, August 1987.

——— (1973). *Gada: Three Approaches of Studying African Society.* New York: Free Press.

Leo Africanus (1550/1956). *Description de l'Afrique.* Translated by A. Epaulard. Paris: Maisonneuve.

Leung, K. (1988). "Some Determinants of Conflict Avoidance." *Journal of Cross Cultural Psychology* 19.

Levine, Donald N. (1972). *Wax and Gold.* Chicago: University of Chicago Press.

LeVine, Robert A., ed. (1961). *The Anthropology of Conflict: Journal of Conflict Resolution.* (Special Issue) 5 (1).

Lewicki, Roy J., et al. (1997). *Essentials of Negotiations.* New York: Wiley.

Lewis, Herbert (1970). "Wealth, Influence, and Prestige among the Shoa Galla," in Arthur Tuden and Leonard Plotnicov, eds., *Social Stratification in Africa.* New York: Free Press.

——— (1966). "The Origins of the Galla and Somali." *Journal of African History* 7.

Lewis, I. M. (1988). *A Modern History of Somalia: Nation and State in the Horn of Africa.* Boulder, CO: Westview Press.

——— (1969). "Nationalism and Particularism in Somalia," in P. H. Gulliver, ed., *Tradition and Transition in East Africa: Studies of the Tribal Element in the Modern Era.* Berkeley: University of California Press.

——— (1965). "Shaikhs and Warriors in Somaliland," in M. Fortes and G. Dieterlen, eds., *African Systems of Thought.* London: Oxford University Press.

Lewis, L. Hall (1988). *Hausa Medicine.* Durham, NC: Duke University Press.

Lienhardt, Godfrey (1963). "The Dinka of the Nile Basin." *The Listener* 69.

Lippman, Thomas (1997). "U.S. Ready to Train African Peacekeepers." *Washington Post,* 30 June.

Little, K. (1973). "The Political Functions of the Poro," in C. Turnbull, ed., *Africa and Change.* New York: Alfred A. Knopf.

——— (1967). *The Mende of Sierra Leone: A West African People in Transition.* London: Routledge and Kegan Paul.

Lofchie, Michael F. (1968). "Political Theory and African Politics." *Journal of Modern African Studies* 6 (1).

Lowi, M., and J. Rothman (1993). "Arabs and Israelis: The Jordan River," in G. O. Faure and Jeffrey Rubin, eds., *Culture and Negotiation.* Newbury Park, CA: Sage.

Lowy, M. (1971). "The Ethnography of Law in Changing Ghanaian Town." Ph.D. dissertation, University of California, Berkeley.

Lyons, Terrence, and Ahmed Samatar (1995). *Somalia: State Collapse, Multilateral Intervention and Strategies for Political Reconstruction.* Washington: Brookings.

Lytton, Earl (1966). *The Stolen Desert: A Study of Uhuru in Northeast Africa.* London: McDonald and Company.

Mail and Guardian (1997). "The Parable of the Bicycle." South Africa, 13 February.

Mair, Lucy (1962). *Primitive Government.* New York: Pelican Books.

Makiya, Kanan (1993). *Cruelty and Silence: War, Tyranny, Uprising and the Arab World.* New York: W.W. Norton and Co.

Makhubu, Lydia (1998). "Bioprospecting in an African Context." *Science* 282 (October 2).

——— (1978). *The Traditional Healer.* Kwalusani, Swaziland: University of Botswana and Swaziland Press.

Makiya, Kana (1993). *Cruelty and Silence: War, Tyranny, Uprising and the Arab World.* New York: W.W. Norton and Co.

Malinowski, Bronislaw (1959). *Crime and Custom in Savage Society.* Patterson, NJ: Littlefield, Adams & Co.

——— (1948). "Anthropological Analysis of War," in *Magic, Science, and Religion.* Glencoe, IL: Free Press.

Manglapus, Raul (1987). *Will of the People: Democracy in Non-Western Societies.* New York: Greenwood Press.

Marchal, Roland (1993). "Un Espace Urbain en Guerre: Les Mooryaan de Mogadiscio," *Cahiers d'Etudes Africains* (October).

Martin, Doris M., and Fatuma O. Hashi (1992). *Women in Development: The Legal Issues in Sub-Saharan Africa Today.* Working Paper No. 4. Washington: The World Bank.

Marwick, M. (1965). *Sorcery in Its Social Setting.* Manchester: Manchester University Press.

Mastenbroek, Willem (1989). *Negotiate.* London: Basil Blackwell.

Mattei, Ugo (1990). "Socialist and Non-Socialist Approaches to Land Law: Continuity and Change in Somalia and Other African States." *Review of Socialist Law* 16.

Mattingly, G. (1962). *Renaissance Diplomacy.* New York: Russell and Russell.

Mazrui, Ali A. (1990). *Cultural Forces in World Politics.* London: Heinemann.

Mbigi, L. (1995). "Ubuntu." *Enterprise* (November).

Mbigi, L. and J. Maree (1995). *Ubuntu: The Spirit of African Transformation Management.* Randburg, S.A.: Knowledge Resources (Pty) Ltd.

Mbiti, John S. (1969). *African Religions and Philosophy.* New York: Praeger Publishers.

McCormick, Shawn H. (1994). "Zaire II: Mobutu, Master of the Game." *Current History* 93.

McDonald, John, and Diane Bendahmane, eds. (1987). *Conflict Resolution: Track Two Diplomacy.* Washington: U.S. Government Printing Office.

McGary, Howard, and Bill E. Lawson (1992). *Between Slavery and Freedom.* Bloomington: Indiana University Press.

Medani, Khalid (1993). "Sudan's Human and Political Crisis." *Current History* 92.

Megerssa, Gemechu (1994). "Knowledge, Identity and the Colonizing Structure." University of London. Unpublished manuscript.

Melbaa, Gadaa (1988). *Oromia*. Khartoum.
Memmi, Albert (1968). *The Colonizer and the Colonized*. Boston: The Beacon Press.
Menkhaus, Ken (1999). *Peacebuilding in Collapsed States: Dynamics of Local-Level Reconciliation in Somalia 1991–1995*.
Menkhaus, Ken, and Lou Ortmayer (1999). "Somalia: Misread Crises and Missed Opportunities," in Bruce Jentleson, ed., *Preventive Diplomacy in the Post–Cold War World: Opportunities Missed, Opportunities Seized, and Lessons to Be Learned*. Lanham, MD: Rowman and Littlefield.
——— (1996). "International Peacebuilding and the Dynamics of Local and National Reconciliation in Somalia." *International Peacekeeping* 3 (1).
Merry, Sally Engle (1989). "Mediation in Nonindustrial Societies," in Kenneth Kressel and Dean G. Pruitt, eds., *Mediation Research: The Process and Effectiveness of Third-Party Intervention*. San Francisco: Jossey-Bass Publishers.
——— (1982). "The Social Organization of Mediation in Non-industrial Societies: Implications for Informal Community Justice in America," in Richard Abel, ed., *The Politics of Informal Justice*. Vol. 2. New York and London: Academic Press.
——— (1979). "Going to Court: Strategies of Dispute Management in an American Urban Neighborhood." *Law and Society Review* 13.
Merry, Sally Engle, and Neal Milner, eds. (1993). *The Possibility of Popular Justice: A Case Study of Community Mediation in the United States*. Ann Arbor: University of Michigan Press.
Michalowski, R. (1985). *Law, Order, and Crime: An Introduction to Criminology*. New York: Random House.
Middleton, John (1966). "The Resolution of Conflict among the Lugbara of Uganda," in Marc J. Swartz, Victor W. Turner, and Artheu Tuden, eds., *Political Anthropology*. Chicago: Aldine.
Middleton, John, D. Tait, and Laura Bohannan (1956). *Tribes Without Rulers*. London: Rouledge and Paul.
Mike, C. K. (1937). *Laws and Authority in a Nigerian Tribe*. London: Heinemann.
Milner, Neal (1996). "Mediation and Political Theory: A Critique of Bush and Folger." *Law and Social Inquiry* 21 (3).
Mitchell, Christopher (1981). *Peace Making and the Consultant's Role*. New York: Nichols Publishing Company.
Montague, A. M. F., ed. (1978). *Learning Non-Aggression: The Experience of Non-Literate Societies*. Oxford: Oxford University Press.
Montagne, Robert (1973). *The Berbers*. Translated by David Seedon. London: Frank Cass.
Montville, Joseph, ed. (1990). *Conflict and Peacemaking in Multi-Ethnic Societies*. Lexington, MA: Lexington Books.
——— (1987). "The Arrow and the Olive Branch: A Case for Track Two Diplomacy," in John McDonald and Diane Bendahmane, eds., *Conflict Resolution: Track Two Diplomacy*. Washington: U.S. Government Printing Office.
Moore, C. (1987). *The Mediation Process: Practical Strategies for Resolving Conflict*. London: Jossey-Bass Publishers.
Moore, Sally Falk (1995). "Imperfect Communications," in Pat Caplan, ed., *Understanding Disputes: The Politics of Argument*. Providence: Berg Publishers.
——— (1978). *Law as Process: An Anthropological Approach*. London: Routledge & Kegan Paul.

——— (1977). "Individual Interests and Organizational Structures: Dispute Settlement as 'Events of Articulation.'" *Social Anthropology and Law.* ASA Monograph 14. London: Academic Press.

Morgan, G. (1986). *Images of Organization.* Beverley Hills, CA: Sage.

Mortabau Degbe, Faustin (1991). "Contribution à l'étude de la pharmacopée traditionnelle au Benin." Pharmacy thesis, University of Dakar.

Movich, Randy (1997–1998). *Traditional Medicine. Institute for Current World Affairs Letters* l, 3, 6. Hanover, NH: Crane Rogers Foundation.

Msabaha, Ibrahim (1995). "Negotiating an End to Mozambique's Murderous Rebellion," in I. William Zartman, ed., *Elusive Peace: Negotiating an End to Civil Wars.* Washington: Brookings.

Mukenge, L. (1967). "Croyances religieuses et structures socio-familiales en societe Luba." *Cahiers Economiques et Sociaux* 5 (1): 3–94.

Nadel, S. F. (1952). "Witchcraft in Four African Societies." *American Anthropologist* 54 (1): 18–29.

——— (1942). *A Black Byzantium: The Kingdom of Nupe of Northern Nigeria.* London: Oxford University Press, for International African Institute.

Nader, Laura (1994). "Civilization and Its Negotiators," in P. Caplan, ed., *Understanding Disputes: The Politics of Argument.* Oxford: Berg Publishers.

——— (1990). *Harmony Ideology. Justice and Control in a Zapotec Mountain Village.* Stanford: Stanford University Press.

——— (1989). "The ADR Explosion: The Implications of Rhetoric in Legal Reform," in *Windsor Yearbook of Access to Justice.* University of Windsor, Ontario.

——— (1979). "Disputing without the Force of Law," *Yale Law Journal* (Special issue on dispute resolution) 88 (5).

Nader, Laura, and H. Todd (1978). *The Disputing Process: Law in Ten Societies.* New York: Columbia University Press.

———, eds. (1969). *Law in Culture and Society.* Chicago: Aldine.

Natsoulas, Theodore (1981). "Ethiopia: The Anatomy of an Indigenous Colonial Empire." *Horn of Africa* 3.

Ndiaye, Moctar Justin (1977). *Contribution à l'étude de al pharmacopée traditionnelle au Sénégal oriental.* Pharmacy thesis, University of Dakar.

New Nation (1997). "Long Wait for Reparation," South Africa, 31 January.

——— (1996). "TRC a Breeding Ground for Bitterness?" South Africa, 20 December.

N'Gaide, Abdarahmane (1996). "Conquete de la liberté, mutations politiques, sociables et religieuses en Haute Casamance: Le cas des anciens maccube de Fuladu (Région de Kolda-Sénégal)." Paris: O.R.S.T.O.M.

——— (1995). "Stratégies d'occupation de l'espace et conflits fonciers: les marabout Gaabunke et les Peuls Jaawaringa." (October) Paris: O.R.S.T.O.M.

Niblock, Tim (1987). *Class and Power in the Sudan.* London: Macmillan.

Nicolson, H. (1954). *The Evolution of Diplomatic Methodology.* London: Oxford University Press.

Norbeck, E. (1963). "African Rituals of Conflict." *American Anthropologist* 65 (6).

Nukunya, G. K. (1992). *Tradition and Change in Ghana: An Introduction to Sociology.* Accra: Ghana University Press.

Nyang, Sulayman S. (1994). *Islam, Christianity, and African Identity.* Brattleboro, VT: Amana Books.

OAU/STRC/DEPA/KIPO (1997). *Policy Issues on Ownership, Access and Conservation.* Workshop on Medical Plants and Herbal Medicine in Africa. Cameroon: BDCP Press.

Offiong, D. O. (1989). *Continuity and Change in Some Traditional Societies of Nigeria.* Zaria: Ahmadu Bello University Press.
Okenge, Osokonda (1984). "La Dynamique du magico-religieux dans l'exercise du pouvoir politique traditionel chez les Tetela." Ph.D. dissertation, University of Lubumbashi, Lubumbashi, Zaire.
Okere vs. Nwoke (1991). 8 *Nigerian Weekly Law Reports* Prt. 209.
Olson, Thomas, and Stephen John Stedman (1995). *The New Is Not Yet Born.* Washington: Brookings.
Orijini, J. N. (1978). "A Reassessment of the Organization and Benefits of the Slave and Palm Product Trade among the Nigerian Igbo." *Canadian Journal of African Studies* 16.
Osaghae, Eghosa E. (1995a). *Ethnicity, Class and the Struggle in Liberia.* Dakar: CODESRIA Monograph Series l/96.
——— (1995b). "The Fire Behind the Smoke: External Sources of Ethnic Conflicts in Africa." *Forum for Development Studies* 1.
——— (1989). "The Passage from the Past to the Present in African Political Thought: The Relevance Question," in J. A. A. Ayoade and A. A. B. Agbaje, eds., *African Traditional Political Thought and Institutions.* Lagos: CAAC.
Otite, O., ed. (1978). *Themes in African Social and Political Thought.* Enugu, Nigeria: Fourth Dimension.
Ou, C. Jay (1996). "Native Americans and the Monitored Retrievable Storage Plan for Nuclear Waste: Late Capitalism, Negotiation, and Controlling Processes," in Laura Nader, ed., *Essays in Controlling Processes.* Kroeber Anthropological Society Papers, No. 80.
Packard, Randall (1981). *Chiefship and Cosmology: An Historical Study of Political Competition.* Bloomington: Indiana University Press.
Parkin, David (1995). "Disputing Human Passion: The Negotiation of the Meaning of Love among the Giriama of Kenya," in Pat Caplan, ed., *Understanding Disputes: The Politics of Argument.* Providence: Berg Publishers.
Parmelee, Jennifer (1993). "Waltzing with Warlords." *Washington Post,* 25 June.
Parsons, Talcott (1937). *The Structure of Social Action.* New York: McGraw-Hill.
Peires, J. B. (1987). "The Central Beliefs of the Xhosa Cattle Killing." *Journal of African History* 28 (1).
Penel, Jean-Dominique (1997). "Epistomological Reflections on Hausa Zoological Names," in Paulin Hountondji, ed., *Endogenous Knowledge: Research Trails.* Dakar: CODESRIA.
Perham, Margery (1969). *The Government of Ethiopia.* Evanston: Northwestern University Press.
Peters, P. E. (1984). "Struggles over Meaning, Struggles over Power: Cattle, Water and the State in Botswana." *Africa* 54 (3).
Plowden, W. (1868). *Travels in Abyssinia.* London: Longman.
Pompa, G. G. (1987). "The Community Relations Service," in D. Sandole and I. Sandole, eds., *Conflict Management and Problem Solving.* New York: Oxford University Press.
Popkin, Samuel L. (1979). *The Rational Peasant: The Political Economy of Rural Society in Vietnam.* Berkeley: University of California Press.
Prendergast, John (1994). *The Gun Talks Louder than the Voice: Somalia's Continuing Cycles of Violence.* Washington: Center of Concern.
Présence Africaine (1956). "Culture Peule." 8/10 (Juin–Nov). Paris.
Pruitt, Dean G., and Peter J. Carnevale (1993). *Negotiation in Social Conflict.* Pacific Grove, CA: Brooks/Cole.

Pye, L. (1986). *Chinese Commercial Negotiating Style.* Cambridge, MA: Oelgeschlager, Gunn and Hain Publishers.

——— (1982). *Chinese Commerical Negotiating Style.* Cambridge, MA: Oelgeschlager, Gunn and Hain Publishers.

Qangule, Z. S. (1979). "A Study of Theme and Technique in the Creative Works of S.E.K.L.N. Mqhayi'." Ph.D. dissertation, University of Cape Town, South Africa.

Radcliffe-Brown, A. R. (1952). *Structure and Function in Primitive Society.* London: Cohen and West.

——— (1940). "Preface," in M. Fortes and E. E. Evans-Pritchard, eds., *African Political Systems.* London: Oxford University, for International African Institute.

Radji, A. (1987). "Médecine et pharmacopée traditionnelle en République populaire du Benin." *Bulletin de liaison ACCT* 1 (1).

Reefe, Thomas Q. (1981). *The Rainbow and the Kings: A History of the Luba Empire to 1891.* Berkeley: University of California Press.

Reisman, Paul (1977). *Freedom in Fulani Social Life.* Chicago: University of Chicago Press.

Rey, C. F. (1927). *In the Country of Blue Nile.* London: Duckworth.

Roberts, Simon (1971). "The Settlement of Family Disputes in the Kgatla Customary Courts: Some New Approaches." *Journal of African Law* 15.

——— (n.d.). *Arable Land Disputes and Administration and Administrative Change in the Kgaleng.* Ann Arbor: Land Tenure Center, University of Michigan.

Robarchek, Clayton A. (1994). "Ghosts and Witches: The Psychological Dynamics of Semai Peacefulness," in Leslie E. Sponsel and Thomas Gregor, eds., *The Anthropology of Peace and Nonviolence.* Boulder, CO: Lynne Rienner Publishers.

Rose, Laurel L. (1996). "Are Alternative Dispute Resolution (ADR) Programs Suitable for Africa?" Ithaca: Cornell University Africa Notes.

——— (1992). *The Politics of Harmony: Land Dispute Strategies in Swaziland.* Cambridge: Cambridge University Press.

Rothenberger, John E. (1978). "The Social Dynamics of Dispute Settlement in a Sunni Muslim Village in Lebanon," in Laura Nader and Harry F. Todd, eds., *The Disputing Process in Ten Societies.* New York: Columbia University Press.

Rubin, Elizabeth (1997). "An Army of One's Own: In Africa, Nations Hire a Corporation to Wage War." *Harpers Magazine,* February.

Sacco, Rodolfo (1996). *Il diritto africano.* Torino: UTET.

Saeed, Abdelbasit (1982). "The State and Socioeconomic Transformation in the Sudan: The Case of Social Conflict in Southern Kordofan." Ph.D. dissertation, University of Connecticut.

Sahnoun, Mohamed (1994). *Somalia: The Missed Opportunities.* Washington: United States Institute of Peace.

Said, Edward (1995). *Peace and its Discontents.* London: Vintage.

Salem, R. A. (1982). "Community Dispute Resolution through Outside Intervention." *Peace and Change* 8 (2/3).

Salibi, Kamal (1988). *House of Many Mansions.* Berkeley: University of California Press.

Schapera, L. (1955). *A Handbook of Tswana Law and Custom.* London: Oxford University Press.

Schmitz, J. (1986). "Project d'Irrigation de Kaskas et Situation des Perimetres Villageois de la Zone." (December) Paris: O.R.S.T.O.M. [Study of the Podor region in Senegal].

Schusky, E., and D. Abbott (n.d.). "Misperception and Misdirection in the Sahel." Paper presented at a Symposium on Hunger, Work, and the Quality of Life. ICAES Post Plenary Session. Hyderabad.

Scimecca, J. (1991). "Conflict Resolution the Bases for Social Control or Social Change?" in Kevin Avruch, P. Back, and J. Scimecca, eds., *Conflict Resolution: Cross-Cultural Perspectives.* Westport, CT: Greenwood Press.

——— (1987). "Conflict Resolution the Bases for Social Control or Social Change?" in D. Sandole and I. Sandole, eds., *Conflict Management and Problem Solving.* New York: New York University Press.

Scoones, Ian, ed. (1994). *Living with Uncertainty: New Directions in Pastoral Development in Africa.* London: Intermediate Technology Publications.

Scott, James C. (1990). *Domination and the Arts of Resistence.* New Haven: Yale University Press.

Selassie, Bereket Habte (1980). *Conflict and Intervention in the Horn of Africa.* New York: Monthly Review Press.

Shack, William (1976). "Occupational Prestige, Status and Social Change in Modern Ethiopia." *Africa* 46. London.

Shriver, Donald W., Jr. (1991). "Theological Reflections," in Brian Frost, *The Politics of Peace.* London: Darton, Longman and Todd, Ltd.

Siegal, Bernard, and Alan Beals (1960). "Conflict and Factionalist Dispute." *Journal of the Royal Anthropological Institute* 90.

Simbine, Antonia (1997). "Role of Nigerian Women's Associations in Urban Conflict Management." Paper presented at seminar on Ethnic and Religious Conflicts in Nigeria, University of Ibadan (29–30 January).

Sindane, Jabu (c. 1995). *Democracy in African Societies and Ubuntu.* Pretoria: HSRC.

Slim, R. (1993). "Turkey, Syria, Iraq: The Euphrates," in Guy Olivier Faure and Jeffrey Z. Rubin, eds., *Culture and Negotiation.* Newbury Park, CA: Sage.

Smith, M. G. (1960). "The Beginnings of Hausa Society," in Jan Vansina, R. Mauny, and L.V. Thomas, eds., *The Historian in Tropical Africa.* London: Oxford University Press.

Smith, R. (1977). *Warfare and Diplomacy in Precolonial West Africa.* London: Methuen.

Smock, David R., ed. (1993). *Making War and Waging Peace: Foreign Intervention in Africa.* Washington: United States Institute of Peace.

Smock, David R., and Chester A. Crocker, eds. (1995). *African Conflict Resolution.* Washington: US Institute of Peace.

So, Alvin Y. (1990). *Social Change and Development.* Newbury Park, CA: Sage Publications.

Soga, J. H. (1931). *The Ama-Xosa Life and Custom.* Lovedale, South Africa: Lovedale Press.

Somali Development and Relief Agency (SDRA) and Mennonite Central Committee (MCC) (1994). "Proceedings of the Erigavo Peace Conference, Sanaag Region, Somalia." Djibouti: SDRA.

Soros, George (1997). "The Capitalist Threat." *Atlantic Monthly,* February.

Southall, Aidan (1995). "Courts of Death among the Alur of Uganda," in Pat Caplan, ed., *Understanding Disputes: The Politics of Argument.* Providence: Berg Publishers.

Spear, Mary, and Jon Keller (1996). "Conflict Resolution in Africa: Insights from UN Representatives and US Government Officials." *Africa Today* 43 (2): 121.

Sponsel, Leslie E., and Thomas Gregor, eds. (1994). *The Anthropology of Peace and Nonviolence.* Boulder, CO: Lynne Rienner Publishers.

Starr, J., and B. Yngvesson (1975). "Scarcity and Disputing on Compromise Decisions." *American Ethnologist* 2 (3).

Stedman, Stephen John (1991a). *Peacemaking in Civil War.* Boulder, CO: Lynne Rienner Publishers.

——— (1991b). "Conflict and Conflict Resolution in Africa," in Francis M. Deng and I. William Zartman, eds., *Conflict Resolution in Africa.* Washington: The Brookings Institution.

Sunday Times (1997). "Reconciling Our People," 23 February.

——— (1997). "Killing Fields," 16 March.

——— (1996). "Healing Our Land through the Truth," 8 December.

——— (1995). "The Gallows Make Way for Ubuntu," 11 June.

Suret-Canale, Jean (1969). "Essai sur la signification social et historique des hegemonies Peuls (17è–19è siècles)." *Recherches Africaines* 1 (janvier–mars).

Susskind, L. (1981). "Environmental Mediation and Accountability Problem." *Vermont Law Review* 6 (1).

Sutherland, Alistair J. (1981). "Local Level Dispute Processes in Botswana: The Jeyi Moot Encapsulated." *Journal of African Law* 25.

Swartz, Marc J. (1966). "Bases for Political Compliance among Bena Villages," in Marc J. Swartz, Victor W. Turner, and Artheu Tuden, eds., *Political Anthropology.* Chicago: Aldine.

Talbot, A. (1969). *The Peoples of Southern Nigeria: Linguistics and Statistics.* London: Oxford University Press.

Thakur, R. (1994). "From Peacekeeping to Peace Enforcement; The UN Operation in Somalia." *Journal of Modern African Studies* 32 (3).

Thompson, Leonard (1990). *A History of South Africa.* New Haven: Yale University Press.

Tibebu, Teshale (1995). *The Making of Modern Ethiopia: 1896–1974.* Lawrenceville, NJ: Red Sea Press.

Ting-Toomey, S. (1988). "A Face-Negotiation Theory," in Y. Kim and W. Gudykunst, eds., *Theories of Intercultural Communication.* Newbury Park, CA: Sage.

Tomasic, R., and M. Feeley, eds. (1982). *Neighborhood Justice: Assessment of an Emerging Idea.* New York: Longman.

Touval, Saadia, and I. William Zartman (1989). "Mediation in International Conflicts," in *Mediation Research: The Process of Effectiveness of Third-Party Intervention.* San Francisco: Jossey-Bass.

——— (1985). *International Mediation in Theory and Practice.* Boulder, CO: Westview Press.

Triandis, H. C. (1994). *Culture and Social Behavior.* New York: McGraw-Hill.

Trimingham, John (1965). *Islam in Ethiopia.* New York: Barnes and Noble.

Truth and Reconciliation Commission (1995). *Justice in Transition.* South Africa.

Tsosie, Michael (n.d.). "Traditional Culture: Issues of Power and Control within Native American Communities." Mimeo.

Turner, Thomas (1988). "Decline or Recovery in Zaire?" *Current History* 87 (529).

Turner, Victor (1957). *Schism and Continuity in an African Society: A Study of Ndembu Village Life.* Manchester: Mancheser University Press.

Turney-High, Harry Holbert (1949). *Primitive War.* Columbia: University of South Carolina Press.

Tuso, Hamdesa (1987). "The Survival Of Oromo Nationalism." Paper presented at the second Annual Conference on the Horn of Africa: "The Ethiopian Revolution and Its Impact on the Politics of the Horn of Africa." New School for Social Research, New York (29–30 May).

——— (1982). " 'Minority' Education in Ethiopia." *Africa* 37 (3). Rome.
Uchendu, V. C. (1965). *The Igbo of Southern Nigeria*. New York: Holt, Rienhart and Winston.
U.S. Department of Defense (1995). *United States Security Strategy for Sub-Saharan Africa*. August.
United States Institute of Peace (1994). "Restoring Hope: The Real Lessons of Somalia for the Future of Intervention." Special Report of the United States Institute of Peace. Washington: USIP.
Ury, William L. (1990). "Dispute Resolution Notes from the Kalahari." *Negotiation Journal* 6 (3).
Uwazie, E. (1994). "Modes of Indigenous Disputing and Legal Interactions among the Igbos of Eastern Nigeria." *Journal of Legal Pluralism* 34.
——— (1991). "Disputing Modes and Strategies among the Igbo of Eastern Nigeria: Perspectives on Legal Pluralism." Ph.D. dissertation, Arizona State University.
Van Rouveroy van Nieuwaal, E. A. B. (1981). "In Search of Justice: Different Levels of Dispute Settlement among the Anufom in North Togo." Documentary film. Leiden: Afrika-Studiecentrum.
Vansina, Jan (1983). "The Peoples of the Forest," in D. Birmingham and P. Martin, eds., *History of Central Africa*. New York: Longmans, Inc.
——— (1966). *Kingdoms of the Savanna*. Madison: University of Wisconsin Press.
Van Velsen, J. (1964). *The Politics of Kinship: A Study in Social Manipulation among Lakeside Tonga*. Manchester: Manchester University Press.
Vilakazi, H. (1991). "The Roots of Ubuntu/Botho." Paper delivered at seminar organized by SECOSAF, Johannesburg, October.
Vinogradoff, P. (1925). *Custom and Right*. Oslo: Instituttet fur Sammenlignende Kulitursforskining.
von Clausewitz, Carl (1832/1968). *On War*. New York: Pelican.
Waldansso, G. (1980). "Toward Understanding the Gada System." *Journal of Oromo Students Union in North America* 4 (1).
Waldron, Sidney R. (1983). "Ethnicity as Epiphenomenon: Foundation of Harai-Oromo Relations under the Empire." Unpublished paper.
Wall, J., and M. Blum (1991). "Community Mediation in the People's Republic of China." *Journal of Conflict Resolution* 35 (1).
Walshe, Peter (1991). "South Africa: Prophetic Christianity and the Liberation Movement." *Journal of Modern African Studies* 29 (1).
Walter, E.V. (1969). *Terror and Resistance: A Study of Political Violence*. New York: Oxford University Press.
Walton, Richard, and Robert McKersie (1965). *A Behavioral Theory of Labor Negotiations*. New York: McGraw-Hill.
Waltz, Kenneth (1954). *Man, the State and War*. New York: Columbia University Press.
Wanitzek, U. (1988). "Legally Unrepresented Women Petitioners in the Lower Courts of Tanzania: A Case of Justice Denied?" Paper presented at the International Congress of Anthropological and Ethnological Sciences, Zagreb.
Warwick, D., and Herbert Kelman (1973). "Ethical Issues in Social Intervention," in G. Zaltman, ed., *Process and Phenomena of Social Change*. New York: Wiley.
Watson, Alan. (1974). *Legal Transplants*. Charlottesville: University Press of Virginia.
Weber, Max (1954). *On Law in Economy and Society*. New York: Simon & Schuster.

Weeks, Dudley (1992). *The Eight Essential Steps to Conflict Resolution.* New York: Putnam's Sons.

Weschler, Lawrence (1990). *A Miracle, a Universe: Settling Accounts with Torturers.* New York: Penguin Books.

White House (1996). *A National Security Strategy of Engagement and Enlargement.* February.

Williams, Gerald R (1996). "Negotiation as a Healing Process." *Journal of Dispute Resolution* 14 (1): 1–66.

Wilmer, Frank (1993). *The Indigenous Voice in World Politics.* Newbury Park, CA: Sage Publications.

Wilmot, W., and J. Hocker (1978). *Interpersonal Conflict.* Iowa City: W.M.C. Brown Publishers.

Wilson, G. (1937). "Introduction to Nyakusa Law." *Africa* 10.

Wilson, Wendy (1996). *Institutional Analysis of Women's Associations in Kolda.* Dakar: WINROCK.

——— (n.d.). *Trip Report: Fouta Djallon, Guinea: Some Observations in Relation to Research and Development Issues.* An appendix to the main report by Moudou Sene. Project NRBAR, Institut Senegalais de Recherche Agricole. Dakar: USAID.

——— (forthcoming). "The Fulani Model of Sustainable Agriculture: Situating Fulbe Nomadism in a Systemic View of Pastoralism and Farming." *Nomadic Peoples.*

——— (1984). "Resource Management in a Stratified Fulani Community." Ph.D. dissertation, University Microfilms.

Wiredu, Kwasi (1990). "An Akan Perspective on Human Rights," in A. An-N'aim and F. Deng, eds., *Human Rights in Africa: Cross-Cultural Perspectives.* Washington: The Brookings Institution.

Wittie, Cathie J. (1980). *Mediation and Society: Conflict Management in Lebanon.* New York: Academic Press.

Wolfers, Arnold, ed. (1956/1976). *Alliance Policy in the Cold War.* Westport, CT: Greenwood Press.

Workie, Abaineh (1979). "Minority Group Perceptions of the Amahras, Tigres, and Oromos," in Robert L. Hess, ed., *Proceedings of the 5th International Conference on Ethiopian Studies.* Chicago: University of Illinois.

Worsley, Peter (1984). *The Three Worlds: Culture and World Development.* Chicago: University of Chicago Press.

Yakubu, Derry-Joe (1995). "Conflict Resolution in Traditional African Societies and Present Day Realities: The Tiv Experience." Unpublished paper for the USIA- Africa Exchange Program (May).

Yetman, Norman R., and C. Hoy Steele (1975). *Majority and Minority.* Boston: Allyn and Bacon.

Zahan, Dominique (1979). *The Religion, Spirituality and Thought of Traditional Africa.* Chicago: University of Chicago Press.

Zahar, R. (1974). *Frantz Fanon: Colonization and Alienation.* New York: Monthly Review Press.

Zaltman, Gerald, ed., (1973). *Process and Phenomena of Social Change.* New York: Wiley-Interscience Publication.

Zartman, I. William, ed. (1997). *Government as Conflict Management: Politics and Violence in West Africa.* Washington: Brookings.

———, ed., (1996). *Elusive Peace: Negotiation an End to Civil Wars.* Washington: Brookings.

———, ed. (1995). *Elusive Peace: Negotiating an End to Civil Wars.* Washington: Brookings.
——— (1994). "Local Negotiations in South Africa," in Stephen John Stedman, ed., *South Africa: Political Economy of Transformation.* Boulder, CO: Lynne Rienner Publishers.
Zartman, I.William, and Maureen Berman (1982). *The Practical Negotiator.* New Haven: Yale University Press.
Zartman, I. William, and J. Lewis Rasmussen, eds., (1997). *Peacemaking in International Conflict.* Washington: United States Institute of Peace.
Zoga, Olana (1993). *Metcha Tulema's Association* (in Amharic). Addis Ababa.
Zvarevashe, Ignatius M. (1988). "Shona Religion," in Clive and Peggy Kileff, eds., *Shona Customs.* Gweru, Zimbabwe: Mambo Press.

The Contributors

Mohammed Abu-Nimer is assistant professor at the School of International Service at American University in Washington, D.C.

Francis M. Deng (Ambassador) is senior fellow and head of the African studies branch of the Foreign Policy Studies program of the Brookings Institution. He has served as Sudan's Ambassador to Canada, the Scandinavian countries and the United States of America, and Minister of State for Foreign Affairs.

Guy Olivier Faure is associate professor of sociology at the Sorbonne University, Paris, where he teaches international negotiation.

Ben K. Fred-Mensah is lecturer and researcher in African and international studies, as well as a consultant in international development.

Laurie King-Irani is editor of *Middle East Report,* the quarterly publication of the Middle East Research and Information Project (MERIP), and is completing a doctoral dissertation in sociocultural anthropology.

Edmond Kwam Kouassi is professor of law and political science at the University of Benin, Togo.

Nomonde Myaluza Masina is lecturer in the Sociology Department at Fort Hare University.

Ken Menkhaus is associate professor of political science at Davidson College.

Eghosa E Osaghae teaches political science at the University of Ibadan, Nigeria. He was until recently professor and head of Political Studies at the University Of Transkei, South Africa.

Hamdesa Tuso is associate professor in the Department of Conflict Resolution at Antioch University.

Ernest E. Uwazie, a mediation trainer and practitioner, is director of the Center for African Peace & Conflict Resolution and associate professor, Division of Criminal Justice, California State University at Sacramento.

Wendy Wilson-Fall is director of the West Africa Research Center (WARC) in Dakar, Senegal, and a social/economic anthropologist.

I. William Zartman is the Jacob Blaustein Professor of International Organizations and Conflict Resolution, director of African studies and conflict management programs at the Paul H. Nitze School of Advanced International Studies of the Johns Hopkins University in Washington, D.C., and the general editor of the SAIS Studies on Africa series.

Index

About the Book

Medical science has taken a new look at indigenous African healing practices, asking whether unique knowledge exists in traditional societies or whether Western and traditional societies developed the same knowledge with different names. In a similar vein, this study considers traditional African conflict management practices.

The authors identify the contributions of traditional mechanisms for conflict management in Africa and elsewhere, seeking to determine what is new and different. With African conflicts today eluding both international and domestic efforts to bring them under control, their work is guided by this crucial question: Can traditional methods yield insights and approaches that might help to end the persistent violence?

I. William Zartman is Jacob Blaustein Professor of International Organization and Conflict Resolution and director of African Studies at the Paul H. Nitze School of Advanced International Studies, Johns Hopkins University. His most recent publications include *Sovereignty as Responsibility: Conflict Management in Africa* and *Collapsed States: The Disintegration and Restoration of Legitimate Authority.*

■ Other *SAIS African Studies Library*— Lynne Rienner Publications

Democracy in Africa: The Hard Road Ahead, Marina Ottaway, editor (1997).

Collapsed States: The Disintegration and Restoration of Legitimate Authority, I. William Zartman, editor (1995).

South Africa: The Political Economy of Transformation, Stephen J. Stedman, editor (1994).

Botswana: The Political Economy of Democratic Development, Stephen J. Stedman, editor (1993).

Europe and Africa: The New Phase, I. William Zartman, editor (1993).

Ghana: The Political Economy of Recovery, Donald Rothchild, editor (1991).

Tunisia: The Political Economy of Reform, I. William Zartman, editor (1991).